IN STEP WITH THE GOD OF THE NATIONS

A BIBLICAL THEOLOGY OF MISSIONS

PHILIP M. STEYNE

ISBN # 1-880828-75-8

Library of Congress Catalog Card Number: 92-60720

Published by Touch Publications, Inc.
Box 19888, Houston, TX 77224
(713) 497-7901
Fax (713) 497-0904

Printed in the Republic of Singapore
by BAC Printers
Fax (65) 296-5588

TABLE OF CONTENTS

FOREWORD

The worldwide missions movement rides the crest of a mighty wave of optimism and growth. Not only are American churches and agencies investing more people and money in missions, so are our brothers and sisters in other lands.

In fact, looking at the status of global mission in 1991, researcher David Barrett counts 4,050 foreign mission sending agencies, 3.9 million national Christian workers, and 296,700 foreign missionaries. His numbers are broadly inclusive, that is, they are not limited to evangelicals. But by the very nature of their commitments, evangelicals stand at the forefront of this worldwide movement.

At the same time, Larry Pate, who tracks Two-Thirds World missionaries, claims they now number 46,157, compared to 13,238 a decade ago. He concludes that the Two-Thirds World missions movement in the last decade has grown more than five times as fast as the Western missions movement.

These stunning facts show why a biblical theology of missions like "In Step with the God of the Nations" is so keenly needed. If the worldwide missions movement is to sustain its momentum and maintain its vitality, it must be anchored in Scripture. Nothing will sink the movement faster, or detract it from its sharp focus, than a sub-biblical outlook.

Side-by-side with missionary expansion moves a powerful worldwide movement to eradicate all of the distinctions between world religions. Eminent theologians plead for interreligious harmony and understanding. Religious leaders of all stripes gather at convocations intended to downplay their theological and traditional distinctives. Participants in the World Council of Churches seventh assembly in February, 1991, watched in amazement while a keynote speaker called on the spirits of the dead.

Christians who take the Bible seriously realize that only a thorough grounding in Scripture will be sufficient to resist this worldwide effort to subvert the uniqueness of Christ and the clear call to salvation in no other name but his. Dr. Steyne's careful work is such a foundational study. It arrives at a critical time when the forces of syncretism and universalism must be encountered.

When many people are taught that evangelical missionary thrust must be dismissed as so much intolerance and pure proselytism, the church needs a book like this one. Dr. Steyne painstakingly traces the major biblical themes of world missions. He thoroughly documents each point with scriptural evidence. No one can miss the impact of the arguments he marshals for a biblical missionary faith.

Perhaps most distinctively, he pays strict attention to Old Testament themes related to missions. This is important, because too often we miss the thread of God's universal appeal in the Old Testament.

Writing with careful reason, and also aggressive passion, Dr. Steyne shows how the biblical texts meet modern objections to world missions. He also draws in current issues such as power encounter, the occult, and social and political ramifications of the gospel.

Having mastered this work, readers will have not only a valid checkpoint by which to test missions movements, they will also learn how the God of history has faithfully sustained his own obedient children who have followed his call to be faithful witnesses to a lost world.

—Jim Reapsome, Editor
Evangelical Missions Quarterly

INTRODUCTION

The battle for the allegiance of man's mind is more evident than ever before. No longer is Islam, Hinduism, Buddhism or some tribal religion confined to a distant Third World country. Each world religion and its derivations as well as the cults, the occult, and Satanism, claims the right to capture man's allegiance. A formerly secular Western world is rapidly exchanging its romance with materialism for the pursuit of spiritual realities. Many claim to have entered new dimensions of spiritualism. Among Americans surveyed, 78 percent expressed their belief that there is a place where people who have lived good lives go to be rewarded, while 60 percent believed there is a place where the bad go and are eternally damned. Most who believe in heaven expect to go there (U.S.News & World Report, March 25, 1991:57).

But by what authority may a religion or spiritual pursuit claim the right to be universally valid? Surely a matter of such eternal consequence is *"either true for all men, whether they know it or not, or it is true for no one, not even for those people who are under the illusion it is true"* (Vidler 1950:10, emphasis added). What is truth? How is it established? Basic issues ought to be addressed in the search for truth: to what purpose was the world created? What is the purpose of man's existence, and what is his relationship to the rest of creation? Is this world all there is to life? If there is another dimension to life, how does man gain access to it? Do spirit beings influence man, his relationship to others and to the environment? What is man's destiny? How will it be fulfilled? Every religious movement maintains that it adequately responds to these basic questions of life. Why else would they seek to win over others to accept their dogmas? But do they truly respond to man's search for spiritual reality? Do they truly speak peace to man's heart?

Among the religions of the world, Christianity stands in a category by itself. The Bible allows for no other claimants to God's truth. The God of the Bible is without peer as Creator and Redeemer. He created with purpose and wants creation to realize its full potential. Man is the crown of creation, created with special abilities to be God's vice-regent—the administrator of creation. But man alienated himself from God, abdicating his responsibilities. The Bible exposes man's insensitivity to God and the

13

judgment awaiting unrepentant man, but it also underscores God's desire to deliver man from judgment and to restore him to Himself. Moreover, the Bible affirms the final outcome of history—the eventual restoration of man and creation. No other religion comes close to having this comprehensive a view of God, creation, and man.

Yet 2,000 years after Christ's resurrection there are at least 3 billion people who have had little or no exposure to the biblical message. World evangelization remains the concern of a few voices crying in the wilderness. If the biblical message is unique, and if it is true, then surely the mission of all God's people should be to reach those who are alienated from God. Could it be that the average Christian sees a very different purpose for the Church? Is the Church a haven from the wilderness of the world? Is is a place where we gather to perform religious rituals at regular intervals in order to get in touch with God? Is it a retreat full of programs intended to animate spiritual life? Or is it the place where God's people are equipped for ministry in the world of darkness and alienation?

To have a proper biblical view of the church is to have a proper understanding of her task.

> The church is not a third class waiting room where we twiddle our thumbs while we wait for first class accommodations in heaven. It is a new dynamic community, winsome and attractive, and with eternal significance in the purpose of God. The Bible makes it clear that the church is God's goal for mankind (Griffiths 1978:9).

The Church is God's vehicle through which He will bring every knee to bow and every tongue to confess that Jesus Christ is Lord, to the glory of God. As Newbigin says, "The church is the pilgrim people of God. It is on the move—hastening to the ends of the earth to beseech all men to be reconciled to God, hastening to the end of time to meet its Lord who will gather all into one" (Newbigin 1953:25).

It is my conviction that only an understanding of the biblical message will counteract the indifference to world evangelization that characterizes the average church. It is also my conviction that the biblical message must be derived from both the Old and New Testaments. One without the other is incomplete and leads to aberrant living. Indeed, the apathetic attitude of the average Christian toward world evangelization may very well be due in part to a misunderstanding of the Old Testament foundation for New Testament truth.

14

All too often Christians spend most of their study time in the New Testament, only occasionally making forays into the Psalms and Proverbs, or now and then into the Prophets. The result is that many Christians fail to understand the whole scope of God's revelation of Himself—they have an incomplete picture of God's purposes (Dyrness 1979:15).

For this reason, our study will begin with an exploration of God's purpose in calling a people to Himself, as is revealed in the Old Testament, and then go on to show the continuity and consummation of that purpose in the New Testament.

Explanation of Approach

This study is divided into three sections. The first section (chapters 1 through 7) introduces the basis of a biblical theology of missions. It is partly an apologetic for biblical faith, based on an overview of the first eleven chapters of Genesis relative to world evangelization. These chapters are indispensable for the development of a biblical theology of missions. They trace man's establishment as God's vice-regent over creation, his alienation from both his Maker and his fellow-man, his regression, judgment, renewal, and finally his cultural and linguistic diversity. Without these essentials we may miss God's heart's desire to bring man back into a relationship with Himself.

The second section (chapters 8 through 19) looks at Israel, God's Old Testament people, on mission. It covers the call of Abram; the significance of the patriarchs; the deliverance of the people of Israel, their nationhood, their rebellion, judgment, exile, and subsequent restoration to the land; and the role of the prophets. These factors are evaluated in respect to the purpose of Israel's election as the people of God. The section concludes with a brief summary of the incompleteness of the Old Testament.

The third section (chapters 20 through 25) reviews the mandates on mission entrusted to the Church, God's New Testament people, looking at the New Testament's emphasis on the Great Commission. After examining God's three models of ministry, it reviews the mission of Jesus Christ, evaluates His summons, highlights the themes coursing through His teaching, and demonstrates the burden of the Gospel writers. It also examines the Apostle Paul's theology of missions and surveys the goal of the Church. A brief look at Revelation underscores the fact that no power can withstand the Lord of the Church, who promised that He would build His Church in the face of all opposition. He will lead His people in triumph.

Throughout this study, the plural term *missions* is used to define the task of the Church. Most American evangelicals think of missions as the ministry and witness of a church beyond its own community to persons who will most likely not become Christians without someone specifically going to present the gospel. European scholars and those associated with the ecumenical movement insist on the singular *mission*. It is argued that the Church has but one task, which should not be fragmented. Thus, all the Church does, regardless of the goal, is the mission of the Church. My preference is *missions* because it stresses that the main purpose of the church is the communication of the gospel of Jesus Christ to otherwise unreachable people, to bring churches into being.

I credit my initial interest in this subject to Professor Arthur F. Glasser, former dean of the School of World Mission, Fuller Theological Seminary. It was his motivational lectures that caused me to reconsider my traditional non-missionary approach to the Bible, particularly the Old Testament. I am indebted to him for his careful attention to the biblical text.

This study is the product of the combined labors of a number of very special people. Jeanne, my wife, spent many hours working on the original outline. A dear friend, Lamar Brown, who like Timothy (Phil.2:20-21) has a servant's heart, worked on the expanded outline and printed several trial manuscripts. Drs. Alex Luc and Ferris McDaniel, my colleagues, expended precious time and provided many helpful corrections and theological insights which added to the value of this study. Stan Guthrie, a former student and dear friend, and Elizabeth Layman, a fellow missionary, provided capable editing skills. Others helped more indirectly, yet without them this project would not have been completed. All these served without personal consideration. I thank them and pray God's blessing upon them. I also thank the administration of Columbia Bible College and Seminary for making it possible for me to give time to this study.

Unquestionably, the ministry of every Christian everywhere is to participate in making Christ known to all people in all geographic areas. It is my prayer that this volume will not only add to the understanding of our sacred task, but also encourage many believers around the world to fall in step with the God of *all* nations.

PART I

THE BASIS OF BIBLICAL

THEOLOGY OF MISSIONS

Chapter 1

WHY EVANGELIZE

THE NATIONS?

It has become commonplace to refer to all religious systems as living faiths (Stowe 1967:176-177,184). Many believe that there are many ways for man to come into a meaningful relationship with God, and Christianity is thought to be but one such religious option. However, none of these "living faiths" agree on who God is or what He is like, how man should relate to Him, or who or what comprises the world of the supernatural. Nor do they agree on what constitutes a meaningful relationship with the supernatural—not even those who espouse the same religion!

Is Biblical Faith Unique?
Throughout history, even from within organized Christianity, some have maintained that all religions have equal validity, that each religion offers its own way of salvation, its own entrance into an eternal relationship with God. Others have said that all mankind will ultimately know God's salvation, if not as a result of God's unchanging love, then through the substitutionary death and victorious resurrection of Jesus Christ. Some claim that even if people never hear of this salvation, still they will not come under God's judgment (Griffiths 1982:115-128).

But when any of these positions are taken, the following questions inevitably arise: "If all religions are equally valid, and if every person will ultimately have a relationship with God, what is the need for world evangelization?" "Does evangelism bring mankind into a distinctive relationship with God, or is it at best a misguided venture, a wasted effort?" Thus a growing number of Christians are discounting evangelism! Is Christianity distinctive, or is it only one among several religions of equal validity? Are there religious commonalities which annul any need for evangelism?

The Sociopsychological Functions of Religion

Centuries ago King Solomon observed, "I have seen the task which God has given the sons of men with which to occupy themselves. He has made everything appropriate in its time. *He has also set eternity in their heart...*" (Eccl.3:10-11, emphases added). Man was created with a longing for fellowship with his Creator. According to St. Augustine, man has an insatiable desire for God which He alone can fulfill.

Aside from this real need for a relationship with his God, man has other physical and emotional needs which all religions meet one way or another. Every religion fills very specific sociological and psychological functions in the lives of its practitioners. All religions provide a point of reference beyond the practitioner to which he may resort for self-validation as a member of a specific community. This reference point supplies both man and his community with a sense of identity and mutual affirmation.

Man cannot function normally without a standard which establishes a sense of right and wrong for all his relationships with his world, his fellows, and the supernatural world. His very human nature demands some measure of morality. Of course his concept of morality may be severely limited by cultural and personal factors, but it exists nonetheless, and is essential in that it enables every man to function meaningfully and "morally" within society.

Bombarded by anxieties, man also needs a source of power beyond himself to maintain a certain equilibrium, both in times of crisis and peace, of need and abundance. Then, too, religion also establishes symbolic explanations for life's mysteries, which bring meaning to life and enable man to face life's unknowns. Thus, religion becomes the integrator of all of life, binding it together into a meaningful experience.

Christianity does share these indispensable sociopsychological factors with all other religions, and this may be the reason that some believe all religions to be equally valid. Unfortunately, many Christians practise their religion in such a way as to make such an evaluation appear accurate.

Are not the objectives of other religions equally satisfactory? These matters demand investigation. Surely the millions subscribing to the many other religions accept them as the truth, even to the point of commending them to potential converts from other religions. Recent converts to these other religions often speak highly of the positive values they find in their newfound faiths. Trained specialists in all world and tribal religions, including Christianity, seek to instruct converts to realize the full benefits of the sociopsychological functions of their faith, expending much effort to help devotees experience the benefits of their religion. It is no longer uncommon to hear of various religions sponsoring programs for children, young people and senior citizens, modeled after their Christian counterparts. Sometimes other religions encourage involvement and offer services that appear to differ in no way from those offered by the church. In some respects their programs are far more intensive, demanding and (by all appearances) more effective. An encounter with a committed Muslim, Buddhist, Hindu, or Shintoist would testify to the effectiveness of their efforts. Furthermore, devotees of other religions appear to be more dedicated to their faith than do most Christians.

But *is* Christianity just one way among many other religions, satisfying man's sociological and psychological needs and providing meaning and tools with which to deal with life's mysteries? Is it only different to the degree that it claims to offer a better quality of life? Is Christianity (as well-intentioned communicators frequently proclaim) merely an escape from an impending judgment of man for sinful living? Certainly, the fear of God's judgment is very often an important factor in a Christian conversion, but is it the sole valid motivation for becoming a Christian?

What, if anything, makes Christianity different? In what way can Christianity claim to be truly unique? If the Christian faith does not differ radically from all other religious faiths, it is unable to answer the life and death questions it has historically claimed to answer from the day of Pentecost on. Jesus Christ said, "And this is eternal life, that they may know Thee, the only true God, and Jesus Christ whom Thou hast sent" (Jn.17:3). If this statement is true, then the Christian faith stands apart from—yes, towers over—all other living faiths!

A Misdirected Focus

In order to comprehend the Church's task more clearly, we must understand that God has revealed Himself to man in the context of a world composed of many nations. At one time, these nations had a knowledge of the one true God, however:

> though they knew God, they did not honor Him as God, or give thanks; but they became futile in their speculations, and their foolish heart was darkened. Professing to be wise, they became fools, and exchanged the glory of the incorruptible God for an image in the form of corruptible man and of birds and four-footed animals and crawling creatures. (Rom.1:21-23).

In the garden man deliberately replaced God's omniscience with his own paltry, finite knowledge. This he promptly proceeded to submit to the authority of another god, "the prince of the power of the air" (Eph.2:2), who deceived him into thinking of himself as at the center of the stage, and of the spirit world as his servant. Subsequently man has come to believe that correct words, works, or rituals can be used to manipulate the spirit world to respond to his desires. Hence, the religious specialist is viewed as the facilitator of man's will, not God's.

The rational thinker creates a philosophical framework with a "god in a box" who relates or does not relate to the world in the terms assigned to him. The hedonist, on the other hand, does not even bother to ask himself "the God question," but simply clamors, "Eat, drink and be merry, for tomorrow we die!" Thus, both the rational and the irrational worldviews by which man orders his life have, in the words of Van Til, agreed to "a secret treaty... a treaty against God." As Van Til put it, "the very idea of pure factuality or chance is the best guarantee that no true authority, such as that of God as the Creator and Judge of man, will ever confront man" (Van Til, 1963:26).

Though man is incorrigibly religious, he constantly seeks to approach God on his own terms. This is why he composes his own scriptures and structures his own response to his own concepts of God. It is, therefore, not surprising that all religious systems other than Christianity (and, all too frequently, Christianity as it is practiced) allow, if they do not presuppose, the sovereignty of man rather than of God. It is assumed that man will be saved by knowledge, especially secret, elitist knowledge. This assumption explains in part the diversity of religious faiths. Each claims its right to man's unquestioned devotion. Indeed, man is hailed as God; he is thought to design and create his own destiny, to be his own master. He assumes that his accountability begins and ends with himself.

Man's search for peace brings him no peace, as he focuses on himself, not on God. But his religion of works does provide him with a sense of self-worth, achievement, and self-actualization. Thus, he persuades himself that he has a right standing before God. How unlike the biblical message, which tells of the God who acts in grace and receives man, not because of any good he has done, but because of His own great mercy (Tit.3:4-6)!

In revealing Himself, God's purpose was not merely our personal salvation; He has also given us the responsibility to be our brother's keeper and guardian of the earth. Furthermore, God earnestly desires the salvation of *all nations*, and has entrusted to the redeemed the ministry of reconciliation of all those peoples yet far away from Him, their Creator, who desires to be their Savior and Lord!

A Distinct Message

What makes the Christian faith distinct from all others? Christianity claims to be distinctively historical, founding its claim in the biblical record of creation. The Bible reviews the introduction of sin into the world and man's response to God in the garden, at the time of the flood, at Babel and throughout history. It recounts God's redemptive program (mentioned first in Genesis 3:15) as it is revealed through Abraham, Moses and ultimately Jesus Christ and His Church. It describes the pilgrimage of the people of Israel, the character and attributes of God and the record of the prophets' interaction with divine mandates. It describes the birth, life, work, teaching and death of Jesus Christ, the Messiah for all nations, the birth and growth of the Church, and the culmination of history itself. The existence of these historical records allows biblical faith to make distinctive claims for itself that no other religion can make. These historical documents should be weighed against the sacred writings of all other religions when one is deciding whether or not Christianity is unique, and whether disregarding it will affect man's eternal destiny.

The most important questions concern the death, resurrection and return of Jesus Christ. How is it that we have precise historical records about the birth, death and life of Christ, but not of Krishna, Buddha, or Muhammed? The Bible says that He is the only mediator between God and man (1 Tim.2:5). Who *is* this Man and what was His purpose in breaking into human history? Did He really come from God to give "Himself as a ransom for all" (1 Tim.2:6)? What other religion dares to make the same claims? Can their scriptures even begin to parallel the Christian message? Can we discount the numerous prophecies, written centuries before Christ's time, which detailed many events that happened to Him? And if this revelation is authentic and is truly divine in origin, what will be the consequences of our withholding it from the rest of mankind? Surely these questions should not be disregarded in the debate about the equality of all religious faiths, about how man can be reconciled to God, and about the purpose of the Church's existence!

Issues of Critical Concern

The disturbing fact is, however, that some "evangelical" scholars are beginning to equivocate about the uniqueness of the Christian faith as universalism in its various expressions reappears in evangelical circles. Generally, the old universalism (which asserts that a loving God will not condemn anyone to eternal separation from Himself) is not the most serious challenge the Church faces. More subtle is the belief that those who seek after God, though they may not know the name of Jesus Christ or be aware of His death and resurrection, will nonetheless be restored to the presence of God. But several passages in both the Old and New Testaments maintain an opposing view (Ps. 5:9; 10:7; 14:1-3; 36:1; 53:1-4; Is. 59:7-8; Rom. 3:9-20; Lk. 24:46-47; Acts 4:12; Rom. 10:9-15).

Some, however, propose that the facts concerning Christ are indispensable elements of salvation, but do not constitute a mandate to bring all peoples to a verdict about the claims of the Gospel. They would agree that Jesus Christ had to atone for the sin of mankind. However, they see the task of the Church not as an evangelizing mission, but rather a heralding mission. While it would be comforting for people to know that through Christ's atonement they have been made acceptable to the Father, they *need* not know it to have an eternal relationship with Him. Whether or not they know it or accept it, they are already reconciled to the Father. Should they receive Christ in this life, it would make no difference in their standing before God, because they are already right with Him through Christ's death. Knowing about and responding to their reconciled state while still in this life would bring many benefits, as Christian history attests; but it certainly is not a *sine qua non* for an eternal relationship with God. Man need not be called to a verdict about his relationship with Jesus Christ. Thus, there is no need to expend one's life in the cause of world evangelization, unless one finds personal fulfillment in doing so. Nevertheless, the work of Jesus Christ on the cross, in His resurrection, ascension and glorification is already effective for all people, regardless of their response to Him while in this life.

When the above beliefs are subscribed to, it does not take a mastermind to conclude that the call to world evangelism is no longer held to be an important mandate for all disciples of Christ. Christian man would be better employed cooperating with other faiths, restructuring society and alleviating social ills because, ultimately, all will be saved. Why confront man with his sinful condition? Why seek to change his understanding of God? And why strive to bring him to a personal encounter with his Creator? Social structures may need to be changed, but not man, who is now (through Christ's redemptive work) essentially good. It is his environment that makes man respond negatively to society, not his being a sinner in need of regeneration. Tragically, this nonbiblical thinking is widespread today and undergirds most liberation theologies.

The biblical mandate, however, instructs Christians to bear the Gospel to all mankind, to all people groups. All barriers must be crossed: geographic, political, social, economic and ethnic. No boundary should block the taking of this Gospel to all peoples in every land throughout all generations! Furthermore, humble, obedient believers, empowered by the Holy Spirit, will often transform the societies in which they minister the Word, as history has so often attested.

But how do we reconcile the biblical evangelistic mandate with the luxurious lifestyle and lackadaisical commitment of the average Christian today? For years, the Church has seemed uneasy with, if not outright indifferent to, the significance of the Great Commission. Could it be that the unique message and mission of the Church have been lost as people seek to embrace the benefits Christian faith provides? Are we so worried about keeping our relationship with the Shepherd that we forget the lost sheep dying out on the rugged peaks? Are we so busy attending seminars on fulfilling relationships that we have no time for those who are still outside the family of God?

A Unique Mission

We return to the question: "Why is the Christian church unique?" The straightforward answer in the Bible is that it is unique because its task is to "Tell of His glory among the nations...the glory due His Name" (Ps.96:3,8). For that purpose Israel was established as a model nation within the arena of nations. By contrast, all other nations were directed and motivated by self-knowledge, not revelation knowledge. They had rejected the revelation which came from a self-disclosing God (Rom.1:18-32). While the Church is a called-out community (modeling by word and deed the glory of Jesus Christ in His crucifixion, resurrection, ascension, and glorious return), the purpose remains the same: that the church be God's messenger of reconciliation bringing every knee to bow, every tongue to confess that Jesus Christ alone is Lord of all nations (2 Cor.5:11-20).

The biblical message emphasizes that a relationship with God cannot be separated from involvement with God's purpose of bringing the nations to faith in Christ. This is unlike all self-oriented religions, which seek after God in order to know security, success, and happiness. Earthly security, success, and happiness may or may not be by-products of Christian faith, but they are not at its heart. The Christian message points to a blessed life and future, in part realized here through kingdom living (Mt.5:3-12), but only fully in the kingdom to come (Jn.16:33; 18:36).

The Bible claims that all sin is committed not only against human beings, but essentially against God. (The Bible claims that man is accountable and responsible for his sin). Sin is not merely a social inconvenience; it is a transgression of God's laws, deserving judgment and eternal separation from Him. Furthermore, Christianity declares that in Jesus Christ's death and resurrection God has graciously provided the propitiation for man's sin so that he may experience forgiveness, both now and in the day of judgment.

Man must appropriate God's gift of salvation in order to experience deliverance from judgment. This deliverance involves repenting and turning to God in faith, receiving the free gift of salvation (Acts 3:19; Eph.2:8,9). Although this personal relationship with a living God is foundational, it is not the complete purpose of the Christian life. Upon man's salvation, God commissions him to take this message of salvation to all peoples (Mt.28:19-20).

How unlike the message of any other faith, living or dead! At best, devotees of other systems have to strive for the god's approval. Even those religions which are perverted forms of Christianity cannot approximate the assurance expressed by the Apostle Paul: "I know whom I have believed and I am convinced that He is able to guard what I have entrusted to Him until that day" (2 Tim.1:12). Other religions strive for man's contentment and enjoyment and not for God's eternal purposes. Sin may be committed against a deity, but in the end good deeds may outweigh bad deeds. Even then, bad deeds and attitudes may be blamed on another person's actions, rather than on self. At best, religious activity suppresses guilt, but guilt then surfaces through emotional, physical, and spiritual problems. Even if a people practices community, there is a one-on-one approach to the deity, rather than corporate worship and service. The concept of a people of God is at best sectarian. The all-encompassing goal of declaring the glory of God for His name's sake is lost.

Israel drifted into the error of believing that God's blessings were for her alone (i.e. "particularism"). God's intention for Israel and later for the Church, was to place before the watching nations a true model of what it means to be the people of God. God's people were to demonstrate and proclaim before all nations the majesty, honor, power, and might of the only all-glorious God revealed in the Bible (Mal.1:11, 14). Israel was reminded:

> You are *a holy people* to the LORD your God; the LORD your God has chosen you to be *a people for His own possession* out of all the peoples who are on the face of the earth.... Know therefore that the LORD your God, He is God, the faithful God.... You shall not be afraid of them.... You shall not dread them, for the LORD your God is in your midst, *a great and awesome God* (Dt.7:6,9,18,21, emphases added).

The Apostle Peter affirms:

> You are a chosen race, a royal priesthood, a holy nation, a people for God's own possession, that you may proclaim the excellencies of Him who has called you out of darkness into His marvelous light (1 Pet.2:9).

Biblical theology reveals that whatever else the people of God are to do, they are to proclaim and manifest the excellencies of the only true God. And what is His excellence?

> For the LORD your God is the God of gods and the Lord of lords, the great, the mighty, and the awesome God who does not show partiality, nor take a bribe [will not be manipulated]. He is your praise, and He is your God (Dt.10:17,21).

Bearing witness to this God was the mission of Israel, and it is still the mission of the Church. Wherever God does not receive the praise of men, there the people of God are called to declare His glory. What an awesome responsibility! How unfortunate that this mission has so often been deflected.

An Unstoppable Mission

The Old Testament shows how God worked in and through Isrāel. Not even Israel's decline could prevent God from achieving His purposes among the nations (Dan.6:26-27). This is the witness of the Old Testament and also the foundational truth for understanding the New Testament. The repeated themes of the Old Testament (also reiterated in the New) highlight that God is a God for all nations. He is also the liberating and saving God for all peoples, and He calls on His people to be His witnesses. But *while making Him known*, there will be conflict. Jesus affirmed, "I will build my church and *the gates of Hades shall not overpower it*" (Mt.16:18, emphasis added). The powers of darkness will oppose the growth of the Church. They will do whatever they can to destroy both man and the Church and to keep Christians from implementing the Great Commission. But the command stands. His followers are to go to all people groups. He Himself will be with them in the midst of all circumstances (Mt.28:20). Not Ephesus' lack of love, not Laodicea's coldness of heart (Rev.2,3), not any power on earth or in heaven will prevent the God above all gods from achieving the redemption of mankind.

The last chapters of history are already recorded fact. Those redeemed by the blood of the Lamb will be there on that great day of His revelation (Rev.7:9). They will come from every tongue, tribe, and nation no matter what we do or do not do. The question which should concern us, however, is whether we will participate in God's program. How should Christians respond to the challenge posed by the Apostle Paul, who believed that his mission, like that of Israel and also of the Church, was to bring the nations to faith in Jesus Christ (cf. Rom.1:5)? Paul's fear was that he, like Israel, might miss God's purpose through involvement in the inconsequential. He reminded himself, and us, that:

> *We have as our ambition*, whether at home or absent, to be pleasing to Him.... For the love of Christ controls us, having concluded this, that one died for all, therefore all died; and He died for all, *that they who live should no longer live for themselves, but for Him who died and rose again on their behalf* (2 Cor.5:9,14,15, emphases added).

A thoughtful journey through the Bible soon reveals that God's purposes go far beyond our personal salvation, important as that is. He wants His people to model before the watching world who He is and what His purposes are for all mankind; He has ordained that they do so in a community of believers committed to this task.

The Bible is indeed God's casebook, a record of His actions for the salvation of mankind. "The stamp of the missionary purpose is on its every part" (Carver 1921:13). Said Carver:

> In all stages of His revelation as it was making and in every book of it when recorded God has been asserting His claim upon the whole human race; proclaiming His love to all mankind; urging His worshippers to "declare his glory among the nations" (Ps.96:3); asking ever "whom shall I send and who will go for us?" and waiting until men would answer, "Here am I, send me" (Isa.6:8) (Ibid.:22).

The result of God's mission will be the glorification of Himself and His Church through a people who have been called to the praise of His glory (Eph.1:6,9,11).

Biblical Theology Defines Biblical Christianity

There is a marked difference between biblical Christianity and other religious systems. Christianity concerns an almighty, active Creator God Who has called to Himself a people for a unique mission. Only this God expects His followers to do works of righteousness and model a unique lifestyle, not in order to gain their salvation, but as a consequence of their personal relationship with Himself (Eph.2:10; Tit.2:14; 3:8). Through what observers may call "weakness" they are to overcome life's challenges. Through their delegated authority they are to challenge all power structures working for the dehumanization and destruction of humanity (Eph.6:12). Biblical Christianity is committed to the worldwide mission of bringing every knee to bow and every tongue to confess that Jesus Christ is Lord, to the glory of God (Is.45:23; Rom.14:11; Phil.2:10).

Biblical Christianity is not imprisoned in any culture, although in varying degrees it will reflect the host culture. It not only concerns itself with certain cardinal truths but also embodies them in the warp and woof of life. Biblical faith, as shown in both Old and New Testaments, testifies to Jesus Christ as God in human flesh and calls all people to acknowledge that Christ alone is Lord, Sovereign of the universe (Phil. 2:6-11).

Biblical theology reveals the larger purposes of God for His people as they relate to all nations, and can deliver a self-centered and somewhat impersonal church from privatism (particularism) in its faith.

Whereas systematic theology draws together in logical order the cardinal beliefs which form the foundation of the Christian faith, biblical theology describes the Bible's message in the words and ideas of the writers. Hence, biblical theology seeks to discover more than the cardinal beliefs underlying the Christian faith. It is more bound to the text than systematic theology, yet it looks at the larger picture—the implications of God's self-disclosure and interaction with His creation, specifically with His people. We trust that answers to the important questions we have raised will be discovered when biblical theology is studied in conjunction with systematic theology.

In this study, we will attempt to bring an understanding of the unique message and mission confided by God through the Scriptures to His people, to all true followers of Jesus Christ.

Both biblical and systematic theology reveal that God's people are opposed by a powerful enemy (Peters 1972:85) whose greatest concern is to prevent them from proclaiming His glory among the nations. This enemy will deceive God's people and deflect them from fulfilling their divine mandate. He will do all he can to keep the citizens of his domain in subjection and impede every effort to reclaim from his enslaving grip those who rightfully belong to God.

Biblical theology examines God's purposes for mankind as revealed in the first eleven chapters of Genesis, then moves on to define these purposes as they are revealed through His interaction with His Old and New Testament peoples. It accepts that man was created by God for a very specific mission.

When we understand God's purposes for man, we will have to exclaim with Paul:

> Oh, the depth of the riches both of the wisdom and knowledge of God! How unsearchable are His judgments and unfathomable His ways! For who has known the mind of the Lord, or who became His Counselor? Or who has first given to Him that it might be paid back to him again? For from Him and through Him and to Him are all things (Rom.11:33-36).

Chapter 2

THE NATURE OF

BIBLICAL THEOLOGY

OF MISSIONS

A biblical theology of missions is a theology of obedience, reflecting the shape of God's commands and promises from the beginning to the end of time.

The Significance of Missions to Theology

Biblical theology underscores that knowing God is not merely a personal mystical experience, but a concrete response in obedience to His commands, including His command to go and make disciples. To know God is to seek His will and do it, and His will is tied to His redemptive purposes for all nations. "God has but one purpose in mind: to glorify Himself, and though there are many facets there is only one history of significance and only one program that God will use to achieve His purpose" (Dyrness 1983:15). The very existence of the Church depends upon its response to the Great Commission. In the words of Emil Brunner: "The Church exists by mission, as fire exists by burning" (Miller 1957:69). Therefore, any theology not formed by and focused on God's redemptive purposes for all nations must be incomplete and unfaithful to God's character and revealed biblical truth.

The theology of the Bible cannot be understood apart from God's mission in the world. The beginning and end of the biblical record presents a God who created a purposeful world. He takes the initiative and accomplishes a purposeful mission in bringing alienated man back into relationship with Himself. God's redemptive mission lies at the core of theology and is rooted in His very character.

This mission is vital for the understanding and the implementation of one's theology because it is the point where beliefs and obedience lead to the concrete application of biblical truth. God's message to men in any generation is that theology must be lived out, not merely known. Therefore, understanding God's redemptive mission to all nations follows, rather than precedes, mission activity, because it flows out of obedience to God.

What is a Biblical Theology of Missions?

A biblical theology of missions establishes the biblical foundation for God's missionary activity and our response to it. The basis for such missionary activity is rooted in all of Scripture rather than specific verses haphazardly found in certain "great commission" passages. A biblical theology of missions identifies various themes as they occur in the course of God's dealings with His people and the nations, in both Old and New Testaments. These themes detail the nature of His mission, reflect His character, and are extensions of His creative work.

A biblical theology of missions reflects a God who has been, is, and will be at work in this world. This theology concerns itself with God's complete program in the world, both the evangelistic and cultural mandates. He approaches man as a total being, in both his physical and spiritual dimensions. God has worked, is working, and will continue working in particular sociocultural realities to accomplish His purposes for all nations.

A biblical theology of missions is concerned with the redemptive activities of the Father, the Son, and the Holy Spirit on behalf of all men throughout history. It deals with God's revelation of His saving purposes in both the Old and New Testaments in His interaction with mankind, and specifically, His own people.

Biblical Theology and History

Biblical theology arises from biblical history, in which God intervenes in history to redeem man and creation. It is historical because it identifies verifiable events in time (e.g., Is.6:1; Heb.1:1).

The first eleven chapters of Genesis are foundational to a biblical theology of missions. The Bible's affirmation of the creation and commission of Adam and Eve, the fall of man into a sinful state, the consequences of man's sin in the flood, and the confusion of languages and dispersion of people at the tower of Babel provide the parameters for understanding God's purposes in creation, which are to be worked out throughout history.

The letter to the Hebrews affirms: "God, after He spoke long ago to the fathers in the prophets in many portions and in many ways, in these last days has spoken to us in His Son...." (Heb.1:1-2). Biblical history records real people and events, such as Abraham and Moses, David and Daniel, Peter and Paul. The Exodus, the conquering of Canaan, the exile to Babylon, and numerous other recorded historical events provide the context of God's purposes in history. Biblical theology maintains that God acted with specific objectives. He took the initiative in seeking out man and in revealing Himself and His redemptive purposes; He communicated with finite man and sought to establish a relationship with him. In His desire to relate meaningfully and purposefully He made specific promises to him, and fulfilled (or will fulfill) these in keeping with His just and righteous character. As the God of promise and fulfillment (Wright 1969:25), He has interacted with man to realize predetermined goals relating to all creation's redemption.

Biblical theology reveals God's intervention and redemptive action in human history. He is distressed over his alienated creation and actively seeks to bring man into a dynamic, purposeful, and intimate relationship with Himself. He spares no means to bring reconciliation between Himself and the crown of His creation, man. God has acted in a dramatic and costly way to restore the crown of His creation to Edenic fellowship with Himself, sparing nothing to effect this reconciliation (Jn.3:16). He seeks to reestablish communion, not only with all men (1 Tim.2:4; 2 Pet.3:9), but also with all creation (Rom.8:21). The redemption of man is centered in a God-provided Savior who reconciles man to Him (2 Cor.5:18-19). This redemptive program was progressive:

> Having *overlooked the times of ignorance,* God is now declaring to men that all everywhere should repent, because He has fixed a day in which He will judge the world in righteousness through a Man whom He has appointed, having furnished proof to all men by raising Him from the dead (Acts 17:30-31, emphasis added).

So God's redemptive purposes relate to specific people, not people en masse. God calls people by name, and concerns Himself with the specifics of their lives. For instance, the Bible notes not only the many genealogies and their tasks, but also records their perversity and frequent rebellion. Scripture does not gloss over man's sin and need of God's redemption (2 Sam.11,12; Ps.51).

A Theology of Participation

Biblical theology reveals the intentions of God for man and all of creation. When God calls man to Himself, the calling is not merely to receive the blessing of salvation, but also to serve in partnership with Him in His purposes for all nations. In the context of receiving salvation, we are reminded that "we are His workmanship, created in Christ Jesus for good works" (Eph.2:10). People are blessed so that they might be a blessing to others (Ps.67:1-2). God does not call and bless so that we may advance our own interests! His call and blessing are always purposeful.

Nor will God share His glory with another. He intends that His name be declared and that His followers be to the praise of His glory (Eph.1:6;12;14). He told Abram:

> Go forth from your country, and from your relatives and from your father's house, to the land which I will show you;... and I will bless you, and make your name great; and so you shall be a blessing; ... and in you all the families of the earth shall be blessed (Gen.12:1-3).

He told Moses, "Therefore, come now, and I will send you to Pharaoh, so that you may bring My people, the sons of Israel, out of Egypt" (Exo.3:10). He apprehended Paul and said of him, "He is a chosen instrument of Mine, to bear My name before the Gentiles and kings and the sons of Israel" (Acts 9:15). Thus, the Great Commission is not optional but mandatory, binding on all who are disciples of Jesus Christ. The Holy Spirit was given to empower Christians as witnesses to Jesus Christ—to His death, resurrection, ascension and glorification. God has extended to man the privilege of working with Himself. In this vein, it has been well said:

> He who is appointed to know God's love is appointed also to share that love. He who is forgiven must forgive and become an ambassador of forgiveness. He who has known God's loving concern for his own brokenness must share that concern for a broken world. He who has known the joy of membership in the people of God is obligated to seek to extend the bounds of God's people until they take in every life in every land. To accept God's covenant is to labor with Him, to suffer if need be, for that grand hour when "at the name of Jesus every knee should bow, in heaven and on earth and under the earth, and every tongue confess that Jesus Christ is Lord, to the glory of God the Father" (Philippians 2:10-11). It is to toil and pray and sacrifice to the end that the "kingdom of the world [shall] ... become the kingdom of

our Lord and of His Christ, and He shall reign for ever and ever" (Revelation 11:15). To accept God's covenant is to serve Him who is the Suffering Servant. To be one of God's beloved sheep whom He calls by name is to go out into the long night with the Great Shepherd searching for those who are lost, "until he finds" them (Luke 15:3-7) (Miller 1957:39).

Biblical history records how man has cooperated or refused to cooperate with God in carrying out His commands. Today God continues to extend that amazing privilege of partnership with Him to redeemed men everywhere.

A Theology of Context

Biblical theology claims no other authority than the text of Scripture itself. The Bible interprets itself. The Bible alone establishes what, why, and how God shall achieve His purposes. For instance, through the study of Jeremiah (25:11), Daniel discovered that the Israelites would be in exile for seventy years:

> I, Daniel, observed in the books the number of years which was revealed as the word of the Lord to Jeremiah the prophet for the completion of the desolations of Jerusalem, namely seventy years. So I gave my attention to the Lord God to seek Him by prayer and supplications, with fasting, sackcloth, and ashes (Dan.9:2-3).

This realization motivated Daniel to ask God to fulfill His promise and take His people back to their promised land. The Bible reveals the scope of God's purposes in history, and their specific application to individuals chosen to carry out those purposes. God delights to work with and through His people in bringing about His divine goals for His creation. The Bible itself establishes the parameters of God's interaction with man on behalf of his redemption.

A Mediatorial Theology

The Bible speaks of a mediatorial, relational covenant which God has established with His people to bring all mankind to Himself. Israel, as recipient of His deliverance from slavery, was called to declare His wonderful deeds (Ps.145:3-13) and call people to His marvelous light through both word and deed. Israel was to be God's priestly nation, standing before Him on behalf of others (Exo.19:4-6, cf. Is.66:18-19). The same applies to God's New Testament people. They, too, have been delivered from bondage in order to serve God's purposes as a royal priesthood, even as they manifest His excellence to all peoples (1 Pet.2:9).

The personal relationship man can have with God, whether in the Old or New Testament era, is to be a mediatorial role. God said to Israel, "the Lord your God has chosen you to be a people for His own possession" (Dt.7:6); and to His New Testament people: "You did not choose Me, but I chose you, and appointed you, that you should go and bear fruit, and that your fruit should remain..." (Jn.15:16). Paul reminded God's people of their mediatorial role in His plan for the world; he taught that they were "God's fellow-workers" (1 Cor.3:9); and again, that they were not to receive His grace in vain (2 Cor.6:1). "He has committed to us the word of reconciliation. Therefore, we are ambassadors for Christ, as though God were entreating through us; we beg you on behalf of Christ, be reconciled to God" (2 Cor.5:19-20). Again and again Paul hammered home the point that we are ambassadors for Christ. The Sovereign Lord has designed that man be in partnership with Himself in bringing to pass His purposes for mankind and creation.

A Theology Conforming to the Bible

Biblical theology is a theology in conformity with the whole Bible. The text is first dealt with on its own terms, rather than by issues raised by philosophical and sociological impositions. It constantly points the student to the central theme of Scripture—God's redemptive mission in, through, and by Jesus Christ. There is no other savior but Jesus Christ. A biblical theology of mission shows that the realization of God's purposes will be fulfilled in none other than Jesus Christ. He is the Way, the Truth and the Life (Jn.14:6). He alone is

> the radiance of [God's] glory, the exact representation of His nature, and upholds all things by the word of His power. When He had made purification of sins, He sat down at the right hand of the Majesty on high;... until I make thine enemies a footstool (Heb.1:3,13).

There is no other source of truth, nor any other way to salvation. Paul could only say, "by Him all things were created, both in the heavens and on earth, visible and invisible, whether thrones or dominions or rulers or authorities—all things have been created by Him and for Him" (Col.1:16).

A Theology of Action

Recognizing that all is God's, the people of God can only humbly and gratefully accept God's mandates to carry the glorious message of salvation to the nations because:

When the kindness of God our Savior *and His love for mankind* appeared, He saved us, not on the basis of deeds which we have done in righteousness, but according to His mercy, by the washing of regeneration and renewing by the Holy Spirit, whom He poured out upon us richly through Jesus Christ (Tit.3:4-6, emphasis added).

A biblical theology of missions is an active theology because it recognizes a God who acts purposefully to redeem people from every tongue, tribe, and nation. The God who speaks in revelation is the same God who acts in human history.

Our understanding of God's redemptive purposes have all too frequently been based on a few select New Testament passages. Even these have been misconstrued to the point that only some of God's people are involved in His worldwide purposes, while others prepare themselves for the "ivory palaces–concentrating on staying well prepared for the second coming of Christ" (Edward Lorek in <u>Pulse</u>, Aug.24,'90). For the most part, Scripture is used primarily as a source book for spiritual diets and successful living. Obeying the statutes and judgments of God brings its own reward, but the idea that God should want His people to impress the world with His glory is a foreign concept to most Christians. It appears that disciple-making is designed mainly to help people live the good life, rather than march in step with the Lord of Glory, calling all powers and people to submit to His Lordship. By and large, the few favorite New Testament Great Commission passages soon lose their power to motivate, and the search for elitist knowledge "to put life together" becomes the major focus of most Christians. Discipling programs, preaching, and all other spiritual activities are generally valued as ends in themselves—accepted as contributions to the development of the spiritual life of the trainee, whether or not the disciple is challenged to encounter a godless world for the sake of Jesus Christ (Rom.1:5). Biblical theology will soon dispel such fallacies.

The observation of George F. Vicedom that "the Bible in its totality ascribes only one intention to God–to save mankind" (Vicedom 1965:4) is alien to most Christians. George Peters poignantly states:

The study of Christian missions has been for centuries a separate and distinct discipline not usually considered to be material for the theologian or the pastor. In fact, most theologians and pastors passed by courses in missions and ignored mission literature and matters of mission organization. The church, the pastor, and the theologian often remained detached, if not aloof, from mission studies and mission movements (Peters 1972:25).

If, however, God has but one intention, the reconciliation of lost humanity to Himself, then we need to ask what He is saying to us as we seek to walk obediently.

God's people in both the Old and New Testaments are commissioned to go into all the world and declare His glory in all nations. The task of the Church is to deploy models who will be effective witnesses to the glory, majesty, and power of the only God. This God was revealed in Jesus Christ our Lord, and is resident in and among His people through the Holy Spirit.

Chapter 3

MISSIONS AND

CREATION

Because God stands before all history and creation, a biblical theology of missions must start with God's intentions in His creative acts. Why did God bring the universe into being? Why did He create the earth and all that dwells on it? To begin to know God and to understand His purposes for creation, we must observe God creating.

Perspectives from Creation

First and foremost, the Bible presents God as dynamic in His creation and in His continuing rule. He has acted and continues to act in His created world. God has by His own authority and power created all things: "Heaven is My throne, and the earth is My footstool...For My hand made all these things. Thus all these things came into being" (Is.66:1-2; cf. Job 38:4-7; Ps. 104:1-30).

God acted on "darkness" and "void." No circumstance was beyond His intervention or is beyond His re-creation. Out of "darkness" and "void" He brought forth "good." All-powerful, He is not limited to mere means to accomplish His purposes. His word was sufficient; He spoke and it was done. The record gives absolutely no hint of an evolutionary process. God "spoke" His creation into being:

> Then God said, "Let there be light"; and there was light.... "Let there be an expanse in the midst of the waters";... and it was so .... "Let the earth sprout vegetation";... and it was so .... "Let the waters teem with swarms of living creatures, and let the birds fly above the earth".... "Let the earth bring forth living creatures after their kind";... and it was so (Gen.1:3-24).

Again, when God created man, He gave no indication of any sort of evolutionary process. On the contrary, it is precisely stated that He created man "of dust from the ground" (Gen.2:7) in His own image: "Let Us make man in Our image, according to Our likeness; and let them rule ... over all the earth";.... And God saw all that He had made, and behold, it was very good (Gen.1:26-31).

The Creator wanted only the best for His creation. It was flawless as He originally planned and produced it. "And God saw all that He had made, and behold, it was very good" (Gen.1:31). In His creative act as owner of the universe, He assigned each element its place; as each element reflected its meaning in relationship to the whole, it fulfilled the purpose for which God made it. None dared stand apart from each other, yet each one had its own kind of life. While creation displays the unity of a vast, inter-related and interdependent cosmological system, it also possesses a seemingly limitless variety of forms and functions, both organic and non-organic. By looking at its different parts, we see the limits, but also the tremendous potential of creation. We see this clearly in the mandate given to Adam and Eve and their posterity before the Fall to "tend the garden" and rule over the earth as stewards of God. "Fill the earth, and subdue it; and rule over ... every living thing that moves on the earth" (Gen.1:28).

God's response to His world was to observe. Once He had completed His creation, He assessed His work. He saw it to be well-suited to the purpose for which He had created it: "And God saw all that He had made, and behold it was very good" (Gen.1:31). Furthermore, He expected His creation to be an ongoing expression of His wisdom and glory. Submitting to its God-given potential, it reflects the wisdom and majesty of its Creator. The Psalmist declared: "The heavens are telling of the glory of God; and their expanse is declaring the work of His hands. Day to day pours forth speech, and night to night reveals knowledge"(Ps.19:1-2). He blessed His creation, giving man, beast and field the power to reproduce and the energy to grow and develop—all to the praise of His glory! Paul observed, "For by Him all things were created, both in the heavens and on earth, visible and invisible, whether thrones or dominions or rulers or authorities—*all things have been created by Him and for Him*" (Col.1:16, emphasis added).

Creation, however, is not an extension of God's being. He made it to have its own existence. Hence, the Bible totally rejects pantheism. Although creation cannot function apart from God, it stands apart from Him. Paul stated that "He is before all things" but that "in Him all things hold together" (Col.1:17); and the writer to the Hebrews pointed out, "He...upholds all things by the word of His power" (Heb.1:3). The biblical record does not allow creation to be personified and deified. Its goodness flows from the perfection of the One who created it and is realized as it fulfills its intended purpose. Creation is there to serve and not to be served; it is there to benefit man as he fulfills the purpose for which God created him. Thus we read,

> Behold, I have given you every plant yielding seed that is on the surface of all the earth, and every tree which has fruit yielding seed; it shall be food for you; and to every beast of the earth and to every bird of the sky and to every thing that moves on the earth which has life, I have given every green plant for food (Gen.1:29-30).

Creation as the work of God attests to the fact that He is not competing with any other god. He stands before all else. He alone is Creator, sustainer, and planner for His creation. God conquers, forms, and directs powers to accomplish His purposes. The record declares:

> To whom then will you liken God? Or what likeness will you compare with Him? As for the idol, a craftsman casts it, a goldsmith plates it with gold, and a silversmith fashions chains of silver .... Do you not know? Have you not heard? Has it not been declared to you from the beginning? Have you not understood from the foundations of the earth? It is He who sits above the vault of the earth, and its inhabitants are like grasshoppers, who stretches out the heavens like a curtain and spreads them out like a tent to dwell in. He it is who reduces rulers to nothing, who makes the judges of the earth meaningless.... "To whom then will you liken Me that I should be his equal?" says the Holy One. Lift up your eyes on high and see who has created these stars, the One who leads forth their host by number, He calls them all by name; because of the greatness of His might and the strength of His power not one of them is missing (Is.40:18,19,21-23,25, 26).

The Bible rejects any notion of dualism. God alone is Creator, Sustainer, and Master Designer of all of creation!

Although the Bible says God rested from His works, His was not a rest of exhaustion, but of completion. He did not rest out of weakness or indolence, but continued to sustain all He had made by His dynamic power. Resting, He awaits a response from His creation—the realization of its full potential when everything will "ascribe to the Lord glory and strength. Ascribe to the Lord the glory due to His name; ...

41

and in His temple everything says, 'Glory!' " (Ps.29:1,2,9).

God has no intention of abandoning that which He has called into existence out of nothing. He will continue to work within and through creation until the day that it fulfills its intended purpose.

The Mission of God in the Creation of Man

Creation demonstrates that man has a very special relationship to both God and His creation. In God's providence, He has placed man at the center of His purposes for all His creation, appointing him to maintain creation and have dominion over it (Ps.8). Apart from man, creation will not realize its full potential; he has been endowed with the ability to "unwrap" creation's built-in potential. In this respect, man is the steward of all creation. This is a responsibility for which man will be held accountable. Eichrodt observes that "the basic phenomenon peculiar to man is consciousness of responsibility" (1951:9). In order to fulfill his responsibility as "tender of the garden" and "his brother's keeper," man was given the capacity to have a spiritual, personal relationship with God. Moreover, his highest calling was to enjoy deep communion with God Himself. Only when he has this intimate relationship with God and submits obediently to Him does he realize his full humanity.

Made in the image of God, man is to take responsibility, be accountable, plan, love, communicate, create, and re-form his environment, as well as to be mutually accountable and responsible for his fellow man. When he exercises these God-given abilities, man reflects God's wisdom and glory. God's image in man, therefore, endowed him with the potential to be a *co-creator* with God. As man serves obediently in dependence upon God, he will not only know His blessing, but will present all his works, including the works of his hands, as gifts to Him. Thus God, not man, will receive all the glory for whatever he does. In this regard Paul says: "Whether, then, you eat or drink or whatever you do, do all to the glory of God" (1 Cor.10:31).

Man was created immortal, and that immortality draws him to reach for horizons beyond anything known by the rest of creation. When this longing is directed to realizing God's purposes, all creation will benefit. Righteousness and peace will be man's reward in this life, and God's commendation, "Well done," in the life hereafter. The key to all creation's realizing its full potential is man's submission to God's purposes for him and all that is entrusted to his care.

42

Implications for Human Existence

The implications are obvious. We were created to walk with God, but our relationship with Him does not end there. We are to be actively involved in God's purposes for all creation, "unwrapping" creation so it will realize its inherent good, to the glory of God.

A biblical theology of missions propounds God's heart's desire to bring all of mankind back into an intimate relationship with Himself. It calls us back to hear and to heed our Maker's mandate to identify ourselves completely with Him in the accomplishment of this glorious and all-consuming mission.

To believe that we must merely respond to biblical truth in some "religious" way for our own personal benefit is to vitiate biblical Christianity. In a very real sense, we were created for others—to be God's friends and stewards of creation, but never owners or sole beneficiaries of the resources entrusted to our care. Only selfish, anarchical thinking will keep us from accepting our responsibilities and carrying out our proper duties. Of those who reject this responsibility we read, "Depart from Me, accursed ones, into the eternal fire which has been prepared for the devil and his angels;.... And these will go away into eternal punishment..." (Mt. 25:41,46).

God has endowed us with capabilities to be used for others, for His glory. The Owner will hold us accountable for the way we use, or abuse, our position. The parable of the talents graphically illustrates this truth. The concept of stewardship is so important that Jesus Christ associated its implementation with personal service to Him. It is noteworthy that He immediately follows this parable by stating how He expects us as His steward-disciples to respond to those in need:

> For I was hungry, and you gave Me something to eat; I was thirsty, and you gave Me drink; I was a stranger, and you invited Me in; naked, and you clothed me; I was sick, and you visited Me; I was in prison, and you came to me. "Then the righteous will answer Him, saying, "Lord, when did we see You hungry, and feed You, or thirsty, and give You drink? ....And when did we see You sick, or in prison, and come to you?" And the King will answer and say to them, "Truly I say to you, to the extent that you did it to one of these brothers of Mine, even the least of them, you did it to Me" (Mt.25:35-40; cf. Gal.6:10).

That all men will be held accountable for their actions is beyond question, as Jesus proceeds to point out in graphic terms in the verses immediately following:

"Depart from Me, accursed ones, into the eternal fire which has been prepared for the devil and his angels; for I was hungry, and you gave Me nothing to eat; I was thirsty, and you gave Me nothing to drink; I was a stranger, and you did not invite Me in; naked, and you did not clothe Me; sick, and in prison, and you did not visit Me." Then they themselves also will answer, saying, "Lord when did we see You hungry, or thirsty, or a stranger, or naked, or sick, or in prison, and did not take care of You?" Then He will answer them, saying, "Truly I say to you, to the extent that you did not do it to one of the least of these, you did not do it to Me." And these will go away into eternal punishment, but the righteous into eternal life"(Mt.25:41-46).

This theme is constantly reiterated in Scripture. "Behold, the Lord came ... to execute judgment upon all, and to convict all the ungodly of all their ungodly deeds which they have done in an ungodly way...." (Jude 14,15; cf. Ps.92:7-9; Heb.9:27; 10:27; cf. Jer.1:16). Paul reminded Christians, "we must all appear before the judgment seat of Christ, that each one may be recompensed for his deeds in the body, according to what he has done, whether good or bad" (2 Cor.5:10).

Missiological Considerations

Now we begin to see why Israel and the Church received the evangelistic and cultural mandates. Both are rooted in creation: the biblical record describes redeemed man's role in God's ongoing program for all ages. Underlying God's creative acts are some truths which significantly speak to the cause of missions. The following demand careful reflection and application.

Creation, in essence, is *an initial demonstration of God's continuing creative providence.* Following the Fall of man, God's providence centers on His concern for man, that man may be led to trust and glorify His name. God's providence is also redemptive. Respecting Abel, God said to Cain, "Where is Abel your brother?" (Gen.4:9); and then in response to his complaint about his judgment, "the LORD said to him, `Therefore whoever kills Cain, vengeance will be taken on him seven-fold' " (Gen.4:15). When God saw that "the wickedness of man was great on the earth, and that every intent of the thoughts of his heart was only evil continually," (Gen. 6:15) He instructed Noah to build an ark and said, "But I will establish My covenant with you; and you shall enter the ark—you and your sons and your wife, and your sons' wives with you" (Gen.6:18). The Psalmist, reflecting on God's compassionate concern for mankind, observed:

The LORD is gracious and merciful; slow to anger and great in lovingkindness. The LORD is good to all, and His mercies are over all His works. All Thy works shall give thanks to Thee, O LORD, and Thy godly ones shall bless Thee. They shall speak of the glory of Thy kingdom, and talk of Thy power; to make known to the sons of men Thy mighty acts, and the glory of the majesty of Thy kingdom. Thy kingdom is an everlasting kingdom, and Thy dominion endures throughout all generations. The LORD sustains all who fall, and raises up all who are bowed down. The eyes of all look to Thee, and Thou dost give them their food in due time. Thou dost open Thy hand, and dost satisfy the desire of every living thing (Ps.145:8-16).

And Paul declares, "...do you think lightly of the riches of His kindness and forbearance and patience, not knowing that the kindness of God leads you to repentance?" (Rom.2:4)

Creation reveals that *the infinite God is greatly concerned for all His creation.* "And the LORD God planted a garden toward the east, in Eden; and there He placed the man whom He had formed ... to cultivate it and keep it" (Gen.2:8,15). Of the post-Fall earth the Lord said to Himself:

"I will never again curse the ground on account of man, for the intent of man's heart is evil from his youth; and I will never again destroy every living thing, as I have done. While the earth remains, seedtime and harvest, and cold and heat, and summer and winter, and day and night shall not cease" (Gen.8:21-22).

In His concern God established parameters to maintain His creation's welfare.

He Himself gives to all life and breath and all things; and He made from one, every nation of mankind to live on all the face of the earth, having determined their appointed times, and the boundaries of their habitation, that they should seek God, if perhaps they might grope for Him and find Him, though He is not far from each one of us; for in Him we live and move and exist... (Acts 17:25-28).

And yet He is prior to His creation: "Before the mountains were born, or Thou didst give birth to the earth and the world, even from everlasting to everlasting, Thou art God" (Ps.90:2); "He established the earth upon its foundations ... He sends forth springs in the valleys ... He causes the grass to grow for the cattle, and vegetation for the labor of man, so that he may bring forth food from the earth..."(Ps.104:5,10,14).

Standing apart, God cares for His creation which is totally dependent upon Him.

Creation, being of God, *is full of His purpose.* Man, made in the image of God, was to "cultivate and keep" God's creation. Endowed by God with creative abilities, he was to "unwrap" creation's potential— its "good" which God had placed within it. In so doing, man would reflect God's glory. But post-Fall man has abdicated his responsibility for creation in general, and for his fellow man in particular. Thus God repeatedly reminded His people, "I will take you for my people, and I will be your God" (Exo.6:7); with a view "to be a people for His own possession" (Dt.4:20). Being God's possession relates to doing God's will: "And you shall do what is right and good in the sight of the LORD, that it may be well with you...." (Dt.6:18). Paul puts it all in perspective when he tells Christians, "walk as children of light (for the fruit of the light consists in all goodness and righteousness and truth) trying to learn what is pleasing to the Lord" (Eph.5:8-10). He also speaks of Christians as "a people for His own possession, zealous for good deeds" (Tit.2:14). God's ultimate purpose is that all creatures should manifest the Creator's glory and that He should rejoice in His works: "Let the glory of the LORD endure forever; let the LORD be glad in His works" (Ps.104:31). This is the underlying imperative of the evangelistic and cultural mandates to which redeemed men, in obedience, commit themselves. The book of Revelation parts the curtains and shows the accomplishment of that glorious purpose—redeemed mankind and all creation stand before the Redeemer, and all rejoice together.

Creation as recorded in the Bible *reflects a dynamic concept of divine activity.* Step by step God prepares the earth for man. First, God creates light, separating it from darkness; then the land masses surrounded by oceans; next vegetation; the heavenly bodies; animal life in sea and sky, followed by animal life on earth; and finally, man.

The God who creates is dynamic in all He does. He works progressively with man and has not withdrawn from man or the rest of His creation. He is not an absentee god: "The kingdom is the LORD'S, and He rules over the nations" (Ps.22:28); "The LORD has established His throne in the heavens; and His sovereignty rules over all [the universe]" (Ps.103:19). This counters a static view of human existence. In His ongoing program to restore His creation to Himself, He continues to work positively, powerfully, and purposefully among men. He is loving, orderly, and progressive in His activity. Jesus said, "My Father is working until now, and I myself am working" (Jn.5:17).

From the creation account it becomes clear that the central focus of it all is man who is at the center of God's all-encompassing purposes. Creation demonstrates that the infinite God can be and is in relationship with finite man. God and man are able to communicate with each other, an indispensable requirement for establishing relationships. Prior to the Fall, God interacted with man.

> The LORD God commanded the man, saying, "From any tree of the garden you may eat freely; but from the tree of the knowledge of good and evil you shall not eat, for in the day that you eat from it you shall surely die." And the LORD God fashioned into a woman the rib ... and brought her to the man. And the man said, "This is now bone of my bones, and flesh of my flesh" (Gen.2:16,17,22, 23).

Furthermore, the post-Fall account shows that God wants a relationship with man. When Adam and Eve hid from God, "The LORD God called to the man, and said to him, 'Where are you?' And he said, 'I heard the sound of Thee in the garden, and I was afraid because I was naked; so I hid myself' " (Gen.3:9-10).

God's image in man, though marred because of the Fall, further establishes a point of contact with man. Man may therefore achieve, though imperfectly, God's purposes for creation. No other creature bears this distinctive or has been entrusted with God's mandate to tend creation. God, therefore, concerns Himself with man, who is central to His Divine activity.

The creation record, in which man figures so largely, *sets the stage for the whole Bible.* So significant is man to the fulfillment of God's purposes for creation, that it is for man's sake, and for God's reconciliation to man, that the Lamb was "slain from the foundation of the earth" (Rev.13:8 see margin; cf 1 Pet. 1:19-20). Man is of utmost worth to God and His purposes. Therefore, He is "not wishing for any to perish but for all to come to repentance" (2 Pet.3:9).

The creation record does not, however, fall into a humanistic anthropocentrism. Yes, man is central in all ages, but only one Man, Jesus Christ, is central to all ages. Man is to witness to Him and not to himself.

> "You are My witnesses," declares the LORD, "and My servant whom I have chosen, in order that you may know and believe Me, and understand that I am He. Before Me there was no God formed, and there will be none after Me. I, even I, am the LORD; and there is no savior besides Me. It is I who have declared and saved and pro-

claimed, and there was no strange god among you; so you are My witnesses," declares the LORD, "and I am God.... The people whom I formed for Myself, will declare My praise" (Is.43:10-12,21).

The Psalmist points out that even ungodly men know they are held accountable to God:

> But to the wicked God says, "What right have you *to tell of My statutes, and to take My covenant in your mouth*? For you hate discipline, and you cast My words behind you. When you see a thief, you are pleased with him, and you associate with adulterers. You let your mouth loose in evil, and your tongue frames deceit" (Ps.50:16-19, emphases added).

To mankind is committed the stewardship of creation (Gen.1:26,28; Ps.8:6). Supremely, however, Christians are entrusted with "the word of reconciliation. Therefore, we are ambassadors for Christ, as though God were entreating through us; we beg you on behalf of Christ, be reconciled to God" (2 Cor.5:19-20).

Creation emphasizes *the validity of all peoples*. All are of worth to God. Even after Cain murdered his brother, God in mercy kept him from the same fate. Amidst the tragic results of the Fall, God continued to act in restraint and mercy. Before Abraham's posterity would possess the promised land, God decreed a time of grace before judgment came to Canaan, because "the iniquity of the Amorite is not yet complete" (Gen.15:16). God evaluated all mankind impartially (Ps.50:1,4,7,16,17,21; cf. 2 Sam.14:14). The Pauline concepts of the unity and duty of all men are consistent with the creation account. Paul sums it up by saying: "He made from one, *every nation of mankind* to live on all the face of the earth, having determined their appointed times, and the boundaries of their habitation, *that they should seek God*" (Acts 17:26-27, emphasis added).

Creation *rules out all forms of theological dualism and pantheism.* God alone is sovereign over and distinct from His creation. Neither man nor any of the rest of creation are extensions of God, as most other religions teach. God alone is "in the beginning" (Gen.1:1).

The creation account is *basic to understanding God's purposes for the world*. God prepared the world for man and man for the world. Within that context, man's relationship to God is established and man's role in God's mission is determined. Man was made to have fellowship with God—to know Him. He also has been given a mandate of stewardship—to rule over the works of God's hands. His task is to subdue, rule, and maintain God's creation and in the process *to make Him known* for who He is— "you are My witnesses. Is there any God besides Me, or is there any other Rock? I know of none.... I, the LORD, am the maker of all things" (Is.44:8,24).

In His ongoing plan for man and creation, God used neither transitional device nor apology for linking His creative activity by narrative and genealogy to Israel's fathers, the Patriarchs. God's program is continuous and purposeful. He alone is sovereign and directs history to accomplish His purposes. Says the Psalmist, "The earth is the LORD'S, and all it contains, the world and those who dwell in it" (Ps. 24:1). He, the Creator, Owner and Director, will bring about His program for all creation, in spite of man's willful disregard of God and His plans. Thus the Psalmist could declare:

> By the word of the LORD the heavens were made, and by the breath of His mouth all their host.... Let all the earth fear the LORD; let all the inhabitants of the world stand in awe of Him. For He spoke, and it was done; He commanded and it stood fast. The LORD nullifies the counsel of the nations; He frustrates the plans of the peoples. *The counsel of the LORD stands forever, the plans of His heart from generation to generation* (Ps.33:6-11, emphasis added).

God will accomplishes His mission shall be accomplished. His plans for creation cannot be thwarted. Those who respond to Him in faith will know His deliverance: "Behold, the eye of the LORD is on those who fear Him, on those who hope for His lovingkindness, to deliver their soul from death" (Ps.33:18-19). All mankind stands equal before an impartial God. Zephaniah recorded:

> "Indeed, My decision is to gather nations, to assemble kingdoms, to pour out on them my indignation, all my burning anger; for all the earth will be devoured by the fire of My zeal. For then I will give to the peoples purified lips, that all of them may call on the name of the LORD, to serve Him shoulder to shoulder" (Zeph.3:8,9).

He is the God of the nations. He did not create in vain. It is for redeemed man to seek God's counsel, and to attempt to do God's will in all of life.

Yes, God has commanded man to be responsible for His creation. But how can redeemed man be God's effective ambassador? We need to look at the unique nature God has placed within man which makes him a responsible moral being.

CHAPTER 4

MISSIONS AND THE

NATURE OF MAN

Man was created for God's purpose, but even more significantly, man is a representation of God's image. In and through man God would identify more closely with His creation. God determined to have a visible representation of Himself in creation saying, "Let Us make man in Our image, according to Our likeness; and let them rule...over all the earth" (Gen.1:26). Although we may never fully know what the image of God represents, there are characteristics separating man from the rest of creation, causing him to be of great worth to God and His purposes.

A Spirit-Being

Man's creation differs from the rest of creation. "Then the LORD God formed man of dust from the ground, *and breathed into his nostrils the breath of life*; and man became a living being"(Gen.2:7, emphasis added). The difference between animal and human life hinges on God's specific action of breathing into man the breath of life (For a comprehensive discussion on the nature of mankind, see Dyrness 1979:84-96). Man has been given the breath of God—spirit-life. Soul-life gives man emotions, reasoning, and volition. Spirit-life provides the capacity to know, love, worship, trust, and glorify God. Man's body enables him to have world-consciousness. Man's soul endows him with self-consciousness, while the spirit of man gives him a capacity for God-consciousness. When the spirit of man is in a right relationship with God and exercises control over body and soul, man knows wholeness of life. Paul makes this wholeness a prayer focus: "Now may the God of peace Himself sanctify you entirely; and may your spirit and soul and body be preserved complete, without blame at the coming of our

Lord Jesus Christ" (1 Thess.5:23). Although none can fully explain the meaning of "the image of God," it does mean man has more than soul-life. Man's spirit-life reveals an essential nature unlike the rest of the animal kingdom. It puts him in contact with the spirit world and the possibility of fellowship with God.

The Expression of God's Character

God, having made man in His own likeness, enabled him to "mirror" Himself. In spite of his sin nature, man may be *a reflection and expression of God's character*, although finitely. The potential is there, but at best is reflected imperfectly. Because man has some elements of God's nature and is a spiritual as well as a physical being, he wants what provides spiritual satisfaction. So in order to realize his full humanity, man must be in harmony with and dependent on God. Even without that harmony, Paul reminds us, "in Him we live and move and exist" (Acts 17:28). Man was made for God and is totally dependent upon Him. Only God can fill his spiritual void, to make man truly and fully human.

When man reflects his true humanity, in a limited way he expresses God's character. In New Testament terms, man subjecting his spirit to God will walk in the Spirit and be known for the fruit of the Spirit reflected in his life (Gal.5:16-25). But there are also other dimensions which will involve man in God's larger purposes for creation.

To mirror God, man must act like God. He must be "godly" in his actions: "you shall be holy for I am holy" (Lev. 11:45; 19:2; 1 Pet. 1:16). What is God like in His actions toward man? The Bible says God is committed to His creation and seeks only its best, and especially man's welfare. This is seen, first, in the way God set about accomplishing His immediate purposes in creation (Gen.1:31) and then revealed repeatedly throughout biblical history. God acted with great benevolence and restraint toward a creation gone awry. Man's initial rebellion against God received a promise of redemption and the covering of animal skins (Gen.3:15,21). Later, Moses' encounter with God in Exodus 33 and 34 reflected God's benevolent, righteous character. In response to Moses' request to be assured of God's accompanying presence, the Lord descended and called out His own name, which represented His character:

"The LORD, the LORD God, compassionate and gracious, slow to anger, and abounding in lovingkindness and truth; who keeps lovingkindness for thousands, who forgives iniquity, transgression and sin; yet He will by no means leave the guilty unpunished, visiting the iniquity of the fathers on the children and on the grandchildren to the third and fourth generations" (Exo.34:6-7).

To mirror God's character, man must show compassion toward those in rebellion against God. He, too, must be gracious, slow to anger, abounding in lovingkindness, but not sentimentality. God does judge sin, but He desires man's restoration. God's attributes must be reflected in man's response to God's creation and specifically to his fellow man. The reflection of these attributes will at best be imperfect because of sin in man's life. To model God's character, he must be an "imitator...of God ... walk[ing] in love ..." (Eph.5:1-2), manifesting "the sweet aroma of the knowledge of Him in every place. For we are a fragrance of Christ to God among those who are being saved and among those who are perishing; to the one an aroma from death to death, to the other an aroma from life to life" (2 Cor.2:14-16). God desires ongoing fellowship with His creation; even in its rebellion, He still sets about reconciling it to Himself. That same character must be reflected in redeemed man if he claims a relationship with God. Being an expression of God's character is a purposeful activity and not merely the reflection of a godly disposition. To be anthropocentric in his concerns, man must first of all be theocentric in his orientation.

God is relational intrinsically, being Father, Son, and Holy Spirit, and He created man to be relational. The essence of man's humanity reveals that he was created with a capacity to respond to God. Man was made for communication with God, and cannot exist meaningfully without communicating with God and others. From the very beginning in the garden, Adam and Eve knew daily contact with God (Gen.3:3,9,11,13). They talked with Him and He with them. Throughout Scripture God speaks to man and seeks his response. In His desire to re-establish communication, God's mercy will tolerate man's rebellion until all avenues of restoration have been rejected. Thus Moses could reflect on God's concern for the Amorites, "for the iniquity of the Amorite is not yet complete" (Gen.15:16). God's "slowness to anger" has in view man's restoration to Himself (cf. 2 Pet. 3:1-15).

Although God will spare no means to re-establish that contact, man does not have God at his disposal. God initiates, and man is constituted so that he can respond. Man is not fully man without relationship with God—a relationship of total dependency. Only in relationship does man know completeness, bringing peace to himself and his fellow man.

Man's social capacity cannot be experienced apart from God or others. When God is absent from his life, man places an inordinate burden for his personal fulfillment on others, using others to meet his insatiable need for recognition and affirmation, without reciprocating. Adam and Eve could complement one another because they were in fellowship with God. Together, in relationship with God, man and woman formed "Man [mankind]" (Gen.5:2). An animal will never be a suitable companion for man because it cannot complement man—it can at best only supplement man's need to express affection for something outside of himself. This may very well be the reason Satan motivates man to idolatry, in which man lavishes his affection on idols: "He also makes a god and worships it; he makes it a graven image, and falls down before it" (Is.44:15).

Despite the face-to-face intimacy of his imparted life (Gen.2:7) and the security of a garden (Gen.2:8), man also needs recognition from his fellows and the affection of loved ones in order to experience his humanity positively, meaningfully, and constructively. Generally, man may be drawn to others in service, or in search of self-fulfillment. However, when he is in relationship with a God who meets his innate needs, man will serve altruistically, seeking to meet the needs of his fellows.

Man, being in God's image, is more than a social creature in need of meaningful relationships. Though his sin nature has brought restrictions, man has an enormous *spiritual capacity*, and his greatest satisfaction comes from activity expressing it. This kind of activity will stimulate his creativity. God endowed man with creative faculties of far-reaching potential, which are realized in part as he seeks to unlock creation's potential (Gen.4:21-22). More significantly, man gets spiritual satisfaction directing his efforts to the benefit of his fellow man. Man has been created with the potential to care for God's creation that he might be a responsible steward. His nature is to find something or someone and lavish his attention on that thing or person. But he will only realize true spiritual satisfaction when he *fulfills his stewardship*, in the consciousness of God's presence, under God's direction, for God's glory (Ps.8).

Furthermore, *man gets spiritual satisfaction using his intellectual capacity to interact with spirit beings*. In this regard, God gave specific instructions to protect man from exploitation by evil spirit beings (Dt.18:9-15). Scripture recognizes that man is susceptible to spirit-to-spirit communication, especially when he seeks a word on the baffling, the mysterious, or the future. God warns:

"You shall not learn to imitate the detestable things of those nations. There shall not be found among you anyone who ... uses divination, one who practices witchcraft, or one who interprets omens, or a sorcerer ... or a medium, or a spiritist, or one who calls up the dead" (Dt.18:9-11).

Demons work deliberately to overthrow God's Word and work. To consort with them and their human dupes is to enter their conspiracy against God. Man is therefore counseled to interact with God only (Dt.6:4-5). God communicates with His people most frequently than not, through His validated (Dt.18:21-22) agents:

The LORD ... will raise up for you a prophet ... you shall listen to him.... And the LORD said ... "I will put My words in his mouth, and he shall speak to them all that I command him.... But the prophet who shall speak a word presumptuously in My name which I have not commanded him to speak, or which he shall speak in the name of other gods, that prophet shall die" (Dt.18:15,17,18,20).

Such possible interaction between God and man, spirit and spirit, confirms man's enormous spiritual capacity. This spiritual capacity enables intimacy with God and may serve to seal his relationship with God (Dt.6:18;7:6; cf. Ps.27:4-10), but it could also work his downfall (Dt.32:15-18).

The creation account does not provide us with a comprehensive answer to the mystery of the composition of man's nature, but the whole Bible underscores the significance of that nature. Man is shown to be *a psychophysical organism*, not a soul and spirit merely in a body. If the body is not well, the soul is distressed and the spirit hindered. Man is a single being. Man cannot be understood or approached apart from his wholeness as a psychophysical being. In this respect, man reflects the image of God, who is a tri-unity in one person. Any interaction with man must keep this wholeness in focus.

All these attributes set human nature apart from creation and underscore why man may be a reflection of God's character. Man's uniqueness shows that he was made for God. Man is of such great concern to God that God spared no means to reconcile him to Himself. In New Testament terminology,

This is good and acceptable in the sight of God our Savior, who desires all men to be saved and to come to the knowledge of the truth. For there is one God, and one mediator also between God and men, the man Christ Jesus, who gave Himself as a ransom for all, the testimony borne at the proper time (1 Tim.2:3-6).

An Extension of God's Presence

Man also has the capacity to be *God's representative.* Man behaves as truly human only when he consciously functions in the presence of God, accepting himself as God has endowed him for meaningful relationships and service, rejoicing in his potential under God. Man made in God's image, therefore, also represents Him to the rest of creation. God has delegated to man such amazing authority (Gen.1:26), and obedient man, dependent on God, has "presence" in the face of all challenges before him. Such godly presence serves as the "light" and "salt" of the earth. It brings into the human context God's sacred presence of blessing—righteousness, justice, peace, kindness, joy, and grace. Man is thus challenged to do on earth what God does in heaven (Mt.6:10).

Man was placed on earth to be an image bearer of God, to show what it means to maintain this world for God's glory (Gen.1:26-28). God placed man in Eden "to tend and keep it" (Gen.2:15). Before Adam, there was no man to "cultivate" (lit. "serve") the ground (Gen.2:5). The Hebrew text of Genesis 2:15 should better be rendered, "The LORD God ... put him in the garden for serving and keeping." In the context, this applies to taking care of the garden, but more is suggested. Moses used these same words ("serving" and "keeping") when speaking of man's responsibility for serving the LORD (Exo.23:25; Dt.10:20) and keeping His commands (Exo.15:26; Dt.4:40). This suggests a twofold purpose for God's image on earth: man is to *care for* God's physical creation *and serve* God in obedience.

But man's yielding to Satan's temptation has led to selfishness and exploitation; only God's common grace motivates man to a measure of concern for creation and keeps him from destroying everything. Instead of ruling over God's creation as His vice-regent, man is ruled by the creature Satan. Thus man's first purpose, to care for the earth, is rendered difficult, and his second purpose, to serve and obey God, is made impossible. But in providing redemption, God invites man back into a relationship with Himself, a relationship in which the creature finds fulfillment with creation and its Creator. Only then can man effectively serve and obey God and, though imperfectly, represent Him through the Holy Spirit's enabling.

As God's image bearer, man does not have to seek power or exercise self-initiated authority to be God's vice-regent. Rather, he gladly accepts his stewardship of creation and exercises his God-given abilities to serve God and others. *When he serves in utter dependence upon God, he brings God's authority to bear on every situation* (Mt.6:9-10). Thus, Christian man who fulfills the mandate to serve and to keep lives in a relationship that can begin to undo, in part, the effects of the Curse (Gen.3:14-19).

An Exhibit of God's Power

The opening pages of Scripture leave no one in doubt about God's power, and man has been created to exhibit that power. If man is to achieve God's purposes for man and for God's creation, he must have power. God certainly intended this when He gave man dominion over all creation (Ps.8). This reference to power is, however, closer to the authority derived from man being God's image bearer. This power is not inherent, but a delegated power which grants man authority to execute his mandated responsibility for God's creation. The theme of power starts in creation and continues throughout the Bible. It has significant implications for a biblical theology of missions. Moses, Gideon, Samuel, David, Elijah, Elisha, Peter, and Paul all confronted spiritual powers and saw them yield. Each acted in the confidence of God-delegated authority and in the process communicated the power of God. God's authority implies power, but only as given by God for His purposes. Moses, responding in obedience to God, could confidently face the gods of Egypt and call them to account before God.

> Magic was inextricably bound up with Egyptian religion, which was demon-controlled idolatry. The miracles performed by the magicians were manifestations of evil supernaturalism, similar to demon powers operative in spiritism and occultism (Unger 1967: 91).

Using delegated authority, Moses brought God's power to bear on each manifestation. Each plague discredited a pagan god. The plagues were power demonstrations which were:

> A series chiefly of natural phenomena, unusual in their severity, in that all occur within one year, in their accurate timing, in that Goshen and its people are spared some of them, and in the evidence of God's control over them, overcame the opposition of Pharaoh, discredited the gods of Egypt and defiled their temples (Tenney 1967:659).

The pagan gods could not withstand God's servant who exposed their weakness when confronted by God's power. The *serpents'* powers (Exo.7:6-13) were defeated when Aaron's rod swallowed them. The gods of the Nile, Hapi or Apis the bull god, Isis the goddess of the Nile, Khnum the ram god and guardian of the Nile, all had their habitat become blood and the living in it die (Exo.7:14-25). Heqet, the frog-headed goddess of birth, could not prevent the appearance of many frogs (Exo.8:1-15). Set, the desert god, could not safeguard the people from gnats (Exo.8:16-19). The Egyptians had to recognize their defeat when they referred to the plague as "this is the finger of God," a reference to the "power of God" brought to bear upon them by God's servants. Re, a sun god, or the god Uatchit, possibly represented by the fly, could not keep people from the misery inflicted by flies (Exo.8:20-32). Hathor, the cow-headed goddess, and Apis the bull god, both symbols of fertility, could not prevent the death of the cattle (Exo.9:1-7, especially verse 6). Sekhmet, the goddess with power over disease, Sunu, the pestilence god, and Isis, the goddess of healing, could not prevent or cure the affliction of boils (Exo.9:8-12). Nut, the sky goddess, Osiris, the god of crops and fertility, and Set, the god of storms, could not control the weather, nor prevent hail (Exo.9:13-35). Nut and Osiris could not save the people from the locust plague, either (Exo.10:1-20). Ra, a sun god, Horus, also a sun god, Nut, and Hathor, also a sky goddess, were unable to prevent darkness from enveloping the land (Exo.10:21-29). Min, the god of reproduction, Heqet and Isis, the goddesses who protected children—even Pharaoh's firstborn son, considered to be a god—were helpless in preventing death, the death of the first born (Exo. 12:29-30). All the gods of Egypt went down in ignominious defeat before God's obedient servants (cf. Unger 1967:91-93).

There is no power, no god, no spirit which can withstand God's power mediated through God's obedient people. Man was created to be an exhibit of God's power, His delegated authority over all God's creation, and the same mandate applies today. Bringing the Gospel to sin-enslaved people demands such delegated authority to confront the powers holding people in bondage (Eph.2:1-2; 2 Cor.4:4) and in the captivity of Satan's domain (Acts 26:18; cf. Acts 13:8-12; 16:16-24; Col.1:13; 2 Tim.2:26).

Appointed to Accountability

Man, with such remarkable potential, *stands under obligation* to carry out his commission (Gen.1:26-28). God has purposed that man take on responsibilities for which he will be held accountable.

Vice-regent: God has called man to act as His vice-regent, under Himself, over all the earth, doing what God would do. He is to direct, develop, and maintain for God's glory God's "good creation." He is to subdue the earth, domesticate it, and fill it with his presence and creativity (Gen.1:23-28 cf. Ps.8:3-6).

Co-operator and co-developer: God enlisted man's co-operation by giving him a "nameless" world and inviting him to complete it (Gen.2:19). That "nameless" world also represents the rest of God's creation, which is to be put to useful purposes. God gave man the ability to unlock the secrets of this world and harness them for God's glory and his own benefit. This started in the garden and is seen in the record of the application of human skills in domesticating physical elements (Gen.4:17-22). Man has enormous creative potential, an innate ability, bestowed on him by God, to be used for God's glory.

Co-creator: Man is to act under God to help uncover and direct the potential of each element of creation, especially the family. He is under obligation to procreate, to spread his influence throughout the earth, to "be fruitful and multiply" (Gen.1:28).

Co-commander: Man is to have authority over the world. The commands of Genesis 1:26-27; 2:15, 18-25 mark the beginning of a stream of obligations for proper administration that widens and deepens as it courses through Scripture. The first obligations God placed on man relate to his social existence: family and community, law and order, culture and civilization. Concerning his environment, man was to subdue, till, and guard it (Gen.1:28; 2:15). In regard to authority structures, including the family, man was commanded to exercise control (govern) over the earth: "rule ... over every living thing that moves on the earth" (Gen.1:28).

After the Fall, another dimension was added to man's responsibility, especially as it relates to his fellow man. It came into greater focus when God commissioned Israel to be His priest nation (Exo.19:5-6). Redeemed man was to be a *"gap-filler," a priest standing before God on behalf of his fellow man.* Man is now under obligation to stand between God and all that is alienated from Him. Man is in touch with earth, but not fully. He is also in touch with God, but not fully. Nevertheless, his role as priest appears frequently in the biblical record. For example, it is referred to in God's promise of a Deliverer (Gen.3:15); in God's enquiry of Cain regarding Abel (Gen.4:9): it is intimated in the Noahic account (Gen. 6, 7; cf. 1 Pet. 3:19-20); in the Abrahamic covenant (Gen.12:1-3); and specifically given to Israel at Sinai (Exo.19:4-6). The prophet Ezekiel also refers to this obligation, "And I searched for a man among them who should build up the wall and *stand in the gap before Me for the land,* that I should not destroy it; but I found no one" (Ezek.22:30, emphasis added).

All men everywhere are held accountable for these obligations—none will be excused, regardless of office in life or sphere of influence. God appointed *all men to be vice-regents* over His creation; all are to participate responsibly. That man will be held accountable is beyond question. There will be a day of reckoning: "Behold, the Lord came with many thousands of His holy ones, *to execute judgment upon all,* and to convict all the ungodly of all their ungodly deeds which they have done in an ungodly way...." (Jude 14-15, emphasis added). Concerning the redeemed through Jesus Christ, we are reminded: "For we must all appear before the judgment seat of Christ, that each one may be recompensed for his deeds in the body, according to what he has done, whether good or bad" (2 Cor.5:10); and "to one who knows the right thing to do, and does not do it, to him it is sin" (Jas. 4:17).

A biblical theology of missions takes man's nature seriously. This nature enables man to respond positively to God's mandates in the opening chapters of Genesis. These instructions are given to men in general—and all will be held accountable. Man cannot abdicate these responsibilities with impunity.

In endowing man with such a unique nature and placing upon him such high obligations, God revealed His universal concern for creation. This concern extended to all people and was reflected from the first in His self revelation (Gen. 6:3-8; ef. Gen. 12:3). Therefore the wrath of God, as expressed in the flood, is not inconsistent with His purposes for man and creation. Man will be held accountable for abdicating his responsibilities.

CHAPTER 5

MISSIONS AND THE

FALL OF MAN

Man's created nature enabled him to have intimate fellowship with God and allowed him to determine his own responses to the world. He was endowed with the ability to choose between good and evil, meaning he had the potential to respond positively or negatively, and become the barrier to fellowship with God and others. God risked creating such a creature because He wanted part of His creation to have meaningful, purposeful fellowship with Himself. If God had not created man the way He did, man could very well deny responsibility for his actions, thereby removing moral responsibility from himself.

The ability to respond volitionally to fellowship with God and others gave man a special place in creation. Man is not a higher primate with more evolved animal instincts. Man is neither in kinship with the world of nature nor an extension of it. Man is uniquely different from the rest of creation (although he may share certain physical and even psychical characteristics with the rest of creation). Man can know genuine volitional interaction with another being. This ability to make choices, to respond volitionally, is the very essence of being a moral agent. Man as a moral being is personally responsible for his actions.

The Option of Choice

The moral capacity to choose, after the Fall, is now enhanced to know good and evil. This is an attribute of God: "Then the LORD God said, Behold, the man has become like one of Us, knowing good and evil" (Gen. 3:22). In recognition of this enhanced moral capacity Paul affirms, "God is now declaring to men that all everywhere should repent, because He has fixed a day in which He will judge the world in righteousness" (Acts 17:30-31). The importance of choice is perhaps even more clearly illustrated in Joshua's counsel to Israel:

> "Now, therefore, fear the LORD and serve Him in sincerity and truth; and put away the gods which your fathers served.... And if it is disagreeable in your sight to serve the LORD, choose for yourselves today whom you will serve: whether the gods which your fathers served ... or the gods of the Amorites ... but as for me and my house, we will serve the LORD" (Josh.24:14-15).

God's redemptive activity centers on His desire that man be liberated from the consequences of wrong choices—choices now strongly influenced by man's sin nature. How can man, subject to a sin nature, ever respond positively to God? Both the Old and New Testaments underscore that God takes the initiative in approaching man and then calls upon man to volitionally respond to Him: "*Turn* to Me, *and be saved*, all the ends of the earth; for *I am God*, and there is no other" (Is.45:22, emphases added); "I take no pleasure in the death of the wicked, but rather that the wicked *turn from* his way and live. Turn back, turn back from your evil ways" (Ezek.33:11, emphases added); and, "But as many as received Him, to them He gave the right to become children of God" (Jn.1:12). God will not violate man's moral capacity. Man must exercise his God-given ability to choose to submit to God. Paul brings in focus man's ability to choose and the need to confront him with a decision:

> "WHOEVER WILL CALL UPON THE NAME OF THE LORD WILL BE SAVED." How then shall they call upon Him in whom they have not believed? And how shall they believe in Him whom they have not heard? And how shall they hear without a preacher? And how shall they preach unless they are sent? (Rom.10:13-15)

These factors are foundational to, and at the heart of, a biblical theology of missions. It is God who seeks man. It is God who sends man to declare His desire for man to be saved. It is God who will work within man but who expects man to respond volitionally to His summons to be saved. God takes the initiative to restore man to Himself, and God has endowed him with the ability to choose for or against Him. The results of choices made have affected the quality of human life, man's search for meaning, and his relationship with his fellow man and the spirit world. Man's choice determines his ultimate destiny. The ability to choose underlies God's determination to effect man's salvation and restoration to fellowship with Himself.

The Moral Test

To establish what kind of nature man had received, the idyllic setting of a garden became the place for testing his morality. The Garden of Eden had beauty, utility, and (of greatest importance) the tree of the knowledge of good and evil. The encounter with another of God's creatures would provide the setting to test man's moral response. This ability made man responsible to and accountable before God, his Creator.

The Probation of Man

God's probation of pre-Fall man involved providing an alternative to fellowship with Himself. God willingly risked that possibility by giving man the potential to reject or obey Him. For the welfare of His creation, God established parameters for man living in His presence. Man was not to be absolute master of all. God gave him a limited commission concerning His creation; man was to carry it out only by God's permission. If man would know God's blessing, then he must live by God's directives:

> Then the LORD God took the man and put him into the garden of Eden to cultivate it and keep it. And the LORD God commanded the man, saying, "From any tree of the garden you may eat freely; but from the tree of the knowledge of good and evil you shall not eat, for in the day that you eat from it you shall surely die" (Gen.2:15-17).

The consequence of the wrong choice is death. Moses appeals to Israel to choose to keep God's statutes and judgments, thereby reflecting the character of God:

> "See, I have taught you statutes and judgments just as the LORD my God commanded me.... *So keep and do them,* for that is your wisdom and your understanding in the sight of the peoples who will hear all these statutes and say, `Surely this great nation is *a wise and under-standing people.*' For what great nation is there that has a god so near to it as is the LORD our God whenever we call on Him?" (Dt.4:5-7, emphases added)

Following man's Fall, God still appeals to man's volition (Gen.9:1-7), affirming man's capacity to respond, even though his sin nature works moral inertia.

The Consequence of Sin

The nature of sin leads man to believe his sin will not have negative consequences. With a choice of a face-to-face relationship with God or a separate existence in defiance of God, man chose the latter without considering the dire outcome. So he would now have to wrestle daily with limited knowledge, the pressures and urges of physical appetites, and values deduced from a created world in defiance of its Creator. The result was not only exclusion from God's presence but death stalking man in all pursuits, both now and in the life to come. Man became hopelessly trapped in his sin and forever beyond the help of anyone save God Himself. Apart from the Creator God intervening to reverse the effects of man's choice, God's purposes for His creation would be lost. But why was it necessary to man's well-being for God to act redemptively?

The Nature of Sin

How does sin reveal itself in a man's life? What is the "fruit" of man's deciding against God? The following characteristics of sin seem to be the most important.

Substitution of Self-Knowledge

The nature of sin was, and continues to be, determined by man deciding what is good and evil, without reference to God. It is an attempt to essentially be "like God, knowing good and evil" (Gen.3:5). When man listened to the serpent, he deliberately "chose" to exercise his own judgment and thus substituted his self-knowledge for God's revelation knowledge. Man was given the option to choose between God's directives or his own understanding. Paul described the negative consequences of sin: "For even though they knew God, they did not honor Him as God, or give thanks; but they became futile in their speculations, and their foolish heart was darkened" (Rom.1:21); and then again, "just as through one man sin entered into the world, and death through sin, and so death spread to all men" (Rom.5:12).

Sin incites man to imagine that with his self-knowledge he can deal with the world on his own terms: he does not need God (Gen.3:5); his own knowledge is sufficient (Gen.3:11, cf. Rom.1:28); his own purposes come first (Gen. 3:6; Is. 53:6); his own rule is adequate (Gen.4:23,24); he is his own master (Gen.11:3-6). When man substitutes his own knowledge, or sight knowledge, for God's revelation knowledge, he sins. By contrast, God's revelation knowledge affirms, "Delight yourself in the LORD and He will give you the desires of your heart" (Ps. 37:4); "The fear of the LORD is the beginning of wisdom, and the knowledge of the Holy One is understanding" (Prov. 9:10).

Moral Inertia

Sin produces within man an apparent inability to do what is right. The nature of sin causes man to blame anyone or anything other than himself. Man denies, or refuses to take, moral responsibility for his actions. As a result, sin has spoiled and soiled a world made good, affecting every area of life. Sin is infectious and progressive, and even as man is made not to live alone, so he does not sin alone. Man's rebellion spreads to all, and all are implicated and contaminated: family (Gen. 4); society (Gen. 6:5); culture (Gen. 9,10); and finally, the whole world stands in rebellion against God (Gen. 11).

Moral inertia characterizes all people, affecting all of life: "All have turned aside, together they have become useless; there is none who does good" (Rom. 3:12; cf. Ps. 53:1-3); "Then Joshua said to the people, `You will not be able to serve the LORD, for He is a holy God. He is a jealous God...' " (Josh. 24:19); "Then the sons of Israel did evil in the sight of the LORD, and served the Baals, and they forsook the LORD ... and they followed other gods from among the gods of the peoples ... and bowed themselves down to them" (Judg. 2:11-12). The emphasis of the biblical record is on temptation now being part of man's environment. Rather than resisting temptation, man usually yields to it. It is as if he cannot keep himself from making wrong choices. The sin principle is deeply entrenched within man: "Then the LORD saw that the wickedness of man was great on the earth, and *that every intent of the thoughts of his heart was only evil continually*" (Gen. 6:5 emphasis added).

Manipulation

Man's thought life and, subsequently, physical appetites, came under both the manipulation of his sin nature and, ultimately, demons: "Sin is crouching at the door; and its desire is for you" (Gen.4:7). Paul spoke of the world, the flesh, and the devil manipulating man to do their bidding (Rom. 12:2; 1 Cor. 2:12; 3:19; Gal. 3:1; 4:3,8,29; 5:17;19-21; 6:8; Eph. 2:2; 6:12; 2 Tim. 4:10; cf. Jas. 4:4; 1 Jn. 2:16-17; 4:1). By yielding to Satan's temptation, man has allowed his thoughts and appetites to be exploited by the demonic:

> And you were dead in your trespasses and sins, *in which you formerly walked according to the course of this world, according to the prince of the power of the air, of the spirit that is now working in the sons of disobedience.* Among them we too all formerly lived in the lusts of our flesh, indulging the desires of the flesh and of the mind (Eph.2:1-3, emphasis added);

> ...they may come to their senses, and escape from the snare of the devil, having been *held captive by him to do his will* (2 Tim.2:26, emphasis added).

In turn, sinful man manipulates his world for his own selfish purposes. In some ways man is also a victim of outside forces encouraging him to express his sinful nature. Man is strongly motivated, if not compelled, to exploit his fellow man (Gen.4:4-10; cf. Dt.15:9-15; 25:13-19); nature (Dt.22:6-7, 9-10; cf. Ps.107:34); and God (Dt.8:1-20; cf. Ps.106:13-39). He wants to overpower everything and everyone for selfish ends.

The Bible is silent concerning the creation of the spirit world, but not man's relation to it. Scripture does not detail much about man and the angelic hosts, whether good or bad. However, it clearly illustrates that the spirit world does influence human government and society.

> And he said to me, "O Daniel, man of high esteem, understand the words that I am about to tell you and stand upright, for I have now been sent to you." And when he had spoken this word to me, I stood up trembling. Then he said to me, "Do not be afraid, Daniel, for from the first day that you set your heart on understanding this and on humbling yourself before your God, your words were heard, and I have come in response to your words. But *the prince of the kingdom of Persia was withstanding me* for twenty-one days; then behold, Michael, one of the chief princes, came to help me, for I had been left there with the kings of Persia" (Dan.10:11-13, emphasis added; cf. Eph.2:2; 6:12; 2 Cor.2:11; 4:4).

There are powers—the world, the flesh and the devil—determined to keep man in bondage to himself, his appetites, his limited self-knowledge, manipulating him to believe he is doing the right thing (Prov.14:12).

Alienation

One of God's creatures set itself against the good purposes of God for creation. By deceit and cunning, he alienated man from God. By contradicting God's instructions, Satan sought to knit a relationship of estrangement which would lead ultimately to death. The devil effectively disguised himself (2 Cor.11:3,14) and approached man with seemingly innocent questions. He cast doubt on God's statutes (Gen.3:1), then drew man into a rational dialogue contradicting God's promise (Gen.3:4-5). Satan's purpose was to draw man to himself, incur God's wrath, and destroy man (Is.14:16-17; cf. Jn.8:44; 1 Pet.5:8). Not only would he rob God of the glory due His name (Ezek. 28:2,6; cf. Ezek. 28:12-17; Is. 14:13,14), but he would set up a counter kingdom to oppose God in everything and ultimately seek to destroy God's creation.

Sin made alienation and estrangement normative. Sinful man approaches others with a sense of alienation already in place, and none escape it. Broken relationships are part of human existence because man became self-centered and sought for self-enhancement, frequently at others' expense. When man seeks relationships and intimacy with others, generally the motive is for others to meet his insatiable thirst for affirmation and approval. Sadly, none are exempt from this motivation. If his will does not triumph, man withdraws from meaningful interaction. This affects man's response to God: he hides from God (Gen.3:8-10), and acts negatively toward his mate (Gen.3:12), and toward his fellow man (Gen.4:8).

Rejection of Responsibility

Man rejected his responsibility, abdicated his role as vice-regent, and allowed evil to prevail. He refused to maintain creation for God's glory. The result? The world began to fall apart. In relationships, man refuses to be his brother's keeper: " 'Where is Abel your brother?' And he said: 'I do not know. Am I my brother's keeper?' " (Gen.4:9) Sin causes man to reject responsibility for others and to believe he is not accountable for them. He stands alone and even thinks he is not responsible for himself. His approach to others and to himself is indifferent.

Sin is under the influence of the powers of darkness, but not to the point that man is absolved of responsibility for his choices. Man's sin nature and its interrelationship with evil powers (Eph.2:2) destroys his "humanness." Cain's response to Abel (Gen.4:7-8), Lamech's perversion of government (Gen.4:23,24), man's rule over creation being constantly challenged and regained at great cost—sweat, toil, thorns (Gen.3:17-19)—and man's humiliating return to "dust" in death (Gen.3:19) all illustrate the tragic consequences of sin.

Man's sin avoids responsibility and accountability. Man accuses others—"*the woman*"—for his failure. He even blames God—"the woman *Thou gavest me*"—believing that the Creator Himself has programed his responses, his sin, his failure, or his obedience and success (Gen.3:12). Ultimately, sin causes man to deny responsibility for his actions.

Willful Rebellion

By willful, deliberate rejection of God's revelation knowledge—His authority——man transfers his allegiance from the God of creation to the worship of creation itself. Behind this idolatry lie the powers of darkness (Dt. 32:15-17; 2 Cor. 4:4). The power of false religion is nothing short of Satan's power through demonic activity (1 Cor.10:19-21). From now on man must not only contend with his own fallen nature, he must reckon with evil powers determined to destroy him.

The Old Testament records the revolt and results of man's choice:

> When the woman saw that the tree was good for food, and that it was a delight to the eyes, and that the tree was desirable to make one wise, she took from its fruit and ate; and she gave also to her husband with her, and he ate. Then the eyes of both of them were opened, and they knew that they were naked ... and the man and his wife hid themselves from the presence of the LORD God (Gen.3:6-8);

> Then he forsook God who made him, and scorned the Rock of his salvation. They made Him jealous with strange gods; with abominations they provoked Him to anger. They sacrificed to demons who were not God, to gods whom they have not known, new gods who came lately, whom your fathers did not dread. You neglected the Rock who begot you, and forgot the God who gave you birth (Dt.32:15-18);

> Has the LORD as much delight in burnt offerings and sacrifices as in obeying the voice of the LORD? Behold, to obey is better than sacrifice, and to heed than the fat of rams. For rebellion is as the sin of divination, and insubordination is as iniquity and idolatry. Because you have rejected the word of the LORD, He has also rejected you from being king (1 Sam.15:22,23).

The New Testament expounds man's subsequent depravity and guilt before God:

> Not everyone who says to Me, "Lord, Lord," will enter the kingdom of heaven; but he who does the will of My Father who is in heaven. Many will say to Me on that day, "Lord, Lord, did we not prophesy in

Your name, and in Your name cast out demons, and in Your name perform many miracles?" And then I will declare to them, "I never knew you; depart from Me, you who practice lawlessness" (Mt.7:21-23);

There is none righteous, not even one; there is none who understands, there is none who seeks for God; all have turned aside, together they have become useless; there is none who does good, there is not even one. Their throat is an open grave, with their tongues they keep deceiving, the poison of asps is under their lips; whose mouth is full of cursing and bitterness; their feet are swift to shed blood, destruction and misery are in their paths, and the path of peace have they not known. There is no fear of God before their eyes ... all have sinned and fall short of the glory of God... (Rom.3:10-18,23).

God's statutes and judgments were never intended to be barriers– legal restrictions to fellowship with God. On the contrary, God's laws defined and protected that fellowship. Those who are to stand in the presence of a holy God must realize that a particular behavior attends and expresses the character of that relationship. The parameters for relationship with God are based on revelation knowledge, which arises with God, not with man. But man's sin nature rejects God's revelation knowledge and establishes its own righteousness in rebellion against God.

The Results of Sin

The judgment on sin is not only a future certainty, but a present reality (Gen.4:14-24). Man may not believe that his sinning brings bad consequences now or hereafter, but sin carries the seeds of dissipation, dissolution, and destruction. The principle "whatever a man sows, this he will also reap" (Gal. 6:7) encompasses all life—present and future. The tragic consequences of sin abound in every sphere of human exis- tence: "every transgression and disobedience receive[d] a just recom- pense" (Heb.2:2). Man receives the just rewards of what he does in and through his own body.

Disruption which leads to Corruption

Man's fall released disruptive tendencies within him which have led to chaos and disintegration: "Then the LORD saw that the wick- edness of man was great on the earth, and that every intent of the thoughts of his heart was only evil continually" (Gen.6:5). Man's sin is in itself God's judgment: "God gave them over in the lusts of their hearts to impurity ... to degrading passions ... to a depraved mind"

(Rom.1:24,26,28). If man does not submit to God's will, he will realize the negative results of his choices. In the process, man destroys himself and everything dear to him. The personal choice to ignore God's will affects not only the individual but everyone else in contact with him.

Man disrupts and corrupts the relationships most important to his existence. *God-ward*, he hides himself (Gen.3:10). *Mate-ward*, he knows a certain amount of tension (Gen.3:12, cf.3:16) and hides behind fig-leaves, symbolizing the many masks he wears even as he blames his mate for his alienation and estrangement. *Toward others* man engages in comparison and competition, which lead to insecurity. Man takes advantage of others, wearing masks, playing games, destroying his own humanity and that of others (Gen.4:5-10; 23-24). *Toward the environment* man neglects his commission to "keep" this earth in God's place. Instead, man either exploits his environment or subjugates himself to it. God gave Israel careful instructions to maintain the environment lest the people destroy it and themselves.

Judgment

The judgments following the Fall demonstrated God's wrath and proclaimed God's continued sovereign control of His creation.

God's judgment of sin brought immediate *humiliation*. The serpent was forced to crawl on its belly (Gen. 3:14). Man, intended for immortality, was humiliated by having his body returned to the earth in death (Gen.3:19). Idolatry, man's substitute self-knowledge for God's revelation knowledge, brought humiliation as man worshiped animals, himself, and perverted appetites (Rom.1:18 ff.)—which was in itself a judgment. Man defamed and defiled himself by responding more to his animal instincts than his God-given spirit (Gen.4:8,23;6:5-12). He became a pathetic spectacle, totally humiliated by sin.

The marriage relationship became prone to *tensions*. Man now became vulnerable to the pressures of lower drives. For the woman, it was the drive of "desire"; for man, the motivation for "domination" (Gen.3:16). Fulfillment was now sought in each other, rather than God. There was confusion of roles; each manipulated the other to realize "fulfillment." The tragic effects of the Fall may be a description of the marriage pattern, but not a biblical prescription for it. [In Christ man and woman can begin to undo, however incompletely, the effects of the Fall (Eph.5:21-33; 1 Pet.3:1-12)]

Life became an unending *struggle* filled with pain, bitterness and hardship. These are a constant reminder of the judgment which came because of man's disregard for God's commands (Gen.3:16-19; cf. Job 5:7).

Even more significant, man's expulsion from the garden was a *dismissal from God's presence* (Gen.3:22-24). Man was created to live in God's presence forever and can never realize full humanity outside of it. Regardless of his many attempts through ritual and liturgy, man is totally unable through his own efforts to re-enter God's presence. Man is a religious being and will be driven to his own approaches to the supernatural, but no amount of religious activity can secure God's presence. Only as God takes the initiative will man be allowed to enter His presence (Gen.6:13-7:4; Gen.12:1-4;cf. Jn.6:35-40; 65). Man is to respond in faith to God. This is to be a deliberate choice on man's part, and only at God's invitation (Jn.5:24-25; cf. Eph.2:8,9). Man's moral failure was to be redeemed by Christ's sacrifice (Jn.12:23-33). Outside of God man lives in a religious vacuum which he desperately tries to fill with almost anything—the material, the physical, the psychological, the spiritual—but all without God.

God created within man a desire for someone greater than himself. Man's inner being has an innate spiritual void—a *dissatisfaction* which only God can fill. This spiritual dissatisfaction sends man on religious pursuits to find sources to meet the inner need. Man senses he is a spiritual being; he has a deeply felt need to relate to a supernatural being. There are spiritual beings ready to fill that vacuum and man, unfortunately, is easily deceived into believing that they intend his welfare. These spirits of deception will do all they can to "steal, kill and destroy" (Jn.10:8-10).

Missiological Considerations

The Fall affects all: innate sin, as well as acts of sin, characterizes mankind. Therefore a biblical theology of missions must take note of the following:

The Fall means that *all are subject to death*. As far back as we can go, man's sin brought death. So death has come to characterize life, literally and figuratively, and man lives in fear of it (Heb.2:14).

Further, man's *defiance and depravity characterize all of life*. Man lives in disregard, indifference and ignorance (if not rejection) of God's love. Man's sinful nature enslaves him to acts of sin (Rom.1:24,26,28). He chooses darkness, suppresses the truth, and persists in sinning; *all he does is influenced by sin.*

In spite of man's defiance and depravity, *God has not withdrawn Himself from the human arena*. He continues to superintend history, not for man's contentment, but for his redemption. The goodness of God, shown in His continued working in human history, is to bring man to repentance (Rom.2:4; Ps.67:1ff). He controls history to give man an opportunity to repent (Acts 17:30; 2 Pet. 3:9).

God's common grace continues to reach out to man. God is long-suffering to the point that society may be humanized, even by unbelievers. God desires that men live in peace that all may seek God (1 Tim.2:2-4). In spite of human depravity and rebellion, God's purposes for His creation will not be frustrated.

God's glory is a basic consideration in calling man to repentance. The Bible never underestimates the sinfulness of man nor the awful consequences of sin. Where there is no repentance, sin will receive its just reward; still God will receive the glory. However, man is called to ascribe glory to God, and only repentant man can do so by offering God the praise due His name (Eph.3:10,21).

God's intervention in the affairs of man reveals the magnitude of His mercy and grace. God has not abandoned human society–the social, economic, and political structures—to be the undisputed domain of Satan. The extent of that mercy and grace can only be appreciated against the backdrop of the horrible picture of sin and rebellion (Rom.3). In spite of man's sinfulness, God persists in entering man's sphere to bring about reconciliation, both vertically and horizontally. God wants man in fellowship with Himself, and He desires that people live together in brotherly kindness. Repentance brings regeneration, which produces transformation, which brings about the humanization of society. Only as man heeds God's call to repent and submits to God does he stop dehumanizing his fellow man and relate properly and purposefully to others and his environment. Because of God's great grace and mercy, *the Great Commandment* (Mt.22:37-38) *is inseparable from the Great Commission* (Mt.28:18-20).

From the start of human history, there have been *forces opposing God and seeking man's destruction.* The Bible shows the reality of forces set against God realizing His purposes. The biblical record recognizes the existence of Satan, demonic spirits, and fallen angels (Dt.32:17) as part of the created order (Mk.5:2-10; 1 Cor. 10:19-21; 2 Thess.2:9). There are the gods of the nations, powers of chaos and evil spirits, false doctrines and teachers, and social structures organized by Satan (Is.41:23; 42:17; Dan.10:12,13). These agents of darkness appear on a continuum from people used by evil powers to actual appearances of Satan (Job 1:12; Zech.3:1; Lk.4:6; 11:17-26). From the Old Testament to the New Testament increasing attention is directed toward the powers of darkness—the gods of the nations, encounters with satanic powers in the thought systems of the world, increasing wickedness, the demonization of people—until the struggle climaxes in the final battle (Rev. 19:19-20). These forces bring great fear upon people (Heb. 2:14-15) and are determined to keep them from God (2 Cor.4:4). They oppose humanity (2 Cor.2:11; Eph.6:11-12) and seek our destruction (1 Pet.5:8).

The above factors give shape to both the message and method for implementing the evangelistic and cultural mandates. They focus on four themes which are traceable throughout the Old and New Testaments: God's concern for all peoples (the nations); His desire to liberate (save) all peoples; His commission to His people to be witnesses to who He is; and the fact of conflict and confrontation with the kingdom of darkness.

CHAPTER 6

MISSIONS AND THE

WRATH OF GOD

The Genesis flood confronts man with the fact that God judges sin (Gen.6-9). When man's sin reached proportions that even the long-suffering God could no longer endure, judgment was inevitable. God's just and righteous character demands a response of wrath to persistent sin. God takes sin seriously in whatever form it may appear—personal or corporate. Yet the wrath of God is not without mercy (Hab.3:2). Before He judges, He warns (Gen.6:1; Jon. 1:2). God commissioned Noah to herald the coming judgment as well as to offer an escape, symbolized by the ark. God desires that none should perish, but should man reject His offer of salvation, God's judgment is inevitable.

The universal flood also foreshadowed another day of universal judgment. Sin does not escape God's attention. Biblical judgment has a moral basis. Man's sin or righteousness affects himself, society, and the environment. Man does not live to himself; through his behavior man impacts others for good or evil (Gen.6:5-22; cf. 2 Cor.2:15-16).

God's Wrath and Man's World

The world operates by laws, both physical and moral. Disregarding either brings negative results and at times dire judgment. Of the two, the moral laws of God are more far-reaching and lasting in their impact on man and his structures. Man cannot escape the consequences of sin unless God intervenes.

Physical Laws

The earth, from its creation to its demise, operates by laws. Although God's creation was perfect, man's sin damaged all of it. All creation "groans and suffers," anxiously awaiting freedom from its slavery to corruption, which will come at "the revealing of the sons of God" (Rom.8:19). Creation now awaits the freeing of man from the curse of sin.

God's laws are subject to God and are not absolutely immutable. In the flood, we see what appears to be the breaking of an immutable law: had not God commanded the dry land to appear and the land to be separated from the waters (Job 38:8-11)? But the depths of the earth were opened, and a "flood against laws" brought God's judgment on all creation. Periodically God intervenes and suspends His own appointed laws in the physical realm to produce the miraculous. God's purpose is man's redemption. The miracles in both testaments relate directly to God's concern to see man delivered from sin.

God's suspending a physical law—the waters overtaking the boundaries of the land—directly resulted from God's concern for creation (Gen.6:9; cf. Gen.8:1). The flood, though enormously negative, was not totally counterproductive. Man's depravity had almost succeeded in insulating him from fellowship with God. In judgment, God suspended a physical law (Job 38:8-11) as "the water of the flood came upon the earth ... all the fountains of the great deep burst open, and the floodgates of the sky were opened. And the rain fell upon the earth for forty days and forty nights" (Gen.7:10-12). Through the flood, God chose to give humanity another opportunity to respond in saving faith. God's invitation to man to enter the ark by faith and escape the flood was an appeal to him as a moral creature made in the image of God. Man was again confronted by choice.

This judgment also demonstrated God's concern for mankind in another way. Without the flood, man would have destroyed himself and his environment. The problem was with man, not the earth. But by giving man a renewed environment, God was willing to place him on probation a second time. Perhaps in a more propitious environment—a renovated earth—man could more readily respond to God. In the same vein, Paul exhorted Christians to pray for all in authority and for all men "that we may lead *a tranquil and quiet life* in all godliness and dignity. This is good and acceptable in the sight of God our Savior, who desires all men to be saved and to come to the knowledge of the truth" (1 Tim.2:2-4, emphases added).

Moral Laws

God's blessing upon His people in every sphere of life has always been contingent upon their active commitment to His statutes and judgments (Dt.5:29; 6:18):

"If I shut up the heavens so that there is no rain, or if I command the locust to devour the land, or if I send pestilence among My people, and My people who are called by My name humble themselves and pray, and seek my face and turn from their wicked ways, then I will hear from heaven, will forgive their sin, and will heal their land" (2 Chron. 7:13,14).

But this principle is not limited to God's people. It is applicable to all mankind. God so structured man's world that there is a relationship between moral and physical laws. The one is contingent on the other. Man's spiritual condition affects his environment. God will turn "a fruitful land into a salt waste, because of the wickedness of those who dwell in it" (Ps.107:34). When man disobeys God's moral laws, physical laws go against him.

God ordered man's interpersonal relationships, even though these are given form by culture, to hinge on moral laws applicable to all men. Man is responsible for his fellow man (Gen.4:9). The prophet Isaiah spoke of the fast God has chosen. Is it not, he asked,

"to loosen the bonds of wickedness, to undo the bands of the yoke, and to let the oppressed go free, and break every yoke? Is it not to divide your bread with the hungry, and bring the homeless poor into the house; when you see the naked, to cover him; and not to hide yourself from your own flesh? Then your light will break out like the dawn, and your recovery will speedily spring forth; and your righteousness will go before you; the glory of the LORD will be your rear guard. Then you will call, and the LORD will answer.... if you give yourself to the hungry, and satisfy the desire of the afflicted ... you will be like a watered garden, and like a spring of water whose waters do not fail" (Is.58:6-11).

Just as physical laws regulate the universe and provide order, so man is controlled by an inherent moral consciousness. This derives from man's God-given conscience, which is now almost totally controlled by the sin nature. When man violates his innate moral law, given for his welfare, he receives negative results within his person, which then affect the larger community. Man neither lives in isolation nor sins in isolation. Moral laws are a safeguard of man's relationship with all of God's creation. If man abuses God's creation, it will cost him. Proper biblical ecological awareness is part of moral consciousness.

Having God's moral law on his conscience, man knows that things such as killing, stealing, and adultery are wrong and violate his dignity and humanity. Deep down he knows he cannot violate these moral laws and escape the penalties. He cannot abuse himself or others without reaping the consequences. God's wrath is built into the moral law and comes into play when that law is violated. No matter how much man is forgiven, he still reaps the negative results induced by sin. For instance, the Bible says honoring parents results in long life; the anger, bitterness, or rebellion (Eph.4:26-27,31) felt while dishonoring parents produce very negative results which affect the quality of physical life . Sin has a built-in negative "reward."

Summary Judgment and Moral Law Judgment

There is a distinction between what may be termed "summary judgment" and "moral law judgment." God judged the earth summarily in the flood and will do so in the future (2 Pet.3:10). But these dire judgments are preceded by warning, as in the sending of Jonah to Nineveh. On the other hand, moral law judgment is part of everyday life. It takes effect immediately, affecting the quality of life of both the sinner and those around him. Indeed, what a man sows he reaps (Gal.6:7). The wages of sin is death, not only in the future, but even in the here and now.

The biblical record also progressively reveals how the "powers of darkness" operate when God's moral laws are disobeyed. Satan exploits disobedience. Apparently he has been given the right to work death when God's moral laws are disregarded. Scripture seems to infer such a process: "and do not give the devil an opportunity" (Eph.4:27); "Be of sober spirit, be on the alert. Your adversary, the devil, prowls about like a roaring lion, seeking someone to devour. But resist him, firm in your faith" (1 Pet.5:8,9). Man is a responsible moral agent who will be held accountable for breaking God's laws, but in a sense he is also a victim of powers seeking to destroy him.

God's judgment is total. The Bible does not support the false dichotomy of saying that God's wrath is only directed against man's sin, not against man the sinner. God hates "all who do iniquity" (Ps.5:5), as the flood shows. His dealings with the Canaanites and later, with Israel, also illustrate this principle. Israel became God's rod of judgment upon the Canaanites. God not only hated their sin, but the sinners as well, and removed them from His presence. In like manner, though Israel was God's special possession, the Lord carried out His threat of judgment against Israel, using other nations to be His rod of judgment. On occasion He simply destroyed them by physical means. He did not allow them to persist in rebellion. The New Testament affirms this principle, even in respect to Christians. Discussing the communion table, Paul warns, "whoever eats the bread or drinks the cup of the Lord in an unworthy manner, shall be guilty of the body and the blood of the Lord.... For this reason many among you are weak and sick, and a number sleep [are dead]" (1 Cor.11:27,30; cf. 1 Jn.5:16).

God's Objective in Judgment

God's sovereign, all-encompassing control of all of His creation never ceases; His purposes will not be thwarted. Though the flood demonstrated the consequences of disregarding God's moral law, it also introduced God's continued intention to redeem. God desires to reverse sin's effects and deliver man from his just dues. He does not desire the death of man nor his separation from His presence. In Jesus Christ God dealt with man's deserved judgment for sin. Though God's righteousness demanded judgment of sin (Prov. 17:15; Exo. 23:7), Jesus Christ Himself paid, in His own body, the just penalty of man's sin. Through His death and resurrection Christ demonstrated His sovereignty over all the consequences of violating His moral law, so that he could absolve man (Is.53; Rom.3:21-26; 4:4-8,25; 2 Cor.5:21; Col.1:20-22; 2:13-14).

In mercy and grace God seeks those who respond to Him in faith by making moral choices. God's election is not apart from man's moral response to abide in the statutes and judgments of God. From all humanity God found but one, Noah, who "found favor in the eyes of the LORD" (Gen.6:8; cf. 2 Pet.2:5). God commissioned Noah to act on behalf of his own family and all creation for their possible salvation. God's election and man's obedient, faithful response to Him are inextricably inter-related. Enoch, Seth, Abraham, Isaac, Jacob, Joseph, Moses and the rest illustrate this. For those who respond in obedient faith, God willingly intervenes in creation, which is why God raised up Israel to be His priest nation to all nations (Exo.19:4-6; cf. Rom.15:16). "I [God] searched for a man among them who should build up the wall and stand in the gap before Me for the land, that I should not destroy it" (Ezek.22:30).

A biblical theology of missions recognizes the partnership between God and man in effecting redemption. Man is not to be passive in his relationship with God, nor in his response to the needs around him. Election and morality demand a faith-obedience response.

The flood demonstrates God's objective in judging. Sin reaped its consequence, but a God of grace sought to provide an environment in which man might respond in faith (cf. Jer.29:5-7,11). God constantly concerns Himself with man's total environment: physical, social, and metaphysical. This is well-illustrated by Malachi:

> "You are cursed with a curse, for you are robbing Me.... Bring the whole tithe into the storehouse, so that there may be food in My house, and test Me now in this, "says the LORD of hosts," if I will not open for you the windows of heaven, and pour out for you a blessing until it overflows. Then I will rebuke the devourer for you.... And all the nations will call you blessed, for you shall be a delightful land" (Mal.3:9-12).

The point is not so much tithing as living in obedience to God and making Him the priority. In turn, God will bless man with whatever is needed to glorify Him.

Missiological Considerations

God does not sit in instant judgment on man and his sinful deeds. He exercises enormous patience (Gen. 6:3; 15:16; 1 Pet. 3:20). Paul said God's kindness, forbearance, and patience should lead to man's repentance (Rom.2:4). But whenever man disregards God's laws, physical or moral, he suffers consequences in the routine of life. This form of judgment is different from God's deliberate acts of judgment.

God will not persevere with those who persist in sin (Gen. 6:5-7; 7:10-12). There is a limit to God's patience (Gen. 6:3). God would cease to be righteous and His love would be mere sentimentality if He did not take sin seriously (Rom. 6:23; 2 Cor. 5:10; Jas. 4:17). R.G.V. Tasker observes, "The wrath of God is the permanent attitude of the holy and just God when confronted by sin and evil" (Tasker 1968:1341).

The whole world is on probation. Man can and must choose moment by moment to obey or disobey God. Every nation and every culture lies under the curse of man's sin, and man's propensity is to live independently of his Creator. He turns from being God-oriented to being man-oriented, replacing God's revelation knowledge with self-knowledge. The results are perversion and depravity (Rom.1:18-32).

God's concerns and purposes cover both the cultural and evangelistic mandates. Man and his created world are interdependent. Sin brings a curse to the environment and a cursed environment brings death. God desires an environment of total welfare—biblical shalom.

Shalom is a comprehensive word, covering the manifold relationships of daily life, and expressing the ideal state of life in Israel. Fundamental meaning is `totality', `wholeness', `well-being', `harmony', with stress on material prosperity untouched by violence or misfortune (Richardson 1950:165).

The reason for *shalom* is so that man can respond positively to God (1 Tim.2:1-6). God, therefore, commands that "all everywhere repent" (Acts 17:30). Man does not sin in isolation nor does the effect of his sin stop with him alone. This ongoing sin principle, initiated by Adam's sinful act of disobedience, continues to bring death to the human sphere: "by the transgression of the one, death reigned through the one" (Rom.5:17). Man dare not disregard any aspect of God's creation and expect to escape the consequences. Man will be held accountable. Only the spirit of anti-Christ could cause Christians to disregard the obligation to be involved in God's concerns for all of man's environment. God's response to Jonah illustrates:

"For I knew that Thou art a gracious and compassionate God, slow to anger and abundant in lovingkindness, and one who relents concerning calamity. Therefore now, O LORD, please take my life from me, for death is better to me than life...." Then the LORD said, "You had compassion on the plant for which you did not work .... And should I not have compassion on Nineveh, the great city in which there are more than 120,000 persons... as well as many animals?" (Jon.4:2-3,10-11)

God always anticipates a new world. He desires to deliver man and earth from all the bondages of sin (Gen.6:8,17-18; 8:1-22; Rom.8:19-20). God's patience may be tested and resisted, but God does not desire the destruction of all mankind or the world (Gen.8:21-22). God anticipates a new "world", a new life for man, even as He provided for Noah and His family. The personal application of the biblical message must anticipate a changed circumstance—a "new world"—which will enhance man's total milieu. Anything less truncates the biblical message and will bring God's judgment.

God gives redeemed man the responsibility to work out his own salvation. This happens first within and then through the individual (Gen. 9:1-27). Personal salvation is the essential beginning but is not an end in itself. Although only Noah is "righteous before God," he bears an influence and responsibility for his family (Gen.7:1; cf. Acts 16:31), and through his family for all others. Redeemed, regenerated man bears a responsibility for others and their environment.

81

God confirms that, though it is delayed, judgment will come. There awaits a specific day of judgment, as is seen in the later curse on Canaan. But even as the flood was total and worldwide, so the coming judgment will be. None will escape. All men stand in peril if God is not their Lord (Jer.25:15-33). However, God is not willing that any should perish, but that all should be saved (2 Pet.3:9). Therefore, both the certainty of God's desire to save man and the inevitability of a total judgment should be incentives for world evangelization.

God's incentive in judgment is mercy. God gives adequate warning; thus His judgment is tempered with mercy. Noah's 120-year preaching ministry (Gen.6:3) testified to God's mercy: "when the patience of God kept waiting in the days of Noah, during the construction of the ark" (1 Pet.3:20). The prophet Ezekiel confirmed God's mercy toward man: " `As I live!' declares the Lord GOD, `I take no pleasure in the death of the wicked, but rather that the wicked turn from his way and live. Turn back, turn back from your evil ways! Why then will you die...?' " (Ezek.33:11) God's wrath towards sin reflects his justice, but it also demonstrates His mercy and compassion by removing a hostile context and making it easier for man to respond in faith. Judgment in itself may motivate man to repentance or create a climate for reflection on God's just character. Judgment is not an end in itself. It envisions the redemption of creation, leading to a new order and environment.

The inescapable truth apparent in all God's dealings is that *God's glory*—all that God is—*and man's welfare cannot be separated.* This is well-illustrated by Christ in the parables, but especially in Matthew 25: "Truly I say to you, to the extent that you did it to one of these brothers of Mine, even the least of them, you did it to Me" (Mt.25:40). Whoever claims to be concerned for God's glory cannot distance himself from seeking man's total salvation—body, soul, and spirit. Man has been created to live in dignity, reflecting the image of God. Anything preventing this is not only an injustice, but an affront to God and can only be attributed to the works of the devil, which are focused on the destruction of man and his world (Jn.8:44; 10:10; cf. Job 1:12ff.; Rev.12:11-12).

The Noahic Covenant

God's concern for man's welfare is illustrated in His covenant with Noah, which revealed that *the whole of creation had been instituted for man.* The Noahic covenant further demonstrated that *redemption is the basis and reward of faith.* By faith Noah responded to God, acting on God's

Word, believing He would intervene in human history (Heb.11:7). Noah firmly believed that judgment was inevitable, even as God had said: "The end of all flesh has come before Me; for the earth is filled with violence because of them; and behold, I am about to destroy them with the earth" (Gen.6:13).

The covenant also attested that *judgment is purposeful.* It is corrective with a view to a new beginning. In grace and mercy God singled out righteous Noah and offered him a new covenant: "I will establish my covenant with you" (Gen.6:18). The covenant pledged to deliver Noah and his family from the flood to give them a new life beyond the flood, and to keep this covenant in force until the final judgment. The rainbow was to be a worldwide constant, a covenant to all nations. It was a reminder of God's concern for all mankind as well as a guarantee of His faithfulness.

The covenant demonstrated that *reciprocity* (man responding to God, and God responding to man) *is the basis of an ongoing moral relationship* with God. Man was expected to believe and obey God. Noah responded in faith, and God acted in grace: "the LORD closed it behind him" (Gen.7:16). By faith and in obedience, Noah and family entered the ark as God commanded, and He Himself shut the door and guaranteed them safety and a life after the flood. After judgment God remembered Noah and safely landed the ark. Noah expressed his gratitude through sacrifice and worship (Gen.8:20). A dynamic, ongoing relationship with God arises from obedient faith in response to God's word.

The covenant was also *an unconditional promise.* God's acceptance of Noah's act of faith was sealed with an unconditional promise. First, there would be no worldwide catastrophe until the final day of judgment (Gen.8:21; 2 Pet.3:6-7). Second, the reproduction of animal life, in abundance, would continue (Gen.8:17). Third, annual seasons would be fixed for man's and creation's benefit (Gen. 8:22). Although Adam's curse remained (Gen.3:17-19), there was a sense in which the curse of the environment was removed: the soil would be productive—"seedtime and harvest ... shall not cease" (Gen.8:22)—if maintained as God ordained (Gen.1:26-29; 2:15; Exo.23:10-11). Non-production would be man's fault, not God's. At times famines were caused by God's judgment through the word of His prophets (e.g. 1 Ki.17:1-14; 18:1-2). God's common grace extends His providence to all, though man's wickedness will not go unpunished: "He changes rivers into a wilderness, and springs of water into a thirsty ground; a fruitful land into a salt waste, because of the wickedness of those who dwell in it" (Ps.107:33-34).

The covenant *heralded a day of new beginnings* by which God's redemptive plan would unfold. Redemption would eventuate in man's renewed enjoyment of God's presence and fellowship. Subsequently, God started anew with Abraham, Jacob, Joseph, Moses, David and many others. There was never a day too dark for God to begin a new thing. Not even impending exile would prevent His day of new things (Is.43:19-21). Although the covenant anticipates another day of judgment, in the interim God exercises mercy on all and calls out a people for His name's sake.

Missiological Considerations

The *God who acts in wrath is the God who delights in mercy.* He continues to ask hiding and fearful man, "Where are you?" in order to deliver him and to offer an intimate relationship with Himself. To facilitate this, God desires a propitious environment for man (Gen.8:1-22; cf. 1 Tim.2:1-5).

God's selection of a particular man is simply one of His secrets (Dt.29:29). From a human perspective, there is no reason why God should elect a flawed character for salvation and service to carry on His mandates (Gen.9:21). The only possible reason is that God desires man's restored fellowship with Himself (Jn.3:16).

In His interaction with man, *the fundamental attribute of God is grace.* In grace He seeks out man, and in grace He elects and delivers him to live and serve in His presence. God sovereignly calls man to himself. He initiated the whole process which would lead to man's restoration. God recreated the earth through the flood and redeemed Noah and his family. In the same way, He regenerates man's depraved nature, gives man abilities to harness nature and reach out to others in ministry, and empowers man to serve Him. But God's selection of man requires a response. Though weak, tainted with sin and depraved, man must respond volitionally to God's call: "Obey my voice, and I will be your God, and you will be my people; and you will walk in all the way which I command you, that it may be well with you" (Jer.7:23). And yet it is God who initiates the whole process and who performs the deliverance which results in the salvation of man (cf. Ezek.37:1-10). The mystery remains because man retains the ability to refuse God's grace.

A covenant initiated by God is based on His faithfulness. Though man may prove unfaithful, God cannot deny Himself (2 Tim.2:13). God's forbearing character impels Him to seek man. He does not desire man's eternal damnation. "For the Lord will not reject forever, for if He causes grief, then He will have compassion according to His abundant lovingkindness. For He does not afflict willingly, or grieve the sons of men" (Lam.3:31-33). Throughout the flood God proved faithful to His creation in spite of man's failure. We may confidently expect, therefore, that though sociocultural structures disintegrate and man hardens his heart toward God, God's Church will remain (Mt.16:18). "The LORD'S lovingkindnesses indeed never cease.... They are new every morning; great is Thy faithfulness" (Lam.3:22-23).

The Noahic Covenant *covers all men*: it is universal; it concerns all peoples and their circumstances (Gen.9:9-10,12-17; cf.Jon.4:11). It extends to every place, as long as rainbows are seen (Gen.9:16-17). God provided common grace for mankind's continued obligation to carry out the cultural mandate (Gen.9:1-9). The amplified cultural mandate covered marriage (Gen.9:1; cf. Gen.1:28); work (Gen.9:3; cf. Gen.1:28); government (Gen.9:2; cf. Gen.1:28); animals as they were given as food (Gen.9:2-4); soil productivity as, in part, the curse of the ground is removed (Gen.8:21-22); and the sacredness of human life as capital punishment is instituted (Gen.9:5-6). Man is unlike the animals; he must bear responsibility and will be held accountable for his actions.

Even though the flood was exceedingly negative, we cannot fail to detect the great love of God for the crown of His creation, man. In grace the Lord extends everything needed to maintain a meaningful relationship with Himself. The reminders of His mercy and grace—the rainbow, the soil that produces, the use of the animal kingdom, and the renewed earth—all testify to a God who constantly seeks to benefit man with His own presence and power.

In spite of God's grace and compassion, man's penchant for evil constantly drives him to be self-centered and self-seeking, as if God has absolutely no right to His own creation. Nevertheless, God persists in seeking man to redeem and liberate him. This covenant stands to the end of time.

CHAPTER 7

MISSIONS AND BABEL

The term "Babel" has several meanings which may bring insight to a biblical theology of missions. The Babylonians named their city "gate of god" (bab-ili), the entry into the presence of god. This describes, in part, man's objective in building the tower: "let us build for ourselves a city, and a tower whose top will reach into heaven.... And the LORD came down to see the city and the tower" (Gen.11:4,5). Looking at it from God's perspective, the Hebrews associated the word Babel with confusion (Hebrew: balal). The record states:

"Come, let Us go down and there confuse their language, that they may not understand one another's speech".... Therefore its name was called Babel, because there the LORD confused the language of the whole earth; and from there the LORD scattered them abroad over the face of the whole earth (Gen.11:7,9).

The difference in perspective reflects those who substitute self-knowledge for revelation knowledge; note how God comes down to the level of man. What were the events that led up to this scattering of people and the confusion of languages?

Prideful Knowledge
Population growth quickly led to an explosion of evil. Immediately following the flood judgment, God observed that "the intent of man's heart is evil from his youth" (Gen.8:21). Man is a willful, perverse being. People choose to be indifferent to God and to act independently of Him—"to walk in their own devices" (Ps.81:12). That was the risk God took in creating man a moral being. In the Babel account we see how man's perversity drove him to elevate himself as his own god. Having substituted his own prideful knowledge for God's design for life, man sought to depend on his own ingenuity to give purpose to life, so he tried to "reach into heaven" (Gen.11:4). Reflecting on man's

perversity, Isaiah observed: "[They] walk in the way which is not good, *following their own thoughts*" (Is.65:2, emphasis added); and again, "*their thoughts are thoughts of iniquity*" (Is.59:7, emphasis added; cf. Rom.3:9-18). But this tragic chapter in man's history allows us see God's compassion. Rather than give man his just due for sin, God confused the people's language, scattered them, and "determined their appointed times, and the boundaries of their habitation, that they should seek God, if perhaps they might grope for Him and find Him, though He is not far from each one of us; for in Him we live and move and exist" (Acts 17:26-28).

Man's Motivation for Life

Rather than respond in obedience according to revelation knowledge, man looked for personal satisfaction and significance apart from God. He sought community as a substitute for the felt need of the creature for God. He pursued uniformity, believing it would bring unity to his broken, sinful world. He craved self-worth by cooperating with others in common pursuits. He strove for dignity even as he yielded his life and labor to what was empty.

First, man *seeks unity in disobedience* because of his strong sense of insecurity in trying to live apart from God. His vanity leads him to believe that he is self-sufficient, but his self-centeredness drives him to find others to rally around him to carry out his objectives. Man's *vanity* drives him to want to appear independent and self-made. He senses his inadequacy due to his creatureliness and projects a false pride of self-sufficiency (Gen.11:4; cf. Rom.1:22: "professing themselves to be wise").

Because of his sin nature man is basically an insecure being who seeks security from others, not God (Gen.11:2-4). Man wants others, not to give of self, but to get for self. Paul described this: "But I hope in the Lord Jesus to send Timothy to you.... For I have no one else of kindred spirit who will genuinely be concerned for your welfare. For they all *seek after their own interests*" (Phil.2:19-21, emphasis added).

Man's sense of insecurity also drives him to *self-centeredness*. To be considered significant, self must be elevated to receive, to give, or to enjoy. This is a subtle way of manipulating or exercising power over others for selfish objectives. Man ends by establishing himself as the object of worship: "For they exchanged the truth of God for a lie, and worshiped and served the creature rather than the Creator" (Rom.1:25).

Second, man *searches for self-fulfillment*. The quest comes from his capacity for God, which as a result of the Fall is empty. Now man tries to fill it through self-preservation, self-gratification, self- actualization, and self-exaltation.

Self-preservation is evidenced in a drive to collectivism ["lest we be scattered" (Gen.11:4)] in deliberate defiance of God's command to "fill the earth" (Gen.9:1). This is a classic example of unity for the wrong motive. Man being the focus, rather than God, is another form of self-centeredness, and this form of fellowship is bound to sour and destroy. Man's sinful nature motivates him to subtly control, manipulate and exercise position over others. People are used, discarded, trampled, and left behind. Ultimately, the few enjoy and the rest struggle to survive. Communism is one contemporary expression of collectivism. Sadly, at times it is reflected in the supposed teamwork of Christian ministry. True fellowship and community are God-focused for God's sake. Only God can remove the walls of partition between people and bind them in common cause without exploitation.

Self-gratification is expressed in the desire for urbanization: "let us build" (Gen.11:4). Sinful human nature disguises its true motives, supposedly seeking to meet others' needs. Inevitably some claim greater needs and satisfy them at the expense of others. Thus, meeting others' needs is seldom, if ever, without a view to gratifying self. When man functions as God intended, he finds dignity and fulfillment serving others. So in that sense man does need others, but his need is to realize his full humanity. Altruistically reaching out to others provides self-worth and dignity, and gratification comes as man fulfills his office of steward, truly being his brother's keeper.

Man also seeks *self-actualization* through personal and social fulfillment. Man's depravity drives him to seek occasions to "make...a name" (Gen.11:4) for himself. He longs for others to appreciate, accept, acknowledge, and fuss over him. This insatiable thirst for recognition leads to frustration. Man is so self-centered that it is hard for him to give or extend appreciation, recognition, acceptance, and genuine love to others. He craves these for himself. Others become man's focus for self's sake.

Self-exaltation rounds out the cycle. In both the Garden of Eden and at Babel, the desire was to be like God. The statement "let us make bricks...let us build...a city, and a tower whose top will reach into heaven, and let us make for ourselves a name" (Gen. 11:3-4) expressed the desire for self- exaltation. The idolatrous, proud elevation of human culture, without recognizing God's enabling grace and providence, shows man's motivation to accept the glory for his accomplishments:

> For since the creation of the world His invisible attributes, His eternal power and divine nature, have been clearly seen, being understood through what has been made.... For even though they knew God, they did not honor Him as God, or give thanks; but they became futile in their speculations (Rom.1:20,21).

Third, *arrogance* characterizes man's approach to life. The tower of Babel itself is a climactic demonstration of man's arrogance and pathos as the creature seeks to deny his creatureliness before his Maker. He is unduly proud of his achievements and believes that temporal things will satisfy. He strives for the impossible, believing that nothing is beyond his ability to achieve. In most non-Western cultures man secures the help of powerful spirits of darkness, while in Western cultures he bows before the shrine of scientific technology. Character-ized by blatant pride, man asserts that he is self-made and can realize all of his goals. His attitude may be summed up: "I can do it myself—I'll go it alone. Who needs God?" The temporary—the makeshift—becomes the focus of his whole life. He flits from one interest to another looking for a more meaningful encounter with the material world or the spirit world. However, man is basically materialistic, so that even in encounters with the spirit world he wants "blessing" upon this mate-rial world. He projects the attitude, "I will make my own world with my own means for my own comfort and pleasure."

Man strives for the impossible, believing that such ventures demonstrate his ability—nothing is impossible to man. The basic motivation is the desire to exercise godlike power. In the process mankind can be discarded, and things become all-important. Man's history reveals that when things become important, man becomes a thing. Exploitation of people becomes normative as man tries to domi-nate the world for his own purposes.

The Babel judgment had universal implications, bringing God's redemptive focus into greater relief, first through Abraham, then Israel, and subsequently the Church.

Judgment at Babel

This judgment resulted in a God-produced linguistic division and national scattering. The linguistic division came about after God said, "let Us go down and there confuse their language, that they may not understand one another's speech" (Gen.11:7). The national division came when "the LORD scattered them abroad from there over the face of the whole earth" (Gen.11:8). But this judgment was tempered with mercy; it was to shield man from the devastating results of his corporate sinful actions. Diversity in culture and language established distinct people groups within their own confines (cf. Acts 17:26-27), showing that God was sovereignly controlling events for man's ultimate benefit.

Fallen, self-centered man had to be protected from himself and all he could achieve for evil through collective efforts (Gen.11:6-9). Corporate man's self-seeking interests can only lead to further perversity, as history so well documents. When nations form socioeconomic and political alliances to promote a common cultural ethos, the consequences are depravity and much human suffering (e.g. the Canaanite peoples, the Solomonic dynasty, Israel's alliances with pagan nations, developments in the 20th century). Our growing global village, in which possessions and appetites rule our morality on a scale unprecedented in history, confirms how we need to be protected from ourselves.

The fragmentation of mankind ushered man into an era of history that will never know full uniformity. There will be commonalities, of course, and as the global village expands, the diversities will lessen. But this world will remain a "babel" of languages and cultures; attempts at unity will continue to be hindered by nationalism and self-centeredness. Alienation, mistrust, and breakdown in communication will characterize interpersonal and, more significantly, international relations. This is God's judgment, but it also protects man from establishing a misdirected prideful unity. Although man seeks to order his own life by ignoring the Lord, God still controls and intervenes in the affairs of man, for man's welfare. God controls His creation in order to redeem and save all nations (Zeph.3:8,9; Ps.86:8-10).

Missiological Considerations

Babel reveals the depth of man's alienation from God and why he so desperately needs to be brought into a vital relationship with God. Babel shows why society, ever facing corruption and disintegration, needs to be brought under the rule of God and why the task of world evangelization lags.

The Babel account shows how uniformity led to a forced diversity as a result of pride. Pentecost reveals how unity, in spite of diversity, becomes reality when God intervenes and regenerates people. God's new creatures in Christ can fulfill their purposes of being in fellowship with Him, being witnesses to Him, and declaring His mighty acts (Acts 2:1-11; cf. Ps.145:5-13). Man demands uniformity, while God delights in unity in the midst of diversity.

The Babel judgment emphasizes that *there is a limit to God's patience*. Though love and mercy are characteristic of God, His Spirit, as the flood narrative showed, will not always strive with man. When God's terms are rejected, God allows man to be foolish in his own eyes and in the eyes of others. Judgment is inevitable if man does not respond to God's goodness. The day of salvation must be heralded while there is opportunity, lest the wrath of God be released. Those who know His mercy and love should proclaim His offer of escape (Gen.6:3; 1 Pet.3:20; 2 Cor.5:11). Joab's message to David through the woman of Tekoa reveals God's heart of compassion: "For we shall surely die and are like water spilled on the ground which cannot be gathered up again. Yet *God does not take away life, but plans ways so that the banished one may not be cast out from Him*" (2 Sam.14:14, emphasis added).

The Babel judgment implies that *the gospel must be proclaimed within the cultural diversity decreed by God*. A theology of missions which seeks to "gather into one the children of God who are scattered abroad" (Jn.11:52) must come to terms with this implication. Cultural diversity will always be part of man's milieu. Uniformity is not necessary for the gospel to be preached and understood. All boundaries—national, cultural, or linguistic—must be crossed to confront man with God's revelation knowledge. The monocultural communicator, who insists on linguistic and cultural uniformity, ignores the consequences of God's judgment at Babel. Not to have cultural sensitivity, appreciation for diversity, and insight into culture dynamics is to be poorly prepared for ministry in a world of cultural and linguistic diversity. God wants unity out of diversity, not a uniformity which ignores the cultural and linguistic differences of people groups. Pentecost demonstrates God's grace and His plan to bring together diverse cultures and languages to reflect His glory. It is a dramatic reversal of the curse of Babel. Homogeneity may be a good starting point in communicating the gospel, but breaking "down the barrier of the dividing wall" (Eph.2:14-16) is the minimal objective.

A fundamental human desire is to claim the glory for self. God says, "I am the LORD, that is My name; I will not give My glory to another, nor My praise to graven images" (Is.42:8). Man seeks the glory through egocentrism, ethnocentrism, and nationalism. He strives to "make...a name" for himself, frequently at the expense of others (Gen.11:4). Man exalts one cultural entity over another and demands that others conform to a given cultural preference. He elevates one nationality above others and assumes that his nationality or country (or church or denomination) is of sole importance to the exclusion of all others. A hostile stance to others is quite common. This is nothing less than idolatry, a worship of self. God delights in unity within diversity and treats all impartially. All cultures, all nations, all people stand equally under the judgment of God.

Further, *universal history underscores dissolution* rather than evolution. Before the flood and Babel this was patently clear. We see dissolution in man's inability, despite his best efforts, to perfect society apart from God. These human attempts tend to corrupt himself and others. Dehumanization always seems to be just below the surface. The more complex the society, the more corrupt it becomes. Wickedness is very contagious; no one escapes its motivations and effects. Under man's control, the environment is either exploited, or man subjugates himself to the world of nature.

Babel also reveals that *humanity learns little from history*. Though the Babel judgment spared man the consequences of his depravity, the long-term effect did not profit him much. God, however, condemns the minimizing of sin. God wants the deliverance of man from the wages of his sin. Yet man, in his continuing alienation from the true God, devises new ways—new theologies—to help him understand God. Such systems are largely extra-biblical, and "for this reason God will send upon them a deluding influence so that they might believe what is false" (2 Thess.2:11). Man deliberately misinterprets God and His commitment to creation (Is.40:27- 31) and misconstrues God's concern for his welfare (Is.40:12-26). He postulates that God is no longer immanent or actively involved with His creation. He may be transcendent but is unconcerned; therefore man must find mediums (spirit or material) who will serve him, rather than seeking to do God's will (Dt.32:15-18).

God's judgment of man clearly indicates that He cares for His creation and wants to restore it to Himself. His purposes cannot be thwarted, even by sinful and unbelieving man. A multicultural world provides an opportunity for at least one society to respond to God's continuing overtures. Man cannot bring unity out of diversity; God alone can do this. Man will realize his God-given potential and significance only when he lives in obedience and is committed to realizing God's purposes for creation.

Following the Babel judgment the unchanging God with an unchanging purpose responded to man's disobedience by selecting an Amorite and calling him out of the idolatrous Sumerian city of Ur. Without transition or explanation God continued His program with no deviation. In the selection of Abram, God demonstrated His unchanging plans for man: "I will make you a great nation, and I will bless you, and make your name great; and so you shall be blessing; ... and in you all the families of the earth shall be blessed" (Gen.12:2-3). In the words of Jeremiah, God always had in mind "plans for welfare and not for calamity to give you a future and a hope" (Jer.29:11), not only for Israel, but for all nations.

In contrast to man's sinful motivations in Genesis 11:3-4, God would do for man what man thought he would achieve by himself. Man sought significance in power, passion, and purpose, but all apart from God. The significance man sought, God would give. Whereas at Babel man proudly tried to ascend to heaven to make a name for himself, God told Abram that He would make the patriarch's name great (Gen.12:2). When God orders a man's reputation, he will have significance. Babel reflected a desire for mutual acceptance and preservation through a collectivized community, whereas God had in mind a great nation, not as an end in itself, but to bring blessing to all nations. Thus, the presumptuous comment at Babel, "lest we be scattered abroad" (Gen.11:4), parallels God's gracious promise to Abram: "I will make you a great nation ... and I will bless those who bless you, and the one who curses you I will curse. And in you all the families of the earth shall be blessed" (Gen.12:2,3). Instead of man foolishly reaching out for unity and self-preservation, God promised to make a great people encompassing the earth to declare His glory (cf. Ps.96:3,8; Gal.3:8). They would live and know fellowship within the orbit of God's blessing and protection as they carried out His mandates for all peoples (Gen.12:2,3; cf. Mt.28:18-20; Eph.3:20-21; 1 Pet.2:9-10). God answered man's desire for purpose by giving him a large enough objective for all of life. "Let us build for ourselves" (Gen.11:4) parallels: "And you shall be a blessing" (Gen.12:2). God's blessing leads in turn to being a blessing. Man was to be a steward of all that God had entrusted to him for the sake of others (Ps.67:1,2). Bringing blessing to others is the very apex of purposeful living achievable by man. In establishing man's purpose for being—to be a blessing—God has allowed man to know personal worth unattainable anywhere in anything, except in obedience to Himself. God called and gave Abram a mission encompassing the earth. In carrying out that mission, man would realize his God-given potential and worth.

The Context of Judgment and Redemption

Throughout this tragic chapter in human history we can almost hear God saying as Jesus did centuries later: "Oh, Jerusalem, Jerusalem.... How often I wanted to gather your children together, just as a hen gathers her brood under her wings, and you would not have it. Behold, your house is left to you desolate" (Lk.13:34-35). The pursuit of perversity prevailed. The descendants of Noah were no different than those living at the time of the flood. Nevertheless God persisted, drawing near to humanity as He came down to intervene redemptively (Gen.11:4-6).

By grace and mercy God mysteriously, sovereignly selected the line of Shem (Gen.11:10) to be His special agent to carry out His redemptive purposes for all nations. Man, who learns best by demonstration, needs to see God's redemptive activity in a particular people (Exo.4:22; 19:4-6; Dt.4:5-7,20; 7:6; 1 Pet.2:9). Thus God purposed to gather many nations to Himself (Ps.67:4; Is. 25:6-7; Zeph.2:11; 3:8,9,10; Mal.1:11; Acts 14:14-17; 15:17-18). Though He selected only one nation, His concern continues to be for all people. Christ said, "Many shall come from east and west, and recline at the table with Abraham, and Isaac, and Jacob, in the kingdom of heaven" (Mt.8:11). Paul reminds the churches that the nations are to be evangelized: "I have placed you as a light for the Gentiles, that you should bring salvation to the end of the earth" (Acts 13:47); and, "to be specific, that the Gentiles are fellow heirs and fellow members of the body, and fellow-partakers of the promise in Christ Jesus through the gospel" (Eph.3:6). He pointedly states that God is our Savior, "who desires all men to be saved and to come to the knowledge of the truth" (I Tim.2:4). The closing chapters of the Bible reveal the result of world evangelization: "and didst purchase for God with Thy blood men from every tribe and tongue and people and nation. And Thou hast made them to be a kingdom and priests to our God; and they will reign upon the earth" (Rev.5:9,10).

Very early in the biblical records God is known and described as "The LORD...is slow to anger and abundant in lovingkindness, forgiving iniquity and transgression; but He will by no means clear the guilty, visiting the iniquity of the fathers on the children to the third and the fourth generations" (Num.14:18). He is the God Who categorically stated "as I live, all the earth will be filled with the glory of the LORD" (Num.14:21). Of this God, Israel was to be a witness to the nations, and He is the One whom Christian believers are to declare among the nations.

PART II

ISRAEL

THE OLD TESTAMENT

PEOPLE OF GOD

ON MISSION

CHAPTER 8

UNIVERSAL

INFLUENCES AND

OBLIGATIONS

The universal scope of the first eleven chapters of Genesis led directly to the judgment of Babel, which brought linguistic and cultural diversity. God now narrowed His focus to one people group in order to extend His salvation to all nations. The nations would see that God's grace can accomplish God's promise—election for salvation. God's righteousness and grace compelled Him to select one nation through which He would continue to confront all nations with the biblical alternative to man's self-indulgence.

Events Leading to the Selection of Israel

As God narrowed His focus to Abram, what was Abram's world like? What kind of a world does the deceitful heart (Jer.17:9) of man produce? All were under the control of powers opposed to God (Rom.1:18-32) and man. Paul explained that unregenerate man "walked according to the course of this world, according to the prince of the power of the air, of the spirit that is now working in the sons of disobedience" (Eph.2:2; cf. Eph.6:12). Man's sight knowledge produced conditions which sought to remove God from His own creation.

The End of the Era of Monotheism

Man's propensity to animism (spiritism), motivated by a demonic appeal for man to be his own God, long preceded the Babel event. Paul suggests that from the Fall man went from bad to worse (Rom.1:18-32). It is likely that all forms of religion were present very early in history, but their full scope only became evident during and after Babel. When God confused man's languages and scattered the people, the monotheistic period of history ended.

Confronted by a searching God, Abram, product of an idolatrous people (Josh.24:2), now had to choose whether to leave his animistic culture. His positive response to God's call led to a distinct division between a monotheistic people, subsequently embodied in Israel, and the nations seeking other gods, such as those kingdoms surrounding Israel. Man, having bartered his birthright as God's vice-regent, yielded to "the serpent of old who is called the devil and Satan, who deceives the whole world" (Rev.12:9). Man now sought his own approach to the spirit world.

The Development of Alternative Religions

After the Fall, and increasingly after Babel, man developed his own religion to contend with his world of insecurity and uncertainty. Today nonbiblical religion generally is characterized by pantheism, reincarnation, moral relativism, and esotericism. Each of these responses is influenced by evil structures and spirit powers. Not all religions subscribe to all of them, but any one is sufficient to set a system apart from biblical faith. Each in its own way appeals to man's sinful nature because each seeks to provide a logical explanation for the human condition.

Pantheism

The appeal of pantheism, "you will be like God," underlies man's motivation to exercise power. In pantheism the spiritual permeates all the world—animate and inanimate. A concentration of spirit power, secured by various means, enables man to exercise control over his life. Through spirit power, man believes he can control his destiny.

Spirit Contact and Reincarnation

Extrabiblical belief systems postulate that there is open traffic between the living and the dead: "you surely shall not die" (Gen.3:4). Man is free to find ways to contact the dead. Along with this is the belief in reincarnation, in which man will come back from the dead in human or some other form. Man never comes into a state of total helplessness, either in death or life. Spirit beings are there to serve man's needs and put him in contact with the right power source. If man should ever need God, it would be for circumstances that spirit beings or man cannot handle. But underlying man's rejection of his finitude is the belief that there is no future accountability to God. Man believes he is not a sinner, but even if he should sin, God does not mind. Sin simply relates to man's poor handling of life.

Relativism

Another characteristic of nonbiblical faith is the aversion to absolutes. Man sees himself as his own standard for all decisions. Absolutes can always be bent. Nothing is intrinsically evil or good except as the occasion dictates. We can trace this relativism directly to the demonic appeal: "knowing good and evil." Morality is defined as what is good for the individual; it has nothing to do with divine standards. Self-indulgence, therefore, is not considered abnormal.

Esotericism

Esotericism, the belief that elitist knowledge is available to deal with all of life, parallels "your eyes will be opened." Sin is simply ignorance of the right ritual, or perhaps a broken custom, or an inconvenience, but not an offense against a holy God. Should sin intrude, there are ways to correct the matter apart from God.

Man-made Divinities

The religious division between Abram [Israel] and the nations surrounding him does not primarily arise from a plurality of gods. Nor does it arise from a struggle between two supernatural realms, but rather from man's defiance and soaring ambitions. To affirm and condone his own perversity, man worships man-made divinities (Rom.1:18-32). Behind these gods are the powers of darkness (1 Cor.10:19-20) determined to dehumanize and destroy man. They do so by clouding man's thinking and seducing him into a lifestyle of self indulgence. Abram himself came out of such a background. Apparently Terah, his father, was a devotee of the moon deity Nanna, patron of the city of Ur. The entire activity of the city—commercial, social, as well as religious—revolved around the worship of Nanna and his spouse Nin-gal (Unger 1967:61). Most likely Terah was involved in such commercial endeavors, and that Abram participated in the industry and its practices through customary apprenticeship in the family business.

Self-Indulgence

Man creates gods in his own image. Since these gods are merely an extension of himself, directly or indirectly man worships himself. He calls upon creation to condone and approve of his depravity through worship of images of "corruptible man and of birds and four-footed animals, and crawling creatures" (Rom.1:23). Of Israel it was said:

> Then he forsook God who made him, and scorned the Rock of his salvation. They made Him jealous with strange gods; with abominations they provoked Him to anger. They sacrificed to demons who were not God, to gods whom they have not known, new gods who came lately (Dt.32:15-17).

When man worships self, he starts seeking to satisfy his animal appetites, which inevitably leads to all kinds of perversion. For one, man will disregard totally the sanctity of sexuality (Rom.1:26-27). Sexual perversion condoned and practiced leads to moral corruption, which in turn affects all of life. When the sacredness of sex is done away, there are no absolutes in other areas of life. Man becomes the measure of all things, but he comes under the control of his appetites. The promptings of the flesh can open the door to demon-inspired and demon-exploited perversities. Man then justifies his immorality, practices it, and is quite offended when his perversity is questioned (Rom.1:28-32).

Ritual Manipulation

The nonbiblical religious devotee conceives himself to be on a par with his gods. He views himself as a helper and partner of the gods, as their sustainer and reviver. He accomplishes this by correct knowledge (usually esoteric), magic and manipulation.

In animism, the routine of life is cyclical; linear history is meaningless. The here and now is all that matters, and man's frequent motivation is simply attaining success, happiness and security in this life: "Eat, drink and be merry, for tomorrow we die" (cf. Is. 22:13; Lk. 12:19) Success, happiness and security are generally achieved by correct knowledge or ritual manipulation. There is no future divine judgment, nor any category in life for a God-mandated mission or purpose. Man has his own mission—getting through life with a minimum of adversity. In the process he hopes to attain wealth and fame, and perhaps some better understanding of life.

Any wrongdoing is readily excused because sin is not an offense against a holy God. Sin is the breaking of custom, or perhaps a person's failure to respond appropriately. Sin can be using wrong means to manipulate the deities, but should one be caught, shame, not guilt, results (cf. Gen.39:9; Ps.51). There is no understanding of forgiveness as described in the Bible. A measure of morality surfaces in the sense that good works should be performed. "Forgiveness" comes through works. Ritual manipulation will appease the spirit world for what even man's seared conscience cannot excuse. So there is a constant need to earn the deity's good will in order to balance the accounts.

There is a driving motivation to seek a deity or spirit being to meet personal (selfish) needs. There is no concept of a covenant community coming before God in worship and humility to seek His will. Corporateness in worshiping or seeking God is generally unknown.

Nonbiblical faith is a presumptuous worship of "no gods," described in the Bible as "vanities" and "lies." By these man imagines himself the conqueror of heaven. In contrast biblical faith confidently asks as it ridicules the religionist:

> "to whom then will you liken God? Or what likeness will you compare with Him?" As for the idol, a craftsman casts it, a goldsmith plates it with gold, and a silversmith fashions chains of silver. He who is too impoverished for such an offering selects a tree that does not rot; He seeks out for himself a skillful craftsman to prepare an idol that will not totter (Is.40:18-20; cf. Is.40:18-26);

> Thus says the LORD, "Do not learn the way of the nations, and do not be terrified by the signs of the heavens although the nations are terrified by them; for the customs of the peoples are delusion; because it is wood cut from the forest, the work of the hands of a craftsman with a cutting tool. They decorate it with silver and with gold; they fasten it with nails and with hammers so that it will not totter. Like a scarecrow in a cucumber field are they, and they cannot speak; they must be carried, because they cannot walk! Do not fear them, for they can do no harm, nor can they do any good..." But the LORD is the true God; He is the living God and the everlasting King. At His wrath the earth quakes, and the nations cannot endure His indignation. Thus you shall say to them, "The gods that did not make the heavens and the earth shall perish from the earth and from under the heavens" (Jer.10:2-5, 10, 11; cf.Jer.10:12-16ff).

Idolatry

The presence of the serpent in the Garden of Eden implies that spirits had access to man's world from the very beginning. (Some hold that Gen.6:2 actually involved the intermarriage of women and angels, a belief commonly accepted by animists). Biblical theology considers idolatry and involvement with spirits synonomous (Dt.32:17; Ps.106:36-38). Idolatry appears immediately after the Babel account before Scripture specifically mentions gods and spirits. Idolatry originated when God was ignored and forgotten (Jer.16:10-13). It is a punishment man brings on himself: "So I gave them over to the stubbornness of their heart, to walk in their own devices" (Ps.81:12); and, "They do not know, nor do they understand, for He has smeared over their eyes so that they cannot see and their hearts so that they cannot comprehend" (Is.44:18). Man is left with the worship of "no-gods" by comparison to God: "Are there any among the idols of the nations who give rain? Or can the heavens grant showers? Is it not Thou, O LORD our God?" (Jer.14:22) Man trusts in his own strength, wisdom, and understanding of life and ignores God (Jer.23:25-28,36-37). Man places his faith in liturgies, rituals, and ceremonies (Jer.7:30-31; 8:1-2; 10:2-5; 18:15; cf. Amos 5:21-23), believing that by these he may manipulate his gods to realize his life's goals.

Idolatry was decreed as a judgment on mankind. Therefore, God cautioned Israel,

> "And beware, lest you lift up your eyes to heaven and see the sun and the moon and the stars, all the host of heaven, and be drawn away and worship them and serve them, those which the LORD your God has allotted to all the peoples under the whole heaven" (Dt.4:19; cf. Ps.81:12; Is.44:17-18; Rom.1:18-32).

Defiance

Man's fundamental sin nature is seen in his rebellion against God. Sin is a defiance of God (I Sam.15:22,23), which simply increases until God deals with it and with the powers motivating and exploiting man's sin nature.

This was the context when God called one man out of an idolatrous city, Ur of the Chaldees. Abram made a moral choice as he elected by faith to walk with God, choosing to believe God's promise and stake his life on it.

The Evidence of God's Common Grace

God's grace was the basis of creation; God's grace was the basis for the continuation of human history; and God's grace was the basis of particularism—the selection of one nation to be His Son (Exo.4: 22; Hos.11:1; cf. Is.45:11), through whom He will call the nations to salvation (Is.45:22-25). Out of one culture at Babel came many nations and languages. Now God would bring through one nation many nations with "purified lips, that all of them may call on the name of the LORD, to serve Him shoulder to shoulder" (Zeph.3:9).

Even though the nations were excluded from God's holiness (and Israel was shown favor), yet all nations remained within the sphere of God's providence and purpose. Isaiah pointed out God's overriding concern for Egypt and Assyria in spite of their idolatry: "Blessed is Egypt My people, and Assyria the work of My hands, and Israel My inheritance" (Is. 19:25).

National Commonalities

All nations continue to stand under God's laws. *All men are still in God's image* in spite of their rebellion. No matter where man is or what he does, the image has not been erased, so the ancient obligations remain. All people have been given dominion over God's creation. Even though they may persist in destroying it, they are still accountable to God. All men still have *the ability to unwrap the potential of creation* and produce the arts of civilization. *God's providence continues to reach all* as He demonstrates mercy and grace in determining the length of life (Ps.90:10), dispersing people over the earth (Gen.11:8-9), and establishing them in their countries for their welfare (Acts 17:26,27).

God chose Abraham to model His grace in order to impress all nations with His concerns:

> "Abraham will surely become a great and mighty nation, and in him all the nations of the earth will be blessed... For I have chosen him, in order that he may command his children and his household after him to keep the way of the LORD by doing righteousness and justice; in order that the LORD may bring upon Abraham what He has spoken about him" (Gen.18:18,19).

But *God continued to keep His eye on all nations* even as He raised up and pulled down and divided to men their possessions: "When the Most High gave the nations their inheritance ... He set the boundaries of the peoples according to the number of the sons of Israel" (Dt.32:8; cf. Dt.2:5,9,19,21f.; Ps.111:6; Is.13-24).

Universal Obligations

God established universal obligations for all peoples. Pagan morality, derived from false premises, is nevertheless grounded in the fear of God, Who still demands that men live by His Law. In this, Abraham was to be God's model. The obligations were to keep man from destroying society and himself. The prohibition of murder is universal (Gen.9:5-6; cf. Gen.20:11). The aversion to adultery, though variously defined, is universal (Gen.39:9). The breach of faith is universally abhorred (Gen.39:8ff.), although keeping faith is frequently limited to the "in group." The concept of benevolence is largely universal (Ruth 1:8-17; 2:10-12; cf. Gen.20:14ff. 2 Chron.20:10-11). Man's motives may not always be beyond question, but should he not show some benevolence, even his manmade gods may punish his selfishness. There is a general concern for the less-privileged among most peoples (Dt.2612-13). All nations seem to have some sense of social justice, even if it is not extended to all peoples. Amalek was condemned for not observing justice (1 Sam.15:2-3). Sexual immorality, though variously defined, is universally censured (cf. Lev.18:6ff.; Lev.20:10ff.) God expelled the Canaanites from their land for disregarding His law (Lev.18:27-28). Practicing cruelty, even in idol worship (Lev.18:21; Dt.18:10-12), is considered reprehensible (Lev.20:2- 5; cf. Amos 1:3-2:3).

Justice and Morality

God's justice and morality are binding on all nations. The Bible always discusses these essentials against a non-Israelite background. For example, the account of Sodom and Gomorrah highlighted issues of immorality, sodomy, and social injustice (Gen.19; Ezek.16:49-50). Job provided the context for discussing suffering and man's ideological, theological, and physical response to it. Proverbs covered most aspects of ethical and moral living, based on the notion that the principles of wisdom are built into the fabric of the universe (Prov.8:22-31). Ecclesiastes spoke of man's foolish ambitions and obvious lack of wisdom. Although man continually seeks to live by self-knowledge, "the Preacher" concluded that the fear of God is wisdom: "The conclusion, when all has been heard, is: *fear God* and keep his commandments, because this applies to every person. *For God will bring every act to judgment*, everything which is hidden, whether it is good or evil" (Eccl.12:13, emphasis added). Jonah was sent to remind Nineveh, a pagan city, that God was about to judge her wickedness. Nahum spoke against Nineveh's sinful excesses. Habakkuk told how God would judge Israel for her perversity and rebellion through the Chaldeans: but he also reminded the Chaldeans that they would not escape God's judgment.

Impartial Response to Wickedness

Israel would be a demonstration of God's impartial response to man's persistent wickedness (Jer.22:13-26). Israel was held up as a model of God's righteousness and justice before all nations. "But I will remember for them the covenant with their ancestors, whom I brought out of the land of Egypt *in the sight of the nations,* that I might be their God. I am the LORD" (Lev.26:45, emphasis added). Israel's calling, commission, inheritance, declension, exile, restoration—indeed, all things in Israel's history—were done in the sight of the nations. Israel was expected to repent and confess before the nations to show that the God of Israel was impartial toward sin (2 Sam.14:14 KJV; Acts 10:34). But He is also unlike all other deities, being merciful and forgiving in response to genuine repentance (Ps.130:4; Is.45:22).

The nations had no such concept of God. Their best hope was that their good deeds would outweigh their bad. Often, if it were possible, they would try to deceive their deities and each other by trying to hide their sin. Repentance and confession are moral unknowns among the religions of the world, except where the devotee hopes to gain merit.

Superintendence of All Nations

Israel was to demonstrate God's ability and determination to superintend His people in all circumstances, whether confronting other nations or enjoying their blessings. God blessed His people but also would chasten them if necessary. Even as He intervened in Israel's history He also desired to bless all nations, though judging their rebellion. Concerning Pharaoh, he said: "For this time I will send all my plagues on you and your servants and your people, so that you may know that there is no one like Me in all the earth.... For this cause I have allowed you to remain, in order to show you My power, and in order to proclaim My name through all the earth" (Exo.9:14,16).

The world would acclaim the LORD God because of His dealings with Israel (Ps.67). God dealt impartially with His model Israel so that the nations would know Who He is and turn to Him (Ps.72). The result would be that "From the rising of the sun to its setting the name of the LORD is to be praised. The LORD is high above all nations; His glory is above the heavens" (Ps.113:3-4). Israel's mandate was to lead the nations to know God's redemption (Num.14:21; Mal.1:11). Thus, the proclamation of the Old Testament gospel was not only an eschatological hope for Israel, but a present, ongoing reality. Israel had a commission from God to be His witnesses at all times (Is.43:10; cf. Jonah). But they also had an eschatalogical hope of seeing the nations respond to God in unprecedented ways and numbers (Is.19:18-25; 25:6-7; 66:18; Zeph. 3:9; Zech.8:20-23; Mal.1:11).

CHAPTER 9

ELECTION AND

PREPARATION

God's call to Abram set in motion a chain of events which would take a people from aimless wandering to purposeful pilgrimage, ultimately bringing the nations to faith in Christ. From the beginning of time, God's "decision [was] to gather nations.... For then I will give to the peoples purified lips, that all of them may call on the name of the LORD, to serve Him shoulder to shoulder" (Zeph.3:8,9; cf. Zeph.2:11). God selected this one people to reach all other groups.

God called Abram to take those first steps leading to that day when "every knee shall bow ... and every tongue shall give praise to God" (Rom.14:11; cf. Is.45:23; Phil.2:10).

The Role of the Patriarchs

God's interaction with the patriarchs revealed His great concern for man. The transcendent God repeatedly disclosed Himself through theophanies and circumstances. His purpose was to raise up a servant-priest people who would declare His mighty acts of righteousness, mercy, and grace to all peoples. His servant people, if necessary would give their life a ransom for others. Through them the nations would see that God is for man. Regardless of their circumstances they could become the sons of God. Each patriarch, in his own way, revealed God's compassion for all humankind.

The Call of Abram

Abram was to be God's model of a servant-priest for all peoples, so

109

that God could manifest His concern for all. The distinction between God-mandated and nonbiblical religious practices would be clear. God's interaction with Abram would reveal God as totally unlike the gods of the nations. His purposes, and the lifestyle reflecting those purposes, would be seen as inseparably related, and distinct from those of the nations.

The Nature of Abram's Call

Abram expressed confidence in God by obeying God's call. He responded in faith, he walked by faith, and submitted in faith to all God's leading. Although at times Abram faltered, he staked his life on God.

From a human perspective, Abram's faith was frequently tested severely. Although his name change from Abram to *Abraham, the father of many nations*, was an embarrassment, he did not doubt God could indeed make him father of many people. The land God promised him was protected by treaties and alliances beyond Abram's ability to conquer, but Abram believed it would be the inheritance of his descendants. By faith he believed that God would indeed fulfill His promises. There were no rituals of manipulation, no sacrifices of appeasement, no attitude of "God helps those who help themselves." (In that respect, Abram tried and failed miserably regarding Hagar and Ishmael.) It was to be a walk of faith in total dependence on God. Humanly speaking, he could do nothing to fulfill God's promises. Either God would fulfill His promise, or man would stand in shame. But Abram's faith was not fatalistic; it was an active waiting upon God in expectation, believing that God's promises would not fail.

Abram's life was a testimony to God's grace, demonstrating that He communicates with man provided man walks in obedience. Everything depended upon God Who initiated, directed, and fulfilled His promise. But man had to respond to God's leading and follow in obedience.

The Elements of the Call

God's promise to Abram (here after Abraham) contained *three elements* which would be realized in Israel's history. Those elements— the reality of descendants (Gen.12:2), a covenant relationship (Gen.12:2-3), and the inheritance of a land (Gen.12:1)—would affect the realization of God's purposes for the nations.

Abraham's *descendants* were to be a blessing to the whole earth, (Gen.12:3; 15:5; 18:18-19; Gal.3:8). Repeatedly, those who comprised the descendants would be in jeopardy, either through their own sin, or onslaughts from the "gods" of the nations, or God's chastisement. But the promise would be sustained. Through them the nations would be brought to faith in the God of Abraham, Isaac, and Jacob. Abraham's descendants had but one reason for being, to participate in God's mission of delivering the nations and reconciling them to Him. Anything less was disobedience and a rejection of their role as priest-nation (Exo.19:6; cf. Rom.15:16). As miraculous as the birth of Isaac and the great numerical growth of his descendants (Gen.13:16) would be the multitudes out of all nations gathered to faith in God (Rev.5:9; 7:9).

Abraham and his descendants were to know the God of *covenant relationship* (Gen.12:2-3; Dt.4:5-7; 7:6-26). God commits Himself to a close and vital relationship with His people and expects the same from them. He desires a heart relationship with Himself, later expressed by the prophet Jeremiah, "Thou art near to their lips but far from their mind [heart]. But Thou knowest me, O LORD; Thou seest me; and *Thou dost examine my heart's attitude toward Thee*" (Jer.12:2,3, emphasis added); and "I will give them a heart to know Me, for I am the LORD; and they will be My people, and I will be their God, for they will return to Me with their whole heart" (Jer.24:7). The God of Abraham promised, "I will establish My covenant between Me and you and your descendants after you ... to be God to you and to your descendants" (Gen.17:7). Moses pointed out that the covenant-making God was the seeking God (Exo.3:2-4); the communicating God (Exo.3:6); the seeing God (Exo.3:7); the delivering God (Exo.3:8); the sending God (Exo.3:10); the ever-present God (Exo.3:12); the God of power (Exo.3:20); and the providing God (Exo.3:21). What God is and does is always integral to reaching the nations (Exo.19:4-6). Says Westermann: "What God did, what He does, and what He will do toward and within His people is always related to other people too, even if this relationship is mostly hidden from us" (Interp.17 [1963]:260).

The *land of the people's inheritance* (Gen.12:1; 13:15; Dt.6:18-25) was to become the stage on which they would model in very practical ways what it meant to be the people of God. Here they could demonstrate the blessedness of being God's people; from here they could launch out on His mission to bring the nations to salvation (Is.45:22-24). Their message would be supported by a living model: "And you shall do what is right and good in the sight of the LORD, that it may be well with you and that you may go in and possess the good land which the LORD swore to give your fathers" (Dt.6:18; cf. Dt.11). Their gospel for the nations issued in practical living which reflected the greatness and glory of their God. Every aspect of this lifestyle was to demonstrate their covenant relationship with God. God Himself gave them a culture He expected them to reflect daily—a culture which touched upon every aspect of life (Dt.4:5-7,14). This model of people and land would draw others to worship God and be a base from which they would confront the gods of other nations (cf. Is.40-48; Book of Jonah).

Israel, God's Model to the World

From the beginning of His dealings with Abraham, God intended His people to reflect visibly what He had always intended for those who walk in obedience (Dt.5:29). Living by God's design brings its own rewards; those who adopt biblical principles prosper. But God's purposes are much greater than merely blessing man. Such blessing is always in order to reconcile the nations to Himself (Ps.67:1,2). Israel frequently concluded that God intended "the good life" for them without responsibility for the nations, as is illustrated by the parable of the wicked tenant farmers (Mt.21:33-45). Too frequently man serves God for his own profit (Job 1:9-11), not to participate in God's purposes for creation.

Abraham's Election Reflects God's Call to All Nations

Abraham is God's specific yet universal message. In and through Abraham (and by extension Israel) all nations would hear (and see) God saying, "I am for you. Believe Me and trust Me. I want to deliver you." "Israel is the opening word in God's proclaiming salvation, not the Amen!" (De Groot 1964:10)

Abraham/Israel shows God's superintendency of all history for the sake of all nations. The nations would see through Israel that God continues to control and guide history and that life has meaning only when linked with the God of history, as illustrated in Daniel. God is moving with purpose and His eye is on the nations. He retains His claim to the nations (Ps.86:8-10).

Abraham/Israel reveals God's unchanging love and mysterious choice of man to participate in His purposes for all of His creation. Israel was not elected above others because of her virtue, but rather to proclaim that God can take the most unlikely people and mold them into a people of God, intent to do His will. Israel was to disclose and unwrap God's redemptive purposes for all peoples. They were reminded of this repeatedly:

The LORD your God has chosen you to be *a people for His own possession*.... The LORD did not set His love on you nor choose you because
you were more in number than any of the peoples.... Know therefore
that the LORD your God, He is God, the faithful God, who keeps His
covenant ... with those who love Him and keep His commandments;
but repays those who hate Him ... to destroy them (Dt.7:6,7,9,10,
emphasis added).

Abraham's/Israel's history underscores the singleness of God's purpose.
God's ongoing purpose is to bring the nations to Himself. Israel, as both
God's model and message bearer, is seen in four generations of patri-
archs planted in two different cultures. Israel was the minority called to
serve the majority. Through the patriarchs and later through Israel,
God discloses His redemptive plan for all nations.

*Abraham's/Israel's election highlights God's great concern for man's
appalling spiritual need.* Abraham's election specifically highlights this
concern. What man strove after in Genesis 11:1-4, God promised
Abraham in Genesis 12:1-3. Thus, to forcefully speak to this sin-blinded
world God raised up a model, first in Abraham, and then through his
physical and now also spiritual descendants (Gal.3:8).

*Abraham/Israel was specifically commissioned to be God's blessing to the
nations.* Abraham could not keep the blessing of God to himself but was
commissioned a steward to share God's redemptive blessings with all
nations (Gen.12:1-3; cf. Gen.18:18,19).

Abraham was the pioneer of missions. God elected to send a man on a
mission to reconcile all humanity with Himself and also with one
another. Lutheran missionary Sundkler observed, "It is the task of
mission to break the curse and replace it by understanding and unity.
When Abraham left his home in faith, not knowing the future, he took
the first decisive step along the road in mission" (Sundkler 1965:12).

Missiological Considerations

What Abraham's call meant to him, to Israel and then to the nations
is applicable to Christians and the Church today. *Every believer has a
responsibility for the salvation of the nations, even as did Abraham and his
descendants.* God's command to Abram to be a blessing was passed on
to all his children, whether physically or spiritually (Gen.12:3; 18:18;
Gal.3:8). That goal can only be sustained by an ongoing relationship
with a covenant-making God Who wants all nations brought to repentance (Is.45:22; 1 Tim.2:4; 2 Pet.3:9).

God desires the intimate fellowship of all men as with Abraham. The one
who claims such a relationship but who is not in tune with God's heart

for all creation does not know the God of the Bible. God's commission to be His witness leads to a message and a lifestyle reflecting that message. The two are inseparable. Abraham's descendants had to live the message if they would speak it; the two together would expose the destructive and dehumanizing ways of the gods of the nations.

Abraham, and by extension Israel, was central to God's redemptive program for the nations. *His election was purposeful:* to bring blessing to all nations. "And in you (and your descendants, Gen.18:18,19) all the families of the earth shall be blessed" (Gen.12:3). Whenever Israel ignored that mandate, they had either forgotten their call to stewardship, exchanging it for a lifestyle of selfishness and greed (Jer.34), or they deliberately followed the gods of the nations, who condoned and encouraged just such selfishness and greed (Dt.32:15-18). This is why God judged the pagan nations and Israel so harshly (Ezek.16:44-52). God had but one purpose, to redeem man. Anything diverting His people from that attacked Israel's commission and was unworthy of the people of the God of Abraham, Isaac and Jacob.

Abraham's/Israel's *usefulness came through encounter with the nations and their gods*, which God used to further His purposes. The nations saw in Israel, whether in battle or exile, the just and righteous nature of a God unlike their own, mighty in power on behalf of His people. At times the nations were considered "spoil" for Israel, or God's "chastening rod" upon Israel. They in turn were judged by God through Israel (Gen.49:10; Exo.3:22; Dt.9:4,5; Jer.51:19-23). Whatever the circumstance, God's purposes were being realized. Whether the nations came to Israel through battle or invasion or the Israelites went to them through compulsion or captivity, the Jews spoke of their God (Jonah; 2 Ki.5:2-4; Dan.4:20-27; 5:17-28). In obedience or disobedience, somehow their God and His gospel entered the picture. The people would cry to Him in their distress (e.g. Judg.3:9,15) and remind themselves of His mighty acts, and through it all the nations were confronted by the God unlike all others (Gen.12:10-20; 14:1-24; etc.; cf. Ps.135; 137).

Central to God's dealings with nations is His justice. He required Israel to wait before taking possession of the land promised to Abraham, "for the iniquity of the Amorites [was] not yet complete" (Gen.15:16). God exercises great patience toward man because He desires that people should turn to Him and be saved (Is.45:22). However, His Spirit will not always strive with man; man's persistent rebellion will bring judgment. Four hundred years later, Israel marched into Canaan to take possession, thus becoming God's rod of judgment upon the inhabitants.

Abraham's/Israel's commission was to be both centripetal (drawing the nations by modeling what it meant to be a God-centered people), and *centrifugal* (going to the nations as His witnesses). Israel's knowing God's blessing and the nations receiving blessing from them affirms the centrifugal and centripetal aspects of her mission. The verbs in Genesis 12:2 and 26:4 are reflexive; verbs in 12:3, 18:18, 28:14 are either reflexive or passive constructions. The Psalmists (66:1-8, note verse 8; 67:1-7; 72:17-19; 96:2-10; etc.) repeatedly reminded Israel of her responsibility to "tell of His glory among the nations, His wonderful deeds among all the peoples" (Ps.96:3; cf. Jonah), as did the prophets. The prophets emphasized that the nations would encourage one another to seek the God of Israel because of what they knew of God through Israel, "for we have heard that God is with you" (Zech.8:22,23 cf. Is.2:2,3; 19:23-25). Although these latter passages point to the future, the seminal notion of Israel's mission to the nations is foundational to biblical truth.

The obedience of a man or nation toward God is not apart from the attitude toward Israel: "the one who curses you I will curse" (in the singular), and "I will bless those who bless you" (in the plural) (Gen.12:3; cf. Ps.87; Mt.25:31-46; Rom.11:25-28). Israel played an important role in God's redemptive program, and to discount her is to call into question God's purposes for the nations (cf. Ps.122:6).

God's agent of mission was called to a pilgrim way, even as she enjoyed God's blessings in any given place. The people were to wield no particular power. Abraham, who modeled what God wanted, had only influence and authority which were delegated by God, through His commission to be a blessing to the nations. Later, unsought promotion came to Joseph, who devoted his energy, wisdom, and influence to maintaining the cultural mandate for peaceful living (shalom) in Egypt (Gen.39-41). The Israelites had to obey local laws and conform to local customs (Gen.21:30; 26:15ff; 14:13-24; 23:4ff; 33:19). But they had to disassociate from intermarrying, immorality, and customs God had proscribed. They had to serve God first, even when called to serve Pharaoh also. Civil service was not necessarily incompatible with being God's servant, although God's concerns were never to be superseded by any earthly interest or duty.

The Israelites were to uphold the cultural mandate contributing to the welfare of others. Patriarchal history supported the general principles of the cultural mandate. For example, human rules were not to be rejected, but accepted as God-ordained ordinances, provided they did not contradict God's statutes (Acts 4:19). Political leaders were regarded as God's servants except when they deliberately dehumanized man. The Jews were to seek the welfare of the people and land (Jer.29:7). But as the people of God they were "aliens and strangers" (1 Pet.2:11) in a foreign land (Heb.11:8-9), "looking for the city which has foundations, whose architect and builder is God" (Heb.11:10). As pilgrims, they did not totally conform to all sociocultural structures in the host country. Wherever possible, they were to be cooperative citizens whose well-doing (1 Pet.2:15) put criticism to silence (Gen.21:22-34; Gen.41).

God's interaction with Abraham/Israel brought the hope of salvation to all nations. God's deliberate encounter with Abraham was the beginning of the Gospel to the nations. The Old Testament Gospel—God seeking man—underlies God's self-disclosure to Abraham. This gospel would extend through a man (Abraham), then a family (Jacob), to a nation (Israel), and then reach all peoples, as Isaiah declared:

> "Turn to Me, and be saved, all the ends of the earth; For I am God, and there is no other. I have sworn by myself, *the word has gone forth from My mouth* in righteousness and will not turn back, that to Me every knee will bow, every tongue will swear allegiance. They will say of Me, '*Only in the LORD are righteousness and strength.*' Men will come to Him, and all who were angry at Him shall be put to shame" (Is.45:22-24, emphasis added).

God alone is God and deserves the praise of all nations: "All the kings of the earth will give thanks to Thee, O LORD, *when they have heard the words of Thy mouth.* And they will sing of the ways of the LORD. For great is the glory of the LORD" (Ps.138:4,5, emphasis added).

The Bible gives no reason for God's sovereign selection of Abraham/ Israel. We are reminded, however, that "the eyes of the LORD move to and fro throughout the earth that He may strongly support those whose heart is completely His" (2 Chron.16:9). God's continued sovereign action in calling out a people is to bring the nations to know that:

> blessed is everyone who fears the LORD, who walks in His ways. When you shall eat of the fruit of your hands, you will be happy and it will be well with you. Your wife shall be like a fruitful vine, within your house, your children like olive plants around your table. Behold, *for thus shall the man be blessed who fears the LORD* (Ps.128:1-4, emphasis added).

Whenever people come to God in faith, it is a result of God's convicting work in their lives for His name's sake (Ezek.36:21-23). God by His Spirit motivates those who come in faith to involve themselves in His purposes, for the sake of His Name (Rom.1:5; 3 Jn.7). God is not only the initiator of redemption, He is also the motivator, the agent, and the culmination of redemption (Col.1:16-17). It is His sovereign grace that elected an Isaac over an Ishmael, a Jacob over an Esau, a Judah over a Joseph. By grace God brought them to Himself and by grace they were to carry out His purposes. But the response to grace includes the communication of that grace to others:

> God be gracious to us and bless us, and cause His face to shine upon us—that Thy way may be known on the earth, Thy salvation among all nations.... God blesses us, that all the ends of the earth may fear Him (Ps.67:1-2,7);

> for all things are for your sakes, that the grace which is spreading to more and more people may cause the giving of thanks to abound to the glory of God (2 Cor.4:15).

God will not be thwarted in His sovereign plan to redeem all nations. God's plans have been opposed repeatedly: by deceit (Gen.20), rebellion (Jacob and his sons), indifference (God's people in Egypt; the times of the judges; the monarchy), disobedience (the wilderness journey; King Saul's time, and many others), and unbelief (at Kadesh-Barnea; Jeremiah's days, and the times of the other prophets), but no opposition can stop God's purpose of redeeming mankind (Rom.8:28-39).

The conflict will be severe—there will be casualties. The confrontations with forces will be many—there will be defections. But the triumph is certain (Mt. 16:16-18). In the words of the Psalmist, "Thy godly ones shall bless Thee. They shall speak of the glory of Thy Kingdom, and talk of Thy power; to make known to the sons of men Thy mighty acts, and the glory of the majesty of Thy Kingdom" (Ps.145:10-12).

CHAPTER 10

REDEMPTION AND

LIBERATION:

THE EXODUS

The Exodus shows God's ability to save man in the context of historical events. Encounters with hostile powers, daily threats and challenges, the manifestation of God and His mighty acts, responding in faith and waiting for God's deliverance: all continue to be examples for God's people in whatever their circumstances (1 Cor.10:1-13).

God does not remove people from difficult circumstances but meets them in those circumstances to demonstrate Who He is. Israel's encounter with Pharaoh shows this: "I have allowed you to remain, in order to show you My power, and in order to proclaim My name through all the earth" (Exo.9:16); and, "Pharaoh will not listen to you, so that My wonders will be multiplied in the land of Egypt" (Exo.11:9); and again, "I will harden Pharaoh's heart, and he will chase after them; and I will be honored through Pharaoh and all his army, and the Egyptians will know that I am the LORD" (Exo.14:4; cf. Exo.14:23-31; Rom.8:37). In difficult circumstances He will proclaim His name and manifest His power among the nations (cf. Jer.33:6-9). He desires that all men may know Him as their deliverer; as the One who sets people free to worship and serve the only true God. His power is sufficient for all man's needs. He is able to deliver both man and nations from all their bondage and to use them as agents of His redemptive mission to all others.

119

The Making of Israel

Genesis ends with a small company of Hebrews living securely in Egypt. But the people had reminders that they were only sojourners: the covenants and promises (Gen.12:1-3; 26:1-6; 28:13-15; 35:9-13; 49:10; 50:24), Joseph's embalmed body—a visible reminder of God's faithfulness—and the promise of a land (Gen.50:25-26; Exo.13:19). These reminders were foundational to Israel's nationhood.

A Distinct Concept of God

In addition, the Hebrews had a distinct knowledge of the God known by the patriarchs as the God of Abraham, Isaac, and Jacob. Israel came to know God as a covenant-maker, unchanging in His glory, wisdom, power, and redemptive purpose. True, He revealed Himself as the God of mighty acts, but He never revealed His acts without first revealing who He was. He was a self-disclosing God who revealed Himself to the fathers. When God disclosed His name to Moses, He said, in effect: "I am the same God your fathers worshiped, but I will give you a new awareness of what I am doing, and who I AM" (Exo.3:13-16). God made no attempt to explain what Yahweh (Jehovah) God meant. He, the ever-present God, was known by His actions. God interacted with Abraham, Isaac, Jacob, Joseph and Moses, who came to know Him as the "God who is there." Unlike the gods of the nations, He never left His people; He was not a god far-removed from His creation. There were no deistic concepts associated with Him. He was the "God in the midst" of His people, at all times and under all circumstances (Exo.33:14-17; Dan.3:24-26; cf. Mt:28:20; Heb.13:5).

The God Israel had come to know was also the God of promise and fulfillment: "God is not a man, that He should lie, nor a son of man, that He should repent; has He said, and will He not do it? or has He spoken, and will He not make it good?" (Num.23:19) As the self-existent God who is never absent from His people, His presence guaranteed that He would keep His promises. He was not a tribal deity restricted to specific activities and regions: "Where can I go from Thy Spirit? Or where can I flee from Thy presence?" (Ps.139:7), "Whatever the LORD pleases, He does, in heaven and in earth" (Ps.135:6). He was the God of mighty acts, intervening in spite of man's indifference or unbelief. He refused to be manipulated by rituals, liturgies, or entreaties. Although He pledged never to be absent from His people, He would not be at their disposal, to suit their convenience (1 Ki. 9:3-9)

A Distinct Sense of Family

Israel had a distinct identity. Amidst strange peoples, the Jews maintained their ethnic and religious distinctives: "For you are a holy people to the LORD your God; the LORD your God has chosen you to be a people for His own possession out of all the peoples who are on the face of the earth" (Dt.7:6). Again:

> "And the LORD has today declared you to be His people, a treasured possession, as He promised you, and that you should keep His commandments; and that He shall set you high above all nations which He has made, for praise, fame, and honor; and that you shall be a consecrated people to the LORD your God, as He has spoken" (Dt.26:18-19).

In Egypt, Israel experienced phenomenal population growth (even as promised to the fathers), which brought resentment and slavery. But though they were dispersed into slave labor gangs among the Egyptians (Exo.1:7-12), throughout their 400-year sojourn they had a sense of family binding them to each other (Gen.46:34; 47:1-6; Exo.8:22-23; 9:26). The promise given Abraham that they would be a blessing to the nations, though not always appreciated or understood, solidified them as a people of God. As His means of redemption, they held a special relationship to God. Thus Jacob could say, "The scepter shall not depart from Judah, nor the ruler's staff from between his feet, until Shiloh comes, and to him shall be the obedience of the peoples" (Gen.49:10).

A Distinct Redemptive Mission

Israel's history was not hidden; it was an enactment before all nations. God used Israel's history to deal with other nations, confronting the world with His glory. Israel had a privileged position; she was to work together with God. This did not, however, give her a privileged claim on God; It was solely due to grace. She was not better than other nations; her election simply bore greater honor and obligation. She was to be the means by which other nations would know God's salvation and through which He would provide the Messiah.

A Distinct Covenant Relationship

God's relationship with His covenant people Israel would be expressed through a covenant, bringing them legal status in relationship with God. This unique bond was unlike anything known by the nations with their gods. The nations tended to regard themselves as extensions of their gods. Should they be defeated, their god was defeated. Their gods were there to condone their beliefs and practices, not establish them. The relationship of God to Israel does not resemble this in the least. His being is not tied to their fate. He is never in jeopardy nor does He suffer defeat. He stands above all nations. "He judges in the midst of the rulers [gods].... Arise, O God, judge the earth! For it is Thou who dost possess all the nations" (Ps.82:1,8). He is the "wholly other" God. The people of God, however, were often afflicted with sickness, hunger, and catastrophes. They were persecuted for their faith and walk with God. They were disciplined by Him for correction. They were delivered but also taken captive through His direction. He delivered them to their enemies and from their enemies "for His name's sake" (Ezek.36:20-23). Observed the Psalmist:

> There is no one like Thee among the gods, O LORD; nor are there any works like Thine. All nations whom Thou hast made shall come and worship before Thee, O LORD; and they shall glorify Thy name. For Thou art great and doest wondrous deeds; Thou alone art God (Ps.86:8-10).

A Unique Position before the Nations

Israel had a unique position before God and the nations. Israel knew that the Glory of God—His name—was at issue in every event in her history. Bearing a responsibility to testify to the greatness and majesty of God, she was remarkably conscious that this position was unique among the nations—the psalmists repeatedly refer to this responsibility). God would use Israel's entire history to reveal Himself to the world. This was true of Israel's defeats and victories (Exo.32:12; Num.14:15-16); her blessedness as God's people (Ps.67:1-2); her sufferings (Josh.7:9); and her deliverances from bondage (Dt.9:26-29; Is.37:20).

Israel had extraordinary motivation to declare God's glory. She was not stirred by the nations' physical and spiritual needs. On the contrary, she believed that "the LORD has made Himself known; He has executed judgment. In the work of his own hands the wicked is snared. The wicked will return to Sheol, even all the nations who forget God" (Ps.9:16,17). Her motivation was rather the concern that all nations recognize that God is Lord of all, and there is no other. Israel could bear anything provided the nations never got the idea that their

God was powerless to deliver His people. Therefore the Psalmist said, "Help us, O God of our salvation, for the glory of Thy name; and deliver us, and forgive our sins, for Thy name's sake. Why should the nations say, 'Where is their God?' " (Ps.79:9-10). "Arise, O LORD, do not let man prevail; let the nations be judged before Thee. Put them in fear, O LORD; let the nations know that they are but men" (Ps.9:19,20; cf. Ps.115:2; Joel 2:17).

Israel was to be concerned with God alone:

> The LORD reigns, let the peoples tremble; He is enthroned above the cherubim, let the earth shake! The LORD is great in Zion, and He is exalted above all the peoples. Let them praise Thy great and awesome name; holy is He (Ps.99:1-3).

She was reminded that she lived in view of the entire world, therefore:

> O clap your hands, all peoples; shout to God with the voice of joy. For the LORD Most High is to be feared, a great King over all the earth. He subdues peoples under us, and nations under our feet. He chooses our inheritance for us, the glory of Jacob whom He loves.... Sing praises to God, sing praises.... For God is the King of all the earth.... God reigns over the nations (Ps.47:1-4,6-8).

God's purpose for Israel was that through her the nations would know that "our God is in the heavens; He does whatever He pleases" (Ps.115:3); and "that our LORD is above all gods. Whatever the LORD pleases, He does, in heaven and in earth" (Ps.135:5-6). He alone is sovereign.

The Context of Liberation

Israel had nothing to commend her to God as His agent of redemption. She was subjected to Egyptian slavery and oppression, a helpless people living under oppressive rulers. All she could do was cry out in distress and anguish (2 Chron.20:12). Remembering that God, who does not forget His covenants and promises, would heed her cry, she was sustained: "I know that the LORD will maintain the cause of the afflicted" (Ps. 140:12). God, who had been preparing Israel as His vehicle of redemption, sovereignly raised up Moses in a face-to-face encounter (Exo.3).

God was about to deliver Israel from the oppression of slavery to a new life. This rescue would ever be the touchstone of Israel's faith.

The people repeatedly would rehearse God's mighty acts of deliverance as the basis of their faith. The events surrounding this deliverance would form a theology of recital of new beginnings that would sustain Israel and motivate her to know and experience God as the God of new beginnings—One who was ever willing to do "something new" (Is.43:19). The creation events of Genesis were a telling account of God's ability to create out of nothing; He would certainly be able to care for His people and accomplish their deliverance now. This deliverance, and God's ability to do something new would also forcefully remind Israel of God's plans of deliverance for other nations (Is.19:19-25; cf. Ezek.36:20-38).

A Confessional Recital of God's Mighty Acts

The Exodus deliverance became Israel's public confession (Exo.15:1-21) before the observing nations and the basis of her worship. The events would be recited in liturgy and be the oft-repeated basis of their faith in Yahweh God (Dt.26:5-9; Josh.24:2-13; Ps.22:4,5; 44:1-7). Narrating these events kept the past alive in the present. There could be no doubt that the God who had promised was the God who fulfilled His promises and would continue to fulfill them: "has He said, and will He not do it?" (Num.23:19) To this day, the commemoration of Passover is a reminder of God's faithfulness.

The recital of the Exodus events gave the nation the identity as a "chosen people." By constantly remembering their supernatural deliverance, the people maintained their self-identity as God's possession. God's intervention crystallized that distinction of being set apart from all other people, not to receive special favor as an end in itself, but in order to be God's blessing to all nations.

The Exodus became the gospel of God's intervention to deliver man from bondage. God Himself intervened in history on behalf of man to deliver him from oppression and slavery. In power encounter with Egypt's gods, God triumphed and effected a remarkable deliverance for Israel from all oppression and slavery.

In brief, Israel's statement of faith reflected a God who would intervene when there was no human possibility of change. He was the God who could deliver even when all the powers of hell were let loose to prevent it. Israel's God could protect with no visible security in sight. He could provide in the midst of utter deprivation. He would act in mercy even when their conduct demanded judgment. He would not forsake His people but would rescue them, even when their own disobedience caused their captivity.

These realities speak significantly to the task of world evangelization. What kind of people does God use? What do they have to commend themselves to God? What do they know and believe? What is their basis of faith—their confessional recital? What is their preoccupation? Did Paul have these people in mind when he penned the description of the kind of people that will be used by God? (1 Cor.1:26-29).

Moses, Mediator of God's Mighty Acts

Whenever God moves in history, He takes one who feels strongly about issues and is willing to take risks while relying on God. In this respect we are told that "the eyes of the LORD move to and fro throughout the earth that He may strongly support those whose heart is completely His" (2 Chron.16:9).

The Man Moses

What characterized Moses? What set Him apart? He felt indignation in the face of oppression (Exo.2:11-13; cf. Acts 17:16). The dehumanization of his people caused him to feel strongly about the oppressors. A man of action, Moses was not beyond taking matters into his own hands. He felt strongly about social issues, even as did his God, who would mandate a just society for Israel (see "The Cultural Mandate," chapter 12).

Moses had a personal relationship with God and came to know Him as the God who spoke with, saw, heard, felt for, sent, and delivered people (Exo.3). He modeled God's desired person-to-person relationship with man which began in the Garden of Eden. Of him it was said, "Thus the LORD used to speak to Moses face to face, just as a man speaks to his friend" (Exo.33:11). Numbers records: "With him I speak mouth to mouth, even openly, and not in dark sayings; and he beholds the form of the LORD" (Num. 12:8). The Living Bible paraphrase reads:

> "Even with a prophet, I would communicate by visions and dreams; but that is not how I communicate with My servant Moses. He is completely at home in My house! With him I speak face to face. And he shall see the very form of God!" (Num.12:8).

Moses' intimacy with God made him sensitive to His desires. Moses discerned God's purpose for people to worship and serve Him.

Even though he doubted his ability to be God's spokesman (Exo.4:10), Moses trusted God's promised presence and power

(Exo.3:14). Thus Moses not only bore a message of truth but also embodied the message God intended (Exo.32:30-33).

Moses, the Missionary Model

Moses was a helpless man of faith who along with God brought liberation to an enslaved people. The Exodus deliverance portrays Moses as "the first missionary" (Rowley 1956:30), sent to bring deliverance to those in slavery. As a missionary he was *called* by God at the burning-bush encounter in the wilderness. *He knew that God had singled him out* as His "sent one." As a missionary *he was sent by God* to Egypt on a very specific mission to declare God's glory, majesty, and supremacy over all powers (Exo.9:16). *He confidently faced enemy territory* under the control of formidable gods and spirit powers, believing that none matched God. As God's missionary *Moses demonstrated the glory of God with great power by challenging the gods* and calling them to account before God. *Moses effected deliverance by bringing the people out of bondage into a new life* with new beginnings. As a missionary *he aligned the delivered people with God's purposes*, serving and worshiping Him (Exo.3:12; 5:1; 8:1,8-20; 9:1; 10:26).

> There was the prophetic personality of the man who appeared in the name of God to promise a deliverance he and the Israelites were helpless to effect; and there was the historic event of the deliverance which responded to his prior promise.... Discount the call of Moses, and we are left with no reasonable explanation of his strange errand, or basis for his confidence of success that no material power was at any point invoked to achieve (Rowley 1956:42).

The Manifestation of God's Mighty Acts

During the protracted power encounter, all the Egyptian gods were exposed as powerless compared to God, although their presence and limited power were not denied. Though the magicians indeed challenged the manifestation of God's power, finally they had to yield, and admit that "This is the finger of God" (Exo.8:19).

God clearly displayed His redemptive activity in the Exodus. In the confrontation with the gods, God's desire to deliver man became progressively evident. No power can retain its hold on man when God acts. In the actual controversy with Pharaoh, there was the hardening of his heart because of his refusal to submit to God. The same principle applied here as in Romans: God gave them up to realize the awful results of perversity. And yet, not even man's rebellion and its consequences could prevent God from realizing His purpose of deliverance.

Behind Pharaoh's hardening of heart was the gods' deception, seeking to keep Egyptians in bondage to false worship and Israelites in slavery. These false gods persisted in misleading man, tempting him to act independently of God, thus creating chaos by threatening God's created order (cf. 2 Cor.4:4). Paul puts this deception in perspective: "you...walked according to the course of this world, according to the prince of the power of the air, of the spirit that is now working in the sons of disobedience" (Eph.2:2). Through power encounter with these gods, God displayed their limitations. In the mounting crises, the plagues singled out the gods of the Egyptians and exposed their powerlessness: "and against all the gods of Egypt I will execute judgments—I am the LORD" (Exo.12:12; cf. Exo.7:7-12).

God revealed that His deliverance was inseparable from the payment of a price. The final deliverance from the power of the gods had to come through a blood confession. Therefore at the climax of God's deliverance was a ransom—the passover lamb. The final confession of the people of God before the Egyptians was with the blood of the passover lamb staining their doorposts and lintels, and by extension covering them (Exo.12-13). This passover lamb foreshadowed another Lamb, slain from the foundation of the earth (Rev.13:8, see margin; Gen.3:15), who would not only reverse the awful consequences of man's sin and bring reconciliation with God, but also destroy the works of the devil (1 Jn.3:8; cf. Col.2:14-15). When Israel obediently sacrificed the Passover (Exo.12:3-28), Passover lamb, God passed over her iniquity and released her from the hold of the gods. Thus through triumph over death God demonstrated who finally has control over all powers, including death. This was the spoiling of the gods of the Egyptians on that "night to be remembered" (Exo.12:27,29-30).

Through faith the promised deliverance became reality. The people acted in faith and God responded in power. No situation was too difficult for God—the Egyptian pursuit and Israel's deliverance at the Red Sea further illustrate this (Exo.14:10-31). Further, God continued to control all the powers which, in spite of defeat, did not stop trying to destroy Israel.

The signs, wonders, plagues and victories over the gods demonstrated to the Egyptians and the other nations that God was more than able to accomplish His objectives (Exo.7:5; 8:10; 9:14,16,29; 14:4,18; 15:14-16; Neh. 9:9-25). Israel now had a history of God's interventions.

The signs and wonders were not primarily that Israel might know God's power, but the nations might know God's power and His desire to deliver man.

Missiological Considerations

The Exodus deliverance testified that salvation was solely an act of God. God took the initiative; God alone delivered. Moses was His prophet, but deliverance was in the name of the Lord God, through His power. Yet man was not simply a passive spectator; he worked with God, being called upon to respond to God's direction. And when he did, God wrought salvation (cf. 2 Chron.20:12-15).

The Exodus demonstrates that there must be a faith response. In the case of the call of Moses, God expected a faith response: a turning aside and an openness to hear and obey God. In the case of the Israelites there had to be a faith response by applying the blood to the doorposts and lintels. Faith honors God; "without faith it is impossible to please Him" (Heb.11:6). Action and faith are inseparable. Through faith in a prophetic word of promise and fulfillment, an enslaved people obeyed God's command, applied the blood, and realized God's deliverance.

From a human standpoint, God suspended "normal" natural laws to bring deliverance. But since God's creation presupposes His supremacy over all forces, there need be no surprise that God performed miracles to deliver man. In signs and wonders God brings His beneficial laws to bear on dehumanizing circumstances. Should the suspension of natural laws be necessary, He will do it (Ps.111:1-6).

The deliverance from Egypt was nothing less than a redemptive activity. God, in grace and mercy, reached into time and space to bring into being a "new people" set apart to seek Him and implement His purposes for all nations: "He has made known to His people the power of His works, in giving them the heritage of the nations" (Ps.111:6). To this day, the deliverance from Egyptian bondage is remembered as an event reflecting God's grace and glory.

Deliverance from the bondage of personal or structural sin is all of grace and for God's glory. Anything less is mere humanism, which ultimately will lead to dehumanization. These are foundational biblical truths which undergird and motivate world mission. It is an injustice to man and an insult to God when man, made in His image, is prevented from being all God designed, in truth and holiness of life. In the Egyptian deliverance, God bought back what was rightfully His; He restored to man the dignity of freedom and choice to respond to Him in faith. God gave man a renewed purpose, for through His redeemed people,

He planned to have His glory cover the face of the earth (Num.14:21; Mal.1:11).

The deliverance from Egyptian bondage emphasized that God watches over the fate of all nations (Amos 9:7; cf. Is.19-22). He moves through history to bring reconciliation until "every knee will bow, every tongue will swear allegiance...[saying]...'Only in the LORD are righteousness and strength' " (Is.45:23,24).

CHAPTER 11

COMMITMENT AND

OBLIGATION

The historic deliverance from Egyptian bondage was not to be an end in itself. God's people, recipients of the mighty saving acts of God, were to bear a new treasure. They were to be witnesses of this great God who desires to deliver all nations from all types of bondage.

The Exodus deliverance, including the events at the Red Sea and at Mount Sinai, emphasizes that election demands response. Israel's relationship with God was to be maintained by accepting God's commission to be His priest-nation to all other nations (Exo.19:3-8; cf. Rom.15:16; Acts 13:47). God had acted on their behalf; as His elect people, they were to act on His behalf. They were to communicate God's world-embracing purposes so that all nations might ascribe Him the glory. The nations would then seek to bring His created order to reflect His glory (Ps.8:6-9; 96:3,8; Is.66:18-19; cf. Eph.2:8-10, especially verse 10).

A Covenant-Law Commitment

Israel was to understand that her relationship to God is founded upon obedience to the covenant. Therefore, in accepting the calling to be His priest-nation, Israel's people agreed to bind themselves to God's covenant with them. From now on, covenant laws would prescribe their relationship to God. Man would know God in a living and personal relationship as he submitted to God's covenant law and responded in faith and obedience to Him. God was not His law, but

God's laws and person were inseparable. His law was the reproduction of His holiness. Israel could not claim the one and reject the other. Israel, therefore, was to be holy, even as He was holy, if she claimed a relationship with Him (Lev.11:45).

A Remembrance of Deliverance

Keeping God's covenant law was to be a remembrance of Israel's deliverance from slavery and oppression, a constant reminder of what they had been and what they had become as God's people:

> "So keep the words of this covenant to do them, that you may prosper in all that you do. You stand today, all of you, before the LORD your God; ... that you may enter into the covenant with the LORD your God, and into His oath which the LORD your God is making with you today, in order that He may establish you today as His people and that He may be your God, just as He spoke to you and as He swore to your fathers, to Abraham, Isaac, and Jacob. Now not with you alone am I making this covenant and this oath, but both with those who stand here with us today in the presence of the LORD our God and with those who are not with us here today" (Dt.29:9-10,12-15).

Identification with God's Mission

The Law was given to define and shape their new life under God. Keeping this covenant law would *qualify them to represent God* among the nations. Their modeling the law would show that they truly knew the Lord God. Justice and righteousness would characterize all areas of their life.

In becoming God's covenant people *several profound relationships were established* which would undergird Israel's mission to the nations.

First, the meaning of their corporate and individual life originated with God, who makes history for His purposes. Meaning came to their life when they followed God's purposes rather than their own, as all of Israel's history illustrated.

Second, man's relationships with God and his fellow man were based primarily on morals and ethics, not rituals. God refused to be manipulated through religious devices, as the nations sought to do. God called His people to focus on Himself, to walk by faith, to maintain truth, to redeem time, and to accept responsibility for all aspects of interpersonal relationships (Exo.20:1-17).

Third, Israel was called to a total allegiance. The people were to keep the law, not in order to become God's people, but because they *were* God's people. Therefore God's demand for total allegiance to Himself and His covenant had to penetrate every facet of their corporate and individual life:

> "You shall be blameless before the LORD your God. For those nations, which you shall dispossess, listen to those who practice witchcraft and to diviners, but as for you, the LORD your God has not allowed you to do so" (Dt.18:13,14).

> "For I the LORD your God, am a jealous God, visiting the iniquity of the fathers on the children, on the third and fourth generations of those who hate me" (Exo.20:5; cf. Exo.34:14-16).

God categorically prohibited the worship of any other god (Dt.5:7).

Fourth, they were called to be a model people. God's call was not so that He could have a people with peculiar culture and customs, nor a people upon whom He merely could shower His blessings, but a people whose individual and corporate life reflected His justice, righteousness, and holiness. They were separated to God for special *service—to model God's kingdom on earth* (Dt.4:5-8), in order to bring the nations to salvation (Is.45:22-24).

Fifth, we see in God's interaction with Israel His untiring commitment to His people. By entering a covenant with His people, God assured them of His continued activity on their behalf.

Sixth, He would retain sovereignty over all situations, exercising His untiring faithfulness to fulfill His promises and so accomplish His purposes. For every generation, the Exodus had a contemporary significance. No national crisis or personal misfortune was beyond the reach of God's mercy and power. From generation to generation fathers told the story to their sons, a story that disclosed who their God was, what He was doing, and what He would do in the future.

Missiological Considerations

Israel's covenant relationship with God, established at Sinai, underscored several significant missiological factors.

The nations were distinguished from Israel as the people whom God does not know (Amos 3:2 KJV; cf. Dt. 7:6). This does not mean that God did not desire their deliverance, but that He had no intimate relationship with them, as He had with Israel. God was dealing constantly with other nations, but they suppressed and aborted His truth.

Israel's election did not mean that God had rejected other nations. God was still concerned about them and desired a close relationship with them. Quoting God, Isaiah said, "Egypt My people...Assyria the work of My hands" (Is.19:25).

Israel's peculiar relationship to all nations was God's primary frame of reference for evaluating her. He spoke of her as "my witness" (Is. 43:10) and "light to all nations" (Is. 49:6) and therefore "the apple of my eye." Israel was His central focus because she was His vehicle to declare His Glory.

The covenant law defined and shaped Israel's mission to the nations. The covenant law, and Israel's modeling of it, were so that the nations would know that God is *sui generis*, totally unlike all other gods. The gods of the nations brought their followers only dehumanization and destruction. They were powerless to deliver from all that enslaved man and powerless to elevate man to his rightful place as vice-regent. On the contrary, they condoned man's perversity and caused their devotees to fear themselves, other men, and the environment. Instead of their followers exercising dominion, they were tyrannized. By contrast, God's encounters with Israel were to let the nations see that He was a God of holiness, righteousness, and justice—totally impartial to all people, including His own.

Through Israel, the nations would see the blessing of living according to God's laws. A life of obedience to God is the life of benediction: "O taste and see that the LORD is good, how blessed is the man who takes refuge in Him" (Ps.34:8); and, "How great is Thy goodness, which Thou hast stored up for those who fear Thee, which Thou hast wrought for those who take refuge in Thee, before the sons of men" (Ps.31:19).

God's dealings with Israel directly concerned other nations: "God blesses us: that all the ends of the earth may fear Him" (Ps.67:7). The nations were free to have a relationship with Israel and share in her salvation and blessing (Exo.12:47-49; Num.9:14; 15:16,29; cf. Dt.23:7-8; Ruth 2:10-12). Israel's history revealed that whenever she disregarded the covenant of God, she walled herself off from those around her and rejected her obligation to the nations.

Israel was to be a model of submission to God's Lordship, representing the Kingship of Yahweh God. She was His first fruits from the nations. For others to follow, they too had to submit to His Lordship: "The LORD will establish you as a holy people to Himself as He swore to you; if you will keep the commandments of the LORD your God, and walk in His ways, *so all the people of the earth shall see that you are called by the name of the LORD*" (Dt.28:9,10, emphasis added).

God's interaction with Israel was *a message to all nations*. The covenant law was not to maintain the status quo, but to help develop right relationships in man's total context. It focused on the restoration and reconciliation of the created order. Living by God's laws was meant to motivate all who were oppressed to seek deliverance.

The covenant law commanded individuals to be just; to deliver the oppressed; to provide for the needy; to lift the burden of the weak; and to deal wisely and justly with the environment. It dealt with both property and people, providing for the settlement of rights and correction of wrongs. Correcting inequities and seeking reconciliation in all relationships were underscored in the giving of the Sabbath, the Seventh Year, and the year of the Jubilee. The covenant law was the mandated approach to God for sinful, self-seeking man. Man had to be made fit to live in the presence of God.

The nations, witnessing Yahweh God's presence and activity in Israel, were summoned to recognize Him as the God of the whole earth (Ps. 86:8-10; 102:15-16). The gods of the nations could not compare with the Lord God. He would not tolerate any distortion or caricature of His character. He alone is Sovereign God, and He alone is able to deliver. Since God was not to be confused with any pagan deity, He provided Israel with everything they needed to exhibit what being a people of God meant (Dt. 33:26-29; cf. 2 Pet.1:3-4).

If the Church is to participate in God's mission in the world, it must take to heart God's working in and through Israel. Although God's Old Testament people had a unique relationship to Him, His New Testament people have the same mandate to declare His glory among the nations, the glory due His name.

CHAPTER 12

ACCOUNTABILITY

FOR CREATION

The "good" that God had built into creation was a potential good, to be used for man's welfare and God's glory, and Israel shared this responsibility with Him. Thus God's delivered, covenant people received specific directions about how to position themselves in regard to the rest of creation, including their fellow man (Exo.20-23; Dt.5-30; Lev.11-27). Kuitert, reflecting on this responsibility, observed:

> We cannot see God in man while man stands still.... The question, then, is what is man for, what is his calling? What is he here for? He is here to reflect God, to reflect God the covenant partner. To be God's image means simply that we as men are to live as covenant partners with God and with our fellows on earth (Mouw 1976:27).

And man must also live as covenant partner in relationship to all creation. Only as man carries out his office of stewardship is he faithful to his covenant relationship with God (cf. Ps.8).

God entered the covenant with His people at Sinai to restore to man, and to require of man, dominion over His creation, which man had squandered in Eden. *Accountability for creation–the cultural mandate is speaking of this stewardship of creation.* In his relationships with creation, man must demonstrate faithfulness to his office of co-regent. Although man's relationship to God is spiritual, and God's Kingdom is first and foremost spiritual, the spiritual dimension is unavoidably reflected in physical categories. Therefore, implementing the cultural mandate will show practically what our Lord emphasized in the Lord's Prayer: "Thy Kingdom come. Thy will be done, on earth as it is in heaven." To realize that Kingdom on earth, though imperfectly, His covenant people had ethical and moral obligations regarding all creation.

To win the nations, God structured a model nation to exemplify His Lordship over creation. As God's model, Israel had to reflect His gracious rule and His just and righteous character. She had to respond in a godly way to those aspects of creation with which she had direct contact, and in a way that the nations would readily observe the distinctions between themselves and those who have God as Lord. How was this to be achieved?

The Divine Strategy

God gave Israel a "heaven-planned culture," which was what He had always intended for all mankind. Of all the nations, Israel was privileged to reflect His Kingdom among the nations by living according to a God-structured culture, to model what it meant to live in a theocracy under Yahweh God, drawing the nations to seek Him. In Israel's obedience to His statutes and judgments, the nations would see the grace, goodness, and wisdom of God who desires justice and righteousness in all of life:

> Take away from Me the noise of your songs; I will not even listen to the sound of your harps. But let justice roll down like waters and righteousness like an ever-flowing stream (Amos 5:23-24).

A Distinctive Lifestyle

At Sinai God gave Israel a distinct identity, giving explicit instructions regarding the distinctive lifestyle He wanted them to adopt. To be "God's people" was an honor. A covenant relationship with the Sovereign God led to abundant blessing and privileged responsibilities in all of life (cf. Tit.2:11-15).

The process of acculturizing the people into a new society with a distinct lifestyle took at least a generation. The majority refused to conform to God's norms for a theocratic society. For 40 years Israel had to wander in the wilderness as the new society took shape with the passing away of the older generation. The younger generation, having accepted God's directives for a God-centered culture, now entered their inheritance and established a kingdom reflecting God's designs for justice and righteousness. Israel's new lifestyle was markedly different from the lifestyles of the nations surrounding her.

The modeling of a theocracy (God's Kingdom among men) demonstrated God's concern for maintaining the cultural mandate for the sake of all His creation (cf. 1 Tim.2:1-4; Rom.8:19-22). The heart of God is reflected in this concern:

> "There shall be no poor among you, since the LORD will surely bless you in the land which the LORD God is giving you as an inheritance to possess, if only you listen obediently to the voice of the LORD your God, to observe carefully all this commandment which I am commanding you today. For the LORD your God shall bless you as He has promised you, and you will lend to many nations, but you will not borrow" (Dt.15:4-6).

Specific Responsibilities

God spelled out some *specific responsibilities* for which He would hold man accountable. These related to land ownership and distribution, slavery, minority peoples, widows, and a variety of other sociocultural issues.

Concerning *land ownership*, God told Israel that she took possession of the land not as owner, but as tenant. The people were expected to pay rent for using the land (Lev.27:30; Dt.26:1-12). The land belonged to God, not to men. "The land ... shall not be sold permanently, for the land is Mine; for you are but aliens and sojourners with Me" (Lev.25:23). As tenants the people of Israel were accountable for the land. All families were to participate equally in the tenancy of the land. Should someone not be able to handle his business affairs properly, losing his inheritance, the land would be returned to him in the Jubilee year. Stewardship of the land and the animal kingdom was emphasized (Lev.25:1-7), as God was recognized as owner and Sovereign Lord over all activities of His people.

> "When you have eaten and are satisfied, you shall bless the LORD your God for the good land which He has given you.... [And] when you have ... built good houses and lived in them, and when your herds and your flocks multiply, and your silver and gold multiply, and all that you have multiplies, then your heart becomes proud, and you forget the LORD your God.... you may say in your heart, `My power and the strength of my hand made me this wealth.' But you shall

remember the LORD your God, for it is He who is giving you power to make wealth, that He may confirm His covenant which He swore to your fathers, as it is this day " (Dt.8:10,12-14,17-18).

This stewardship recognizes that all returns from the labors of man are from God, who is actively involved in providing for His people; He was not some "lord of the castle," unconcerned for and uninvolved in the affairs of the tenants. Since every seventh year the land was would lie fallow, the sixth year would have a larger harvest, after the pattern of the manna in the wilderness (Exo.23:10-11; Lev.25:2-7). Thus the people would not suffer deprivation even though the land was not tilled.

There was a commitment to *land redistribution* (Lev.25) during the Year of the Jubilee. All of the land was "trust" land and was carefully guarded against exploitation. This demanded the practice of soil conservation. Every seventh and 50th year the land was to lie fallow to regain its productivity. Further, original ownership of the land had to be guaranteed. All peasants who had lost their freedom and their land through insolvency were set free. If this had not yet occurred, it was to be done during the Year of Jubilee. The sold lands were to be returned to the original owner or his family:

"If a fellow-countryman of yours becomes so poor he has to sell part of his property, then his nearest kinsman is to come and buy back what his relative has sold.... But if he has not found sufficient means to get it back for himself, then what he has sold shall remain in the hands of its purchaser until the year of jubilee; but at the jubilee it shall revert, that he may return to his property" (Lev.25:25, 28).

God thus showed his impartiality to all and rejected the selfish concept and practice of a land-owning aristocracy: "Woe to those who add house to house and join field to field, until there is no more room, so that you have to live alone in the midst of the land" (Is.5:8).

God gave very specific directives concerning *slavery*. Slaves were considered family rather than aliens (cf. Exo.12:44), not as inferiors, though they had few or no civil rights (cf. Dt.15:16-17). Slaves were not to be treated as material property, even though they may have been acquired by purchase (Gen.17:12), captured in war (Num.31:9), born to slaves already owned (Exo.21:4), gained as payment for debt (Lev.25:39,47), or as a gift (Gen.32:22). The Mosaic Law bound the master to protect the slave and did not allow exploitation (Dt.15:12ff; Exo.21:2-11,20-21, 26-27; Lev.25:39-55). Disregarding these statutes not only led to abuses but also brought God's judgment (Jer.34:8-22). Israel was to be known for her compassion, even as seen in God's giving cities of refuge.

Israel had to accord *minority peoples* special consideration (Exo.12:49; 20:10; 23:9). They were classified with widows, fatherless children, and the needy and given a recognized place in society (Dt.14:29; Ps.146:9). The non-Israelite within Israel's care had certain rights and privileges:

> "For the LORD your God is the God of gods and the Lord of lords, the great, the mighty, and the awesome God who does not show partiality, nor take a bribe. He executes justice for the orphan and the widow, and shows His love (compassion) for the alien by giving him food and clothing. So show your love for the alien, for you were aliens in the land of Egypt" (Dt.10:17-19).

The Israelites were obligated to love them (Lev.19:34), help them, and not oppress them (Exo.22:21), nor neglect them (Dt.24:19-22). Aliens also had social and religious obligations and shared in covenant obligations (Dt.29:10-12; 31:12; Josh.8:33-35).

God did not want people to be poor (Dt.15:4), but if through circumstances they became destitute then Israel had to accept responsibility for them. Israel was to return their land and make loans available interest free. Israel was also to give generously of its means, allowing the poor to glean the fields and reaching out to them in whatever special need they might have (Dt.15:4,7-11). Throughout Scripture, God mandated that His people reflect His compassion for the poor:

> "Is this not the fast which I choose, to loosen the bonds of wickedness, to undo the bands of the yoke, and to let the oppressed go free, and break every yoke? Is it not to divide your bread with the hungry, and bring the homeless poor into the house; when you see the naked, to cover him; and not to hide yourself from your own flesh?" (Is.58:6-7)

The majority of the 205 references to the poor in the Old and New Testaments concern those who are materially poor, emphasizing God's concern for this segment of society.

Widows, though frequently associated with the orphan and alien, stood in their own right in Israelite society. Because traditional cultures made it very difficult for a widow to survive without remarrying or prostituting herself, Israel, as God's model of the cultural mandate, was given very specific directions concerning her welfare. The widow was regarded as a helpless, needy person, unable to protect or provide for herself. "Cease to do evil, learn to do good; seek justice, reprove the ruthless; defend the orphan, plead for the widow" (Is.1:16-17). She is to be given special consideration and treated with justice (Exo.22:22-24; Dt.10:18; 24:17-22; 26:13; Mal.3:5).

Numerous other sociocultural matters came under God's review in the wisdom literature, the prophetic books, the writings of Moses, and the New Testament references to these matters. *Labor* was respected, not despised as among the Greeks and other non-Israelite tribes. *Idleness* was denounced. *Child training* was a family responsibility; parents were required to "train" their children (Dt.6:4-7). Although much of the training was in apprenticeship form, there was also training in the Law of God, in order to observe His statutes and judgments (Dt.4:5-9).

The people were to be *interdependent and responsible for each other*, as pictured in the 12 sons of Jacob who were concerned for one another standing before Joseph in Egypt. The people had to know they belonged to God and to each other. They were corporately the people of God; what affected one, affected all (Josh.7). *Social relationships* were clearly defined and structured to protect the individual and safeguard the welfare of the community. *Sexual concerns* were strictly defined and infractions brought severe judgments. Any stripping of *human dignity* was guarded against and severely censured, even to the point of death. The covenant and commandments of God assured dignity and respect to all within Israelite society (Lev. 19:29-20:23). Even the *animal kingdom* was to be protected from exploitation and cruelty (Exo.23:12; Lev.25:7; Dt.25:4). *Health laws* were given to protect both man and environment.

> "If you will give earnest heed to the voice of the LORD your God, and do what is right in His sight, and give ear to His commandments, and keep all His statutes, I will put none of the diseases on you which I have put upon the Egyptians; for I, the LORD, am your healer" (Exo.15:26).

God's design for life assured "shalom"—genuine welfare for all.

> "But the land into which you are about to cross to posses it ... a land for which the LORD your God cares; *the eyes of the LORD your God are always on it*, from the beginning even to the end of the year. And it shall come about, *if you listen obediently to my commandments* ... that He will give the rain for your land in its season ... that you may gather in your grain and your new wine and your oil. And He will give grass... for your cattle, and you shall eat and be satisfied" (Dt.11:11-15, emphasis added).

Living within the bounds of the cultural mandate was a very significant way in which Israel would model the Lordship of God over all of life, and thus also ascribe Him glory. The mandate for such a different, distinct, non-exploitive approach to man, animal, and plant-life was derived from God Himself.

All God's directives were intended to produce a "kingdom model" before the nations. God spelled out in detail what life under His benevolent rule would be like. His assured presence and Israel's obedient response would bring peace, blessing, and victory in the encounter with the nations. Israel's obedience to God was not confined to merely keeping God's commands (cf. Lk.18:18-25); the people were to truly know God and love Him with all their heart (1 Sam.12:20,24; 2 Chron.15:12; Is.29:13-14; cf. Mt.22:36-38). They were to make Him known to their neighbors, the surrounding nations (Jonah; cf. Lk.10:25-37). The cultural mandate was not instituted simply for man's well-being, but to model God's theocratic kingdom before the watching nations, to draw them to seek God.

Even when Israel failed, there was a way to restoration. In carrying through with the *sacrificial system* Israel acknowledged her own sinfulness and showed the nations that *God provided a way of reconciliation* for man to know fellowship with Himself (Num. 28;29). Acknowledged failure led to restoration. Declaring His glory and testifying to Him through lifestyle were the evangelistic and cultural mandates. By living in obedience to God the Israelites would ascribe Him glory by modeling His wisdom.

> "For what great nation is there that has a god so near to it as is the LORD our God.... Or what great nation is there that has statutes and judgments as righteous as this whole law" (Dt.4:7- 8);

> "And you shall do what is right and good in the sight of the LORD, that it may be well with you and that you may go in and possess the good land.... So the LORD commanded us to observe all these statutes, to fear the LORD our God for our good always ... and it will be righteousness for us if we are careful to observe all this commandment before the LORD our God, just as He commanded us" (Dt.6:18,24,25).

Missiological Considerations

The bearers of the Gospel must demonstrate integrity in all of life if they are to be credible witnesses of God. Biblical faith is more than merely believing certain things about God. It must issue in a total lifestyle which demonstrates the righteousness and justice of God in all of life. Concern for right belief apart from right living contradicts the biblical thrust to ascribe God the glory.

Biblical faith does not separate the spiritual from the physical. Man is not merely a spirit inhabiting a body; he is a whole being made in the image of God (1 Thess.5:23). Western materialists may dichotomize human life, but the Bible does not. It is injustice for anyone made in the image of God to live in any way inconsistent with that image, like a mere animal.

God has supplied the resources to carry through with His mandate to "multiply and fill the earth," so it is imperative that God's co-regents practice stewardship of all He has placed at their disposal. They can never claim ownership of anything. They are to meet needs creatively and direct God's resources to areas of need. They are not only to maintain this world, but also to unwrap its potential for man's benefit in order to ascribe God the glory and make Him known among all nations. He is the God who has provided a design for man's total welfare—spiritual, emotional, physical, and material. In contrast, the destroyer, who would rob God of His glory, will do anything he can to dehumanize man. He does not want man to worship God, give Him thanks, or live his life as an expression of God's image. But God is concerned for the totality of human life. Jesus Christ put it all in biblical perspective when He declared:

> "I am the door; if anyone enters through Me, he shall be saved, and shall go in and out, and find pasture. *The thief comes only to steal, and kill, and destroy: I came that they might have life, and might have it abundantly.* I am the good shepherd; the good shepherd lays down His life for the sheep. He who is a hireling, and not a shepherd, who is not the owner of the sheep, beholds the wolf coming, and leaves the sheep, and flees, and the wolf snatches them, and scatters them. He flees because he is a hireling, and *is not concerned* about the sheep" (Jn.10:9-13, emphasis added).

Implementing the cultural mandate is not an option; it is an imperative that if not put into effect will bring God's judgment (Mt.5,6,7; 25:14-46; Gal.6:7-10; Jas.2; 5:1-6). The cultural mandate is more than social action. It is a life lived in obedience to God's commands, thereby reflecting His kingdom, however imperfectly. It is a life in conformity to the life God intended Israel to live and that Jesus Christ Himself exemplified here on earth.

CHAPTER 13

CONQUEST AND

NATIONHOOD

Israel, constituted a model people before the nations, was now to demonstrate the sovereign grace, power, and purposes of Yahweh God in confrontation with God's enemies. The land, though given, must be taken by confrontation with real enemies. Victory was unquestionable, but man, in faith, must take hold of God's promises. Appropriating God's promises required "battle." Though it may seem contradictory, the promised land had to be fought for.

Preparation for Confrontation

God prepared His people for battle by taking them through the wilderness. If they were to face the armies of Canaanites and their gods, demonstrating by faith that Yahweh God was Lord of all, they needed to know who He was. They had to come to know Him under all circumstances as the faithful, all-powerful, unswerving God who fulfills His promises. The wilderness not only served to acculturate them into God's cultural design, it also trained, tested, and prepared them for battle. Here they got to know themselves and God in an experiential way. The wilderness experience became a foundational factor in their faith. *If the cultural mandate produced a behavioral model, the wilderness experience produced a faith model.*

The people came to know God's *presence, power, and provision* for every circumstance in the wilderness. They came to know God in their midst through the pillar of cloud and pillar of fire, symbols of God's constant presence and guidance. They came to know Him as the immanent God who constantly guided His people, but also as the One

145

upon whom they must wait. They came to know Him as the God of power. No circumstance was too difficult for God. Whether sending manna from heaven, bringing water out of a rock, opening a path through the water, healing people of snake bites, opening the earth to swallow rebels, or dealing with Israel's enemies—all were within God's power. Never would there be a situation in which God could not take care of His people. Further, they came to know Him as the God of unfailing provision, as became evident in His giving manna, meat, water, or clothing that did not wear out.

In the wilderness they learned *total dependence* on God. It was a region of stark destitution—"the howling waste of a wilderness"—where survival depended on someone else supplying provisions from somewhere else. The wilderness taught Israel that following God demanded surrender without visible security. It required total dependence on God for every need. Forsaking all of man's scheming, they had to submit to God in humble and simple faith without any reservations.

God's grace and goodness toward Israel, they learned, were totally apart from the people's righteousness. Israel came to know herself as a murmuring, self-centered, wholly sinful people not deserving God's grace and mercy. Yet God persisted in working in and through her. Israel could never claim that her own righteousness brought her God's blessing: "It is not for your righteousness or for the uprightness of your heart...."(Dt.9:5-7). Israel demonstrated God's compassion and commitment to accomplish His purposes for all nations, in spite of man's frequent rebellion.

A Model for Confrontation

God intended the wilderness experience to produce those characteristics—confidence, assurance, and an anticipation of victory—which would set Israel apart as a community of faith on mission for God. God worked in and through His people who, in faith, were totally dependent upon Him. Joshua and Caleb, true leaders, reflected what all of Israel was supposed to be in confronting God's enemies.

Israel was *a confident people* whose confidence was founded on historical realities. They had experientially known God's mighty acts. They believed God when He said, "No man will be able to stand before you all the days of your life. Just as I have been with Moses, I will be with you; I will not fail you or forsake you" (Josh.1:5 cf. Dt. 31:7-8 Ps. 81:13-14). They had personally experienced God's mighty interventions in their immediate history and confidently anticipated His continued intervention.

As *an assured people*, they had constant reminders of God's unique dealing with them, His covenant people. They were assured of having a working covenant, not only a written record of a covenant. The written word (the statutes and judgments of God) and the living word (the God who promised and fulfilled) undergirded their assurance that God was for them (Ps.56:9-11; cf. Rom.8:31-32). So they believed God's word to Joshua: "You shall give this people possession of the land which I swore to their fathers to give them" (Josh.1:6). As God's delivered people, they believed He would not allow them to be taken into captivity. Their deliverance from slavery, their wanderings through the wilderness, and their impending conquest of the land constituted their confessional creed that God is a God of deliverance. These mighty acts of deliverance became recurring themes throughout the ministry of the prophets, who constantly reminded Israel of God's desire to intervene in His people's history to deliver them.

"By this you shall know that the living God is among you, and that He will assuredly dispossess from before you the [nations] ... Behold, the ark of the Covenant ... is crossing over ahead of you ... and it shall come about when the ... priests who carry the ark ... shall rest in the waters of the Jordan, the waters of the Jordan shall be cut off .... until all the nation had finished crossing the Jordan.... "Israel crossed this Jordan on dry ground" ... that all the peoples of the earth may know that the hand of the LORD is mighty, so that you may fear the LORD your God forever" (Josh.3:10-11,13,17; 4:22,24).

Lastly, they believed *they would be victorious*. They entered the land believing God to secure victory for them. His promise to them was: "Be strong and courageous, do not be afraid or tremble at them, for the LORD your God is the one who goes with you. He will not fail you or forsake you" (Dt. 31:6). And the fulfillment was no surprise:

And the LORD confounded them before Israel, and He slew them ... And Joshua captured all these kings and their lands at one time, because the LORD, the God of Israel, fought for Israel (Josh.10: 10,42);

[And] The LORD gave them rest on every side, according to all that He had sworn to their fathers, and no one of all their enemies stood before them; the LORD gave all their enemies into their hand (Josh.21:44).

147

The Conquest

In conquest, the Israelites simply implemented their confidence in God, who had said that He would fight for them (Exo.14:13-14). They demonstrated their confidence by marching in the vanguard of what God was doing. Beginning about 1405 B.C., utter catastrophe hit the Canaanites, costing them nine-tenths of their land (Tenney 1967:450). Not only was Israel's coming miraculous, but the encounters with their enemies were also miraculous. Numerous events in the invasion made it obvious that a power greater than Israel was present. Their crossing of the Jordan on dry ground was a response in faith to Yahweh God. Jericho falling by the sound of a trumpet was unique. Many a battle in Canaan witnessed the miraculous—for instance, the miraculous defeat of the two gods of Canaan—the sun and moon (Dt.4:19):

> So the sun stood still, and the moon stopped, until the nation avenged themselves on their enemies (Josh.10:13);

> And they came out, they and all their armies with them, as many people as the sand that is on the seashore, with very many horses and chariots.... And the LORD delivered them into the hand of Israel, so that they defeated them.... So Joshua took the whole land, according to all that the LORD had spoken to Moses, and Joshua gave it for an inheritance to Israel.... Thus the land had rest from war (Josh. 11:4:4,8,23).

God had brought them victory as promised.

In rapid succession Israel made three thrusts into Canaan: the central parts (Josh.7-9); the south country (Josh.10); and the far north (Josh.11). In six years (Tenney 1967:450; cf. Josh.14:10) Israel took all the enemy territory except the coastal plain, held by those with chariots which were far superior to foot soldiers. Although Israel conquered the Canaanites, she did not drive them out as commanded by the Lord: "And it came about when the sons of Israel became strong, they put the Canaanites to forced labor, but they did not drive them out completely" (Josh.17:13; cf. Judg.1:28). This toleration of enemy presence became Israel's downfall. God sought to safeguard them from false worship inspired by demonic powers and the consequent destruction which would inevitably follow.

> "You shall make no covenant with the inhabitants of this land; *you shall tear down their altars.* But you have not obeyed Me; what is this you have done?...." Then the sons of Israel did evil in the sight of the LORD, and served the Baals (Judg.2:2,11, emphasis added).

When their faith wavered, the people hesitated to obey God and suffered the consequences. However, at times they were *a people of commitment*. Those who entered the land with Joshua knew a measure of commitment which earned them the commendation: "And the people served the LORD all the days of Joshua, and all the days of the elders who survived Joshua, who had seen all the great work of the LORD which He had done for Israel" (Judg.2:7). As a people committed to God's purposes, they brought fear to the surrounding nations: "When all the kings of the Amorites ... heard how the LORD had dried up the waters of Jordan before the sons of Israel ... their hearts melted" (Josh.5:1; cf. Josh.9:1-14). When the Israelites obeyed, they utterly destroyed the enemy:

> Now Joshua captured Makkedah ... and he utterly destroyed it and every person who was in it. He left no survivor .... Then Joshua ... fought against Libnah.... He left no survivor in it.... And the LORD gave Lachish into the hands of Israel ... and he struck ... every person who was in it .... And Joshua passed on from Lachish to Eglon ... and he utterly destroyed that day every person who was in it ... Hebron ... and he utterly destroyed every person who was in it ... Debir ... and utterly destroyed every person who was in it .... Thus Joshua struck all the land, the hill country and the Negev and the lowland and the slopes and all their kings. He left no survivor, but he utterly destroyed all who breathed, just as the LORD, the God of Israel, had commanded (Josh.10:28-40).

God desired a constant volitional response to His commands. When the people walked in obedience, they knew victory. When they questioned, they suffered defeat. The powers of darkness were constantly trying to deter Israel from fulfilling God's purposes by drawing her into false worship. Thus Joshua, after capturing the land, challenged Israel:

> "Choose for yourselves today whom you will serve: whether the gods which your fathers served which were beyond the River, or the gods of the Amorites in whose land you are living; but as for me and my house, we will serve the LORD" (Josh.24:15).

Short of total obedience, they would be prone to make their own faulty judgments concerning the land and its people (Josh.7;9:3-16).

The Purpose of Canaanite Destruction

God commanded the enemy's destruction to protect Israel from the perverted worship of the gods of Canaan and to safeguard them as His model before the nations.

God also mandated the destruction of the Canaanites because of the evils of their religious forms, and because His patience toward them had ceased (cf. Gen.15:16). God was being just, not cruel. He was not bloodthirsty, but holy and righteous. The dehumanization which issued in all kinds of perversions and murder was opposed to God's design for mankind. Child sacrifice, sexual license, exploitation and dehumanization were all common and accepted as normative. When Israel rejected the covenant, these degradations came to characterize even her life. God wanted all peoples to be freed from the debauchery and degradation of Canaanite culture, so His command to destroy the Canaanites had to be obeyed lest the Canaanites seduce others.

God sought to keep Israel from taking on Canaanite culture. He raised up judges and prophets to warn of the consequences. Even before entering the Promised Land, Moses spelled out the grave consequences of disregarding the covenant (Dt. 27:15-26; 28:15-68).

But Israel did not obey God. She did not utterly destroy the Canaanites, and in time exchanged her covenant religion for that of the nations. Instead of trust and obedience, she settled for rites and rituals of manipulation to excite the gods to do her bidding. Rather than aligning with the purposes of God, motivated by historical memory and moving toward the redemption of all creation, she sought the satisfaction of her appetites. Rather than believing that sin was an offense against a holy God, she viewed sin as the breaking of custom or the use of insufficient use of means to deceive man and the spirit world. Rejecting God, whose compassion would make a way for forgiveness, Israel tried to regain her status through balancing her bad deeds with her good. She exchanged the concept of a covenant community (the corporate serving and worshiping of God) for individual and private esoteric rites seeking to implore deities of caprice. Instead of confessing and repenting only to the one God, the people served many, in case one or several were unresponsive. In spite of God's gracious presence, power, and provision, through her disobedience Israel exchanged the God of glory for demon gods:

"But Israel grew fat and kicked—you are grown fat, thick, and sleek—then he forsook God who made him, and scorned the Rock of his salvation. They made Him jealous with strange gods; with abominations they provoked Him to anger. They sacrificed to demons ... to gods whom they have not known, new gods come lately whom your fathers did not dread" (Dt.32:9-17).

Beyond the sensuality of false religion, the distinction between Yahweh God and the gods is so profound and obvious that Israel's deception could only be ascribed to demons.

God had called Israel to be *a confessing people*, claiming knowledge of and relationship to God, who called all other "gods" and their devotees to account. The God of Israel was the sovereign and delivering God who revealed Himself and acted mightily in redeeming people. The conquest of the land was in the name of the "Captain of the host of the LORD," who was presented as impartial, just, and righteous. He did not take sides but was purposeful in all His actions: "Joshua ... said 'Are you for us or for our adversaries?' And he said, 'No, rather I indeed come now as captain of the host of the LORD.' " (Josh.5:13,14). The battle with the nations (and their gods) was God's, not Israel's, though Israel was to be the agent: "for the LORD your God will deliver it *into your hand*" (Josh.8:7, emphasis added).

Along with the *shema*, "Hear, O Israel, the LORD is our God, the LORD alone is [God]" (Dt.6:4), another major confessional emphasis was Israel's *election* as God's people: "Be silent and listen, O Israel! This day you have become a people for the LORD your God" (Dt.27:9). Israel had a traceable beginning, which started with Abraham and was confirmed at Sinai, initiated by God. Her *deliverance* from Egyptian bondage was a further validation of that election, because God had acted mightily on her behalf. The people could recall and recite specific events to substantiate their faith in the God of deliverance. The tangible evidence of *a land of inheritance* was a visible demonstration of God's fulfilled promise.

> And the LORD gave them rest on every side, according to all that He had sworn to their fathers, and no one of all their enemies stood before them; the LORD gave all their enemies into their hand. Not one of the good promises which the LORD had made to the house of Israel failed; all came to pass (Josh.21:44-45).

Repeatedly Israel stated her confessional creed of election, her deliverance and inheritance, before the nations, testifying to the glory of her God. Without the LORD God, Israel would never have been. This in itself was proof that He alone is God, the One who blesses, who desires the salvation of all peoples (Is.45:22-24), and who sought to keep His people from the corruption and depravity of the Canaanites (Dt.11:16-28).

A Model Land in the Sight of all Nations

The land would be the arena in which Israel would display the character and purpose of God for all nations. Although it was a land flowing with milk and honey, the people were not about to be restored completely to Paradise. Though the land was fertile—Eden-like—sin was still there. Before they entered the land God warned the people that man's sin nature would still be there. The depraved actions of sinful and rebellious man, which had gone to seed in Canaan, would still characterize them. But this land, which was to be their inheritance, was also to be their context of priestly ministry to the nations (Exo.19:4-6). As such, the land was to be a place of *reciprocal relationships* reflecting righteousness and justice, and God would deal thus with His people.

Israel had to respond to God in righteousness and holiness; thus the land was to be a place of righteous living. *Giving and sharing* were to be normative. The people's conduct toward each other had to be just and righteous in all of life. Lack of integrity in any matter would be judged. Sin in any form was intolerable. By word and deed, they were to represent the God of justice, righteousness, and holiness (Dt.16:18-22).

The land was to be a place of obedience issuing in godly religion. It was not only to be a place of blessing, but also of challenge to expose and confront anything contrary to the worship of the sovereign Lord. There would be threats; occult practitioners—agents of the Canaanite gods (Dt.18:9-14); idolatry—the worship of demons (Dt.12:2-4, 29-32; 13:1-18; 32:16-17); temptations to act without recourse to God: "Whatever I command you, you shall be careful to do; you shall not add to nor take away from it" (Dt.12:32). They would have to constantly, deliberately choose between obedience to God and blessings, or disobedience and curses:

> "See, I am setting before you today a blessing and a curse: the blessing, if you listen to the commandments of the LORD your God, which I am commanding you today; and the curse, if you do not listen to the commandments of the LORD your God, but turn aside from the way which I am commanding you today, by following other gods which you have not known" (Dt.11:26-28).

The land was to be *where the destiny of the nations centered*. The nations' future was tied to Israel's obedience or disobedience to God:

"The LORD will establish you as a holy people to Himself, as He swore to you, if you will keep the commandments of the LORD your God, and walk in His ways. So all the peoples of the earth shall see that you are called by the name of the LORD; and they shall be afraid of you.... But it shall come about, if you will not obey the LORD your God ... that all these curses shall come upon you... And you shall be an example of terror to all the kingdoms of the earth.... Because you did not serve the LORD your God with joy and a glad heart, for the abundance of all things, therefore you shall serve your enemies whom the LORD shall send against you" (Dt.28:9,10,15,25,47,48).

Foreigners would then come and ask about the land's desolation:

"Why this great outburst of anger?"... "Because they forsook the covenant of the LORD, the God of their fathers ... and they went and served other gods and worshiped them ... therefore the anger of the LORD burned against that land, to bring upon it every curse which is written in this book" (Dt.29:24-27).

If the God of Israel were merely a territorial deity, there would be no reason to speak of the other nations' response to Israel. But because Israel was to represent Him to the nations, God warned of dire consequences if they played lightly with their commission. Isaiah reminds Israel:

It is too small [light] a thing that you should be My servant to raise up the tribes of Jacob, and to restore the preserved ones of Israel; I will also make you a light of the nations so that My salvation may reach to the end of the earth (Is.49:6).

The Conquest: An Example of Holy War

Holy war is the struggle between God and the powers of darkness—the worship of God or the worship of false deities inspired by demonic powers. Holy war is also the demonstration by God's servants of the incomparably great power of God in confrontation with and victory over the gods of the nations.

The land would be secured by holy war (Dt.2:24; 20:1; Josh.4:13; 11:20; cf. 2 Chron.20:15,17). Even though God promised the land as their inheritance, it would only become theirs as they actually won it through battle. War sometimes becomes the instrument of God's providence, and battle would be a key factor in realizing God's continued blessing. This was not a new strategy; it was disclosed immediately following the Fall (Gen. 3:15; cf. Eph. 6:12; 1 Thes. 2:18; 2 Tim.2:26).

Israel's wars were more than overpowering other nations for land. They had a *unique character*, being wars declared against the evil of nations. God cautioned Israel:

> Do not say in your heart when the LORD your God has driven them out before you, "Because of my righteousness the LORD has brought me in to possess this land," but it is because of the wickedness of these nations that the LORD is dispossessing them before you (Dt.9:4).

God Himself declared these wars (Josh.5:13-15) and sanctioned them: "for the LORD your God is the one who goes with you, to fight for you against your enemies, to save you" (Dt.20:4). The Spirit of the Lord anointed the people for battle (cf. Judg.6:34). The people had to rely on God boldly and with confidence: "[When] you are approaching the battle .... Do not be fainthearted. Do not be afraid, or panic, or tremble before them, for the LORD your God is the one who goes with you..." (Dt.20:3,4). These battles were fought by insignificant people facing enormous odds, totally dependent on God: "The LORD did not set His love on you nor choose you because you were more in number than any of the peoples, for you were the fewest of all peoples" (Dt.7:7). The battle was not theirs but God's. The Psalmist observed:

> Thou with Thine own hand didst drive out the nations; then Thou didst plant them; Thou didst afflict the peoples, then Thou didst spread them abroad. For by their own sword they did not possess the land; and their own arm did not save them; but Thy right hand, and Thine arm, and the light of Thy presence, for Thou didst favor them (Ps.44:2,3).

Israel was merely God's rod of judgment upon the wickedness of Canaan (Gen.12:3; 15:16; cf. Jer.51:20-23).

Israel's wars with the nations were in God's plan to overcome His enemies and were paradigms of the continuing battle God's people would have with the powers of darkness. Therefore these battles were fought, as was the case in Egypt, against the gods of the land (Exo.12:12; Deut.7:16,25; 12:2-3,30-31). The nations had no misconceptions about their encounters with Israel. They understood the battles to be encounters between gods:

> Now the lords of the Philistines assembled to offer a great sacrifice to Dagon their god, and to rejoice, for they said, "Our god has given Samson our enemy into our hands." When the people saw him, they praised their god, for they said, "Our god has given our enemy into our hands, even the destroyer of our country, who has slain many of us" (Judg.16:23,24; cf. 1 Sam.5,6).

Even after the war for the land of Canaan was won (Josh.21:44,45), there remained many skirmishes to be fought against the gods of the land:

> But you have not obeyed Me ... Therefore I also said, "I will not drive them out before you; but they shall become as thorns in your sides, and their gods shall be a snare to you.... I also will no longer drive out before them any of the nations which Joshua left when he died, in order to test Israel by them, whether they will keep the way of the LORD to walk in it as their fathers did, or not" (Judg.2:2-3,21-22).

God was recognized as *a warrior*: "I will sing to the LORD, for He has triumphed gloriously.... The LORD is a warrior.... Who is like Thee among the gods, O LORD? Who is like Thee, majestic in holiness, awesome in praises, working wonders?" (Exo.15:1,3,11); and "The LORD will go forth like a warrior, He will arouse His zeal like a man of war. He will utter a shout, yes, He will raise a war cry. He will prevail against His enemies" (Is.42:13; cf. Rom.8:37; 2 Cor.2:14; 2 Cor.10:4; Col.2:15; 1 Jn.3:8; Rev.19:11-21). Through holy war God would bring His people into "rest" (Josh.11:23). But the ultimate rest would come when every knee bows and every tongue confesses that Jesus Christ is Lord, to the glory of God (cf. Is.45:22-25; Phil. 2:10-11). These wars would cause all wars to cease:

> The nations made an uproar, the kingdoms tottered; He raised His voice, the earth melted.... Come, behold the works of the LORD, who has wrought desolations in the earth. He makes wars to cease to the end of the earth; He breaks the bow and cuts the spear in two; He burns the chariots with fire (Ps.46:6,8,9).

In a remarkable way God accompanied His calling of Israel to be His agent of redemption with His enabling grace and power to

155

accomplish the task. Israel had everything needed to declare God's glory, "the glory due His name." Much later 2 Chronicles 20 illustrated this reality: the Word of God elicited the worship of God which issued in the work of God, and the enemy was routed. Moses said,

> "For the LORD'S portion is His people; Jacob is the allotment of His inheritance. He found him in a desert land, and in the howling waste of a wilderness; He encircled him, He cared for him, He guarded him as the pupil of His eye. Like an eagle that stirs up its nest, that hovers over its young, He spread His wings and caught them, He carried them on His pinions. The LORD alone guided him, and there was no foreign god with him. He made him ride on the high places of the earth, and he ate the produce of the field; and He made him suck honey from the rock, and oil from the flinty rock, curds of cows, and milk of the flock, with fat of lambs, and rams ... and goats, with the finest of the wheat—and of the blood of grapes you drank wine" (Dt.32:9-14).

God called, prepared, commissioned, and sent His people to war against His enemies. Through them, in part, the prophecy of Genesis 3:15 would be realized, and with them the nations would have to acknowledge "Only in the LORD are righteousness and strength" (Is.45:24).

Missiological Considerations

God has called His people to holy war. The gods of this world are deluding the nations into false worship. Behind the destruction and exploitation of God's creation, the perversity of man, and the defiance of nations toward Yahweh God are spiritual powers determined to keep man captive to sensual appetites, to the dehumanization of their fellow man, and to false worship (2 Tim.2:26).

To realize God's promises, to take possession of "the land," to bring the nations to bow before Him, cannot happen without battle. There must be face-to-face encounter, and total dependence on God.

Along with this overriding mission, maintaining all God's creation will remain His people's task. The land is to produce "milk and honey" for the tenants. But God's enemies are determined to deflect God's people from doing His will and are set on destroying creation. Though the battle is fierce, the victory is assured, and God will achieve His purposes.

Amidst the battles, temptations to exchange God's glory for that of demons will ever be present. Idolatry (demon worship) appears in a variety of forms, from the apparently innocent to the bizarre. The counsel of Peter must not be taken lightly: "Be of sober spirit, be on the alert. Your adversary, the devil, prowls about like a roaring lion, seeking someone to devour" (1 Pet.5:8). Satan will not hesitate to deceive and destroy to keep God's servants from declaring God's glory to those in captivity to demons.

Holy war is not an option but an imperative. God's people must engage in spiritual warfare (Eph.6:12-18) to release those captive to demonic powers (2 Cor.4:4; Eph.2:2; cf. Jn.14:30). But with spiritual warfare must be face-to-face encounter (Lk. 9:1-6; 10:1-20; cf. Lk. 11:18-26). And all this must be accompanied by a life consistent with the character of God (Jn.7:37-39; 15; Eph.4:1-6; 5).

CHAPTER 14

CONFEDERATION

TO MONARCHY

The land was given for one purpose: that Israel might reflect and proclaim the grace of God to sinful, lost people. The land was never meant to be a retreat to simply bask in God's blessings. It was to be the crossroads for all nations to encounter God. God's model was brought into the land so that the nations might behold God's glory.

Promise and Fulfillment

The book of Judges begins with the fulfillment of God's promises, noting, "The people served the LORD all the days of Joshua, and all the days of the elders who survived Joshua, who had seen all the great work of the LORD which He had done for Israel" (Judg.2:7). God was faithful to His people, providing them with everything needed to accomplish the task. When God's people submitted to His laws and carried through with His purposes, the nations stood in awe, if not fear. Deborah's song of victory reflects this so well:

> "That the leaders led in Israel, that the people volunteered, Bless the LORD! Hear, O kings; give ear, O rulers! ... I will sing praise to the LORD, the God of Israel. LORD ... when Thou didst march from the field of Edom, the earth quaked, the heavens also dripped ... the mountains quaked at the presence of the LORD.... Thus let all Thine enemies perish, O LORD; *but let those who love Him be like the rising of the sun in its might.*" And the land was undisturbed for forty years (Judg.5:2-5,31, emphasis added).

But the record was not all victory; all too frequently Israel's disobedience marred it. Man's sinful nature made him do "what was evil in the sight of the LORD; and the LORD gave them into the hands of [their enemies]" (Judg.6:1); and "Israel again played the harlot with the Baals, and made Baal-berith their god. Thus the sons of Israel did not remember the LORD their God, who had delivered them from the hands of all their enemies on every side" (Judg.8:33,34). Thus Judges ended in despair: "In those days there was no king in Israel; everyone did what was right in his own eyes" (Judg.21:25).

Repeatedly, God gave them over to their enemies that they might find out what bondage there was when God was not their Lord. But time and again God mercifully intervened and showed Himself Lord over all gods, ready to deliver:

> And the sons of Israel said to the LORD, "We have sinned, do to us whatever seems good to Thee; only please deliver us this day." So they put away the foreign gods from among them, and served the LORD; *and He could bear the misery of Israel no longer* (Judg.10: 15,16, emphasis added).

A Forgotten Mandate

When Israel became prosperous and indolent—"grew fat and kicked," no longer confronted God's enemies, "forsook God who made him, ...scorned the Rock of his salvation ... [and] sacrificed to demons" (Dt.32:15,17)—then God's people forgot their purpose.

Throughout the Bible there is a close relationship between obedience to the Great Commission and faithfulness in walking in the "statutes and judgments" of God. When there is no need of God, there is no life purpose, either. Then indulgence reigns, and depravity becomes acceptable. But man cannot live without purpose, and apart from God there is no purpose significant enough to keep man from self-indulgence. This certainly was true of Israel, who sought after the gods of the nations: gods who would satisfy and justify sensuality (Ezek.33:23-32).

The events in the book of Ruth were to remind Israel of her mission to the nations. God's grace would extend even to Moab, an enemy of Israel. Even in the family's going to Moab, in disregard of God's promised provision, the wholly otherness of the God of Israel was communicated so that a Gentile woman was willing to trust Him. The account illustrates that even when the message of God's glory is carried in disobedience, the nations cannot help but take note. In order to attract Ruth, the family's life must have reflected that Israel was in covenant with a God who is totally unlike other gods (Ruth 1:16-18). As the story unfolds, we can see that God (who provided for Boaz in abundance) expected that Israel would deliberately share her blessings with the nations. God wanted His agent of redemption, Israel, to cover the nations with her skirt of blessing (Ruth 3:9-13). It was up to Israel to exercise the right of kinsman in relationship to the nations. She was to share her inheritance and have them join in being a blessing in the midst of the yet unreached peoples (Ruth 4:9-22).

God's persistent intervention in Israel's history was a witness of the nature of God and of His concern for all nations. If He could persist in working with Israel in the face of deliberate rebellion and perversity, then surely no nation was beyond the pale of God's mercy. Through these encounters with God, the nations would come to know what He was like and what He desired to do for all peoples (Dan.2:47; 3:28-29; 4:34-37; 6:25-27).

The books of Samuel continue to highlight the compassionate heart of God and Israel's continued perversity. The people were constantly drawn to the gods of the nations and their dehumanizing practices. Unlike the gods of the nations, the God of Israel had commanded His people to be holy. He wanted a people who would worship Him, not because He blessed them, but because He was God and longed for true fellowship with them. God, furthermore, had extended to Israel the privilege of being His "priest-nation" to all nations; that privilege ought to have elicited gratitude and humility. God desired all peoples to be redeemed, and Israel was to be both model and message that there is but one God who desires to deliver all people from all bondages:

> "If you will return, O Israel," declares the Lord, "then you should return to Me. And if you will put away your detested things from My presence, and will not waver, and you will swear, `As the LORD lives,' in truth, in justice, and in righteousness; *then the nations will bless themselves in Him, and in Him they will glory"* (Jer.4:1-2, emphasis added).

Why was it so hard for Israel to walk in obedience? Had God not consistently demonstrated His loving concern with mighty power? Much later, Jeremiah spoke for God:

"I brought you into the fruitful land, to eat its fruit and its good things. But you came and defiled My land, and My inheritance you made an abomination".... "Has a nation changed gods, when they were not gods? But my people have changed their glory for that which does not profit.... For My people have committed two evils: they have forsaken Me, the fountain of living waters, to hew for themselves cisterns, broken cisterns, that can hold no water" (Jer.2:7,11,13).

Why did Israel turn from the liberty of serving the Lord God to the enslavement of the gods of the nations? Berkhof insightfully comments, "Man evokes God's anger, yet at the same time His compassion. That he sins is his own fault; yet there is also something in it of being over-powered, which in the Bible is variously designated as ... `slavery,' `the powers,' or `the devil' " (Berkhof 1972:200). There is no other way to account for Israel's ongoing rebellion which seems, at times, to over-reach even the most sinful depravity of man (Ezek.22,23). That all men are sinful and depraved is beyond dispute. But was not Israel a special target of the powers of darkness because of her special relationship to God? Are not God's servants especially targeted by Satan to keep them from declaring God's glory to the ends of the earth? Again Berkhof notes,

> The Apostle Paul speaks of such an overpowering force beside man's guilt ... it is the powers, the exousiai and the stoichea, which so much control men's actions (Eph.2:1f.) that the struggle against sin must as it were be fought in a supermundane realm with these mysterious powers which manipulate man and society (Eph.6:12) [Ibid.].

It is not surprising, therefore, that even after a great victory over the enemy, Israel deliberately turned against God's theocratic rule. Samuel had scarcely raised a memorial stone commemorating God's faith-fulness "thus far the LORD has helped us" (1 Sam.7:12), when Israel asked for a king after the pattern of the ungodly nations. She who was called to be God's blessing to the nations wanted to imitate them. The people wanted a visible king, not the invisible, sovereign God, medi-ated through Samuel, to rule over them:

> Then all the elders of Israel gathered together and came to Samuel.... and they said to him ... "Now appoint a king for us to judge us like the nations"... And the LORD said to Samuel ... "they have not rejected you, but they have rejected Me from being king over them ... they have forsaken Me and served other gods" (1 Sam.8:4,5,7,8).

162

Israel could not deny responsibility for her rebellion. "Have you not done this to yourself, by your forsaking the LORD your God, when He led you in the way?" (Jer.2:17) But Israel may very well have been targeted by Satan to keep her from fulfilling her divine purposes, declaring God's glory to the nations and being the people through whom the Messiah would come (Gen.49:10). History shows that her status as a nation was frequently threatened (e.g. book of Esther). At times only a remnant remained but God remembered His covenant, and to this day He has not forgotten His promises (Is.66).

God's Law of the King

Israel's desire for a king was not outside God's purpose. God had promised Abraham that kings would descend from him (Gen.17:6). Judah was promised a coming king who would wield the scepter (Gen.49:10). The Kingdom concept was not alien to God's purposes for the nations (cf. Jesus Christ's teaching on the kingdom, Acts 1:3).

The reign of the king God ordained would reflect God's own rule. The monarch would be a model of God's character, righteousness, justice, and mercy. The nations had to know of the vast difference between their kings and Israel's. This king was the undying hope of Israel, a hope throughout her history.

Although desiring a king was not against God's plan, the timing of his appointment was motivated by Israel's disobedience, mistrust, and selfishness. Until God installed this king, His rule would be mediated by appointed agents. God's claim to kingship over Israel was twofold: by right of creation and by right of purchase. The time would come when God would appoint an earthly king for Israel—one who would act in His place, leading the people in God's purpose for the nations. This king would foreshadow the Messianic King, who one day would bring complete deliverance to all nations.

God's law of the king (Dt.17:14-20) was unique among the nations. The king was to be chosen and anointed by God to reflect His own merciful rule over His people and to point to the Ruler yet to come. The king was to rule as a brother among brothers, not as a god or an aristocrat, but as a servant to the people. His office was one of stewardship of God's inheritance—not ownership or authoritarian control.

Very strict regulations defined the king's role and relationships to God and the people. By submitting to them he would reflect his commitment to the statutes and judgments of God. First, he was not to multiply possessions or wives, which were signs of wealth and prestige and means to formalize treaties and gain security. God's king was not permitted to enter treaties or seek security from the nations. His interests and efforts were to focus on God and His glory, not on personal gain or prestige. He had to write the law as if it were written just for him. He had to learn to fear the Lord by keeping the law diligently (Dt.17:19-20). The king stood under God, to serve on behalf of God, and was therefore steward of all—the people, their resources and faith, remembering the mandate to declare God's glory (Ps.96:3,8; 1 Chron.16:8,24,28; cf. 2 Chron.19:1-7).

No parallel exists between God's law of kingship and those of the nations. God's king was to be free to serve, committed to a profoundly different lifestyle. God's glory, not man's selfish interests, was at stake and had to be upheld.

The Nations' Law of the King

The nations had laws governing the role of kings. Kingship, to them, was committed to maintaining the status quo of wealth for some and poverty for others, freedom for some and oppression for others, all validated by the gods and a theology supporting perversions (Jer.5:26-28,30-31). In contrast to the law of God, the pagan king operated by custom (1 Sam.8:11-17). Military conscription, personal exaltation, the servitude of fellow-countrymen to facilitate comfortable living, a landed aristocracy, universal, comprehensive taxation, forced labor, and kingly oppression were expected. Hardship and suffering were the unavoidable cost of earthly kingship (vs.18).

Although God warned Israel clearly what it would be like to live under a king of her own choosing, Israel "refused to listen ... and they said, `No, but there shall be a king over us, that we also may be like all the nations, that our king may judge us and go out before us and fight our battles' " (1 Sam.8:19-20). How could Israel reject the beneficent rule of God and look for security in an earthly king?

The Confederation of Israel

During the conquest of the land, Israel was a loose confederation of clans descended from a unified ancestry. They were united through their common faith in God who had called their forefather Abraham and had miraculously delivered them from Egyptian slavery. Without statehood or central government, their focal point was the Ark. The Ark was only a box—not an image as found among the nations—but contained the symbols of their history (Heb. 9:4): the law which defined their faith and lifestyle (Exo. 25:16); a jar of manna, the symbol of God's daily provision for their physical need (cf. Phil.4:19); and Aaron's rod, the symbol of God's authority and power over all forces and a reminder of God's intervention in times of need (Num. 17:10). Thus the Ark and its contents were reminders of God's redemptive and liberating presence, as so well illustrated in the encounter of the Ark with the god Dagon and the gods of the pagan cities (1 Sam.5).

Israel's feast days celebrated the presence of God and sealed the people's allegiance to Him and His covenant. Seven times annually they corporately confessed and celebrated that God alone was their Lord. Three times a year they were to go to a central place to remember His covenant with them. These times also served to bind them into a reciprocating brotherhood—a confederation of clans bound in common interests and concerns.

As a people in submission to God's rule, they rejected the city-state pattern typical of Canaan, each with its localized deity, and opted for a theocracy. Thus they would model God's kingdom before the nations.

They were a people whose commitment God repeatedly tested. "I... will no longer drive out before them any of the nations which Joshua left when he died, *in order to test Israel* by them, whether they will keep the way of the LORD to walk in it as their fathers did, or not" (Judg.2:21,22, emphasis added); and again, "these nations ... were *for testing Israel*, to find out if they would obey the commandments of the LORD, which He had commanded their fathers through Moses" (Judg.3:3,4, emphasis added). Much later it was said concerning Hezekiah, "even in the matter of the envoys of the rulers of Babylon ... God left Him alone only *to test him*, that He might know all that was in his heart" (2 Chron. 32:31, emphasis added). Thus, when the Philistines invaded, Israel's leaders were tested beyond what they thought they could endure. As a result, they believed that, like other nations, their strength must lie in having a monarchy.

In spite of a history replete with the mighty acts of God, the people doubted God's ability to deliver them from the neighboring kings (cf. Jer.2:5-8). They finally drew into question their own historic creed and looked to other gods for deliverance (1 Sam.8:7,8; cf. Jer.2:23-28). They became a vacillating people who forgot their heritage and reaped the consequences of unbelief. First, God gave them Saul as king. Although God changed his heart and even put His Spirit upon him (1 Sam.10:9-10; 11:6), Saul was proud and self-seeking and disobeyed God (1 Sam.13:8-14;15). The people's uniting under a king proved their undoing (1 Sam.28:1-19). The people they sought to conquer eventually dominated them and the land God had given. Instead of God receiving the glory due Him, the nations ascribed praise to their gods:

Thus Saul died with his three sons ... And when the men of Israel who were on the other side of the valley ... saw that the men of Israel had fled and that Saul and his sons were dead, they abandoned the cities and fled; then the Philistines came and lived in them. And it came about on the next day when the Philistines came to strip the slain, that they found Saul and his three sons fallen ... And they cut off his head, and stripped off his weapons ... and sent them throughout the land of the Philistines, to carry the good news to the *house of their idols* ... and they put his weapons in the temple of Ashtaroth (1 Sam.31:6-10, emphasis added).

Thus Israel exchanged the glory of God for the slavery of the nations' gods. And in the lamentation of God's prophet, "A voice is heard on the bare heights, the weeping and the supplications of the sons of Israel; because they have perverted their way, they have forgotten the LORD their God" (Jer.3:21). Nevertheless, God remembered His covenant and invited them to "return, O faithless sons, I will heal your faithlessness" (Jer.3:22). In His mercy, God would give Israel a king, "a man after His own heart" (1 Sam.13:14).

The Transition to the Kingdom

The period from the conquest of the land to the destruction of the first temple (586 B.C.) was characterized by rebellion and judgment (Judg.2:11-13), with only occasional blessing. In spite of all their rebellion, God's concern for His people remained; "For the LORD will not abandon His people on account of His great name, because the LORD has been pleased to make you a people for Himself" (1 Sam.12:22); and, "those whom the Lord loves He disciplines, and He scourges every son whom He receives" (Heb.12:6). He was still willing to work with and through His people:

And when the LORD raised up judges for them, the LORD was with the judge and delivered them from the hand of their enemies all the days of the judge; for the LORD was moved to pity by their groaning because of those who oppressed and afflicted them (Judg.2:18).

But in the people's stubbornness they acted corruptly, more so than their fathers (Judg.2:19), which brought them to seek a king and reject God's rule.

God granted Israel her desire and, through Saul's misconduct, allowed them to learn more clearly what His kingdom was intended to be. This God required unwavering obedience:

166

"Has the LORD as much delight in burnt offerings and sacrifices as in obeying the voice of the LORD? Behold, to obey is better than sacrifice, and to heed than the fat of rams. For rebellion is as the sin of divination, and insubordination is as iniquity and idolatry. Because you have rejected the word of the LORD, He has also rejected you from being king" (1 Sam.15:22-23).

The people's rebellion, however, did not change God's purposes for them or the nations. God, who continued to direct history for His redemptive purposes, set the stage for the king after His own heart. In the fulness of time, He instituted the permanent kingdom: "The LORD has torn the kingdom of Israel from you today, and has given it to your neighbor who is better than you. The Glory of Israel will not lie or change His mind" (1 Sam.15:28,29). The kingdom instituted by God was to be an instrument of redemption as well as the embodiment of the blessedness of Israel.

This kingdom would encompass the messianic expectations of Israel, foreshadowing God's messianic rule on earth, when deliverance would be known in full. This earthly kingdom would be a model to all nations and also point God's people to the future perfected kingdom ruling over all nations (Ps.2). This kingdom was to be deliberately instituted by God, a kingdom of God's design and for His purposes.

The realization of the kingdom was at the heart of Biblical faith. It focused on both God's evangelistic (declaring His glory) and cultural (being the kingdom people of God) mandates. God established, and will more fully establish His kingdom when the Messiah returns. The kingdom, however, was to be a present reality in the lives of His people and touched every aspect of life. The Davidic and Solomonic kingdom in many ways reflected the blessedness of God's presence. The nations could see, in measure, God's glory reflected in the reign of a righteous king. Solomon declared of the king: "May his name endure forever; may his name increase as long as the sun shines; and let men bless themselves by him; let all nations call him blessed," and acknowledging the source of it all, Solomon exclaimed, "Blessed be the LORD God, the God of Israel, who alone works wonders. And blessed be His glorious name forever; and may the whole earth be filled with His glory" (Ps.72:17-19). Thus it was recognized that the kingdom was not to glorify Israel (or the Church), but to be God's vehicle to take His glory to all nations (Ps.67).

The Rise of Prophetism

The purpose of the prophets was to maintain God's people as His redemptive agents: "I will raise up a prophet from among their countrymen like you, and I will put My words in his mouth, and he shall speak to them all that I command him" (Dt.18:18; cf. 1 Sam.12:23-24). The prophet's mission was to affect the destinies of both Israel and the nations: "Now the word of the LORD came to me saying, before I formed you in the womb I knew you, and before you were born I consecrated you; *I have appointed you a prophet to the nations*" (Jer.1:4,5, emphasis added).

Prophetism, which accompanied the coming of the kingdom, was God's instrument to maintain His people in biblical faith. Although Moses was rightfully considered a prophet, prophetism as here described started with Samuel during the beginning of the monarchy and later became the central focus in maintaining Israel's mission to the nations.

The prophets were guardians of God's continued lordship over His people. They went straight to the motives and intents of the heart. Calling for obedience, they consistently challenged Israel's leaders to submit to God's laws. They were a threat to those who sought to usurp the kingship of Yahweh God, and they thundered against those who bowed at the shrines of other gods. The prophets represented and presented God as the only One entitled to rule Israel.

> Hear this, O house of Jacob, who are named Israel ... who swear by the name of the LORD and invoke the God of Israel, but not in truth or in righteousness.... I declared the former things long ago and they went forth from my mouth, and I proclaimed them. Suddenly I acted and they came to pass ... lest you should say, "My idol has done them, and my graven image and my molten image have commanded them." For the sake of my name I delay my wrath, and for My praise I restrain it for you, in order not to cut you off .... For My own sake, for My own sake, I will act; for how can My name be profaned? And My glory I will not give to another. Listen to Me, O Jacob, even Israel whom I called; I am He, I am the first, and I am also the last (Is.48:1,3,5,9,11,12).

The prophets were dominated by God and possessed by His word. Although they did not speak primarily to the political, economic, or social issues of their day, their message radically affected those realms. This happened because God's statutes and judgments affected man's total life. They had an experiential awareness of the righteousness, justice and mercy of God, and therefore faced the depraved customs of their day head-on. Man could not claim a relationship with God and ignore justice and righteousness—the cultural mandate (Is.1:11-26; Amos 5:23,24; Mic.6:8).

God's word, written and spoken, was the prophets' chief instrument. God's word was "a hammer which shatters a rock" (Jer.23:29), and would not return to Him without having accomplished its purpose (Is.55:11). Their reference point was God's word; they constantly proclaimed, "Hear the word of the LORD;" "Thus says the LORD;" "Listen to Me," thus identifying their authority for ministry. The word they communicated was the instrument to relate Israel to her spiritual union with Yahweh God, to both make and keep her as a visible representation of His kingdom.

The prophets upheld biblical principles, which were for all times and peoples. The prophets did not create facts—they upheld what they already knew to be true of God, what He had already given by previous revelation. They kept in focus God's redemptive purposes, as they had occurred in the past, were designed for the present, and would be realized in the future. Throughout, they underscored that God, the King over the earthly king, demands a moral response from all peoples at all times. And should the people not listen, God would still hold them responsible: "it shall come about that whoever will not listen to My words which [the prophet] shall speak in My name, I Myself will require it of him" (Dt.18:19). Obedience was the *sine qua non* for a reciprocal relationship between God and man. "No religious activity avails in the context of a blatantly sinful life" (Motyer, NBD:1043). The prophets were agents of God's revelation; God spoke, and they merely communicated His speech: "Thus saith the LORD." They mediated for the "God Who gives Himself in the word of His mouth" (Vos 1948:205). For example, Hosea spoke of Israel's repudiation of the covenant. God made Hosea share in His grief by marrying an unfaithful woman.

> Hosea provides a new understanding of the treasure committed to Israel, which the NT will develop further. As eroticism stands at the center of Canaanite religion, so a new depth of love stands at the center of God's initiative to Israel (most movingly described in chapter 11).... Once again the promises of God include all creation and the whole human community in its scope and will highlight the interrelated character of creation and re-creation (Dyrness 1983:100).

Amos warned of impending judgment due to the oppression and unjustice festering below the surface of the peace and luxury of the privileged classes (Amos 1:7; 2:6-8; 4:1; 5:7,10-12). Amos also revealed that God would rescue a remnant to carry through with Israel's special role to the nations: "that they may possess the remnant of Edom and all the nations who are called by My name, declares the LORD who does this" (Amos 9:12).

Of Isaiah, Dyrness observes:

> As if to underline this dimension of God's rule, chapters 16 to 24 are given over to prophesying judgment upon the nations, a judgment punctuated with the refrain: "says the Lord of hosts." For God is the God of the nations—after Isaiah there can be no doubt of this. But now Jerusalem and the root of David (see 11:1-9) are more and more involved with the fate of these nations; what he opens none shall shut, and what he shuts, none shall open (22:21,22) [Ibid.:102].

The prophets maintained the biblical faith that places the focus on God, who is above all gods. He alone delivers, saves, and concerns Himself with the destiny of all nations. He established and designed Israel's relationship to the nations. Therefore, through prophetism, biblical faith came into clearer focus as the religion of truth, the religion of the Book, the message for all times and for all peoples. The prophets were the guardians of the truth given by God and delivered in God's historical encounter and interaction with man. They therefore appealed to historical facts and reflected on historical realities. In contrast to the false prophets, they did not ignore what had happened before.

Conversely, false prophets encouraged and maintained false worship (Dt.13:2) and were strongly influenced by the demonic (cf. 1 Cor. 10:20; 2 Thess. 2:9-11). On occasion they evidenced supernatural power through signs and wonders (Exo. 7:11,22,8:7; Dt.13:1-5). They conceived of their rituals as effective means to cajole the spirit world into action (1 Ki.18:26-29). They rejected the biblical record and had no recourse to history, thus having no reference point to evaluate the present or future—merely their own prognostications. They conveniently ignored past actions and laws as they sought to predict the future to please man without regard for God's holy character (1 Ki. 22: 5-28; Jer.6:13-14). What the prophets predicted eventually happened.

> I will put My words in his mouth, and he shall speak to them all that I command him ... And you may say in your heart, "How shall we know the word which the LORD has not spoken?" "When a prophet speaks in the name of the LORD, if the thing does not come about or come true, that is the thing which the LORD has not spoken. The prophet has spoken it presumptuously; you shall not be afraid of him" (Dt.18:18,21,22; cf. 1 Ki.13:1-10).

The prophets did not fill an enviable role in Israel. They were feared and hated, sought but despised, heard but also martyred. These were "men whose vision of God showed evil for what it was and displayed an energizing consciousness of a new order" (Brueggemann 1978:32). Of them the world was not worthy (Heb.11:38). The characteristic sins which the prophets exposed were idolatry—rejecting God for other gods, worshiping demon spirits (Dt.32:15-18), the indulgence of the rich, and the oppression of the poor (Jer.22:13-16). They railed against Israel's neglect of her covenant stewardship and obligations to others. However, throughout all the condemnations they heaped on the people, the prophets kept in focus the coming King, the Messiah who would bear the sins of the people (Is.53), create within them hearts of flesh and remove their hearts of stone (Ezek.36:24-28), and set up an everlasting kingdom (Dan.7:9-14).

The Degeneration of the Kingdom

God's purpose in the monarchy was for His people to reflect His righteousness and have the nations recognize His rightful dominion (Is.45:21,24). There were kings—Asa, Jehoshaphat, Hezekiah, and Josiah—who, though imperfectly, sought to abide by covenant obligations and were recognized as witnesses to God's purposes. Periodically, Israel did reflect God's justice and righteousness, and served Him wholeheartedly (e.g.Neh.8).

Of all Israel's kings, the Davidic dynasty modeled before the nation the coming rule of the Messiah. Although there were similarities between David's and Solomon's kingdoms, there were also significant differences which contributed to the kingdom's division and the nation's captivity. The Davidic kingdom was a constitutional monarchy: God was King and Shepherd and David served as undershepherd. David understood his role of carrying out God's purposes for the land, for His people, and for the nations: all three themes appeared repeatedly in his reflections (1 Chron.16:7-36; cf. 2 Sam.7:18-29; Ps.96). Under David's capable direction, the people recognized God's leadership and their obligations to maintain covenant-relationships.

As a man after God's own heart (1 Sam.13:14), David's history illustrated remarkable humility as well as confidence in God. With God's help, David consolidated his kingdom and rapidly conquered the nations which had caused Israel such great distress. During his reign, the Philistines were defeated; the Canaanite fortress towns were reduced to servitude; Transjordania was made tributary; Israel's territorial power was extended to Syria (2 Sam.8:1-5); Jerusalem became the capital of Israel (2 Chron.6:6); and Israel's treasury was full. The Golden Age, which would extend through the Solomonic kingdom, had begun. The Song of David captured his commitment to God's covenant and his gratitude for God's sustaining grace, faithfulness, and abundant blessings in Israel:

> "For who is God, besides the LORD? And who is a rock, besides our God? God is my strong fortress; ... He trains my hands for battle, so that my arms can bend a bow of bronze. Thou hast also given me the shield of Thy salvation, and Thy help makes me great.... I pursued my enemies and destroyed them, and I did not turn back until they were consumed. And I have devoured them and shattered them, so that they did not rise; and they fell under my feet.... The LORD lives, and blessed be my rock; and exalted be God, the rock of my salvation.... *Therefore I will give thanks to Thee, O LORD, among the nations,* and I will sing praises to Thy name" (2 Sam.22:32,33,35,36,38,39,47,50, emphasis added).

God was the central focus of David's life. David remembered his past with humility (2 Sam.22:5-20), believing all of his accomplishments could only be ascribed to God's intervention. The God who had promised would fulfill His word; David could rely on the Rock of His salvation. Not forgetting God's redemptive plan for all nations, he frequently reminded himself and Israel of the obligation to declare God's glory among the nations. Thus he instructed Asaph:

> Oh give thanks to the LORD, call upon His name; *make known His deeds among the peoples....* Speak of all His wonders.... He is the LORD our God; His judgments are in all the earth.... Sing to the LORD all the earth; proclaim good tidings of His salvation from day to day. *Tell of His glory among the nations,* His wonderful deeds among all the peoples. For great is the LORD, and greatly to be praised; He also is to be feared above all gods. For all the gods of the peoples are idols, but the LORD made the heavens.... Ascribe to the LORD, O families of the peoples, ascribe to the LORD glory and strength.... Tremble before Him all the earth.... And *let them say among the nations,* "The LORD reigns" (1 Chron.16:8,9,14,23-26,28,30,31, emphasis added; cf. 2 Sam.22:50; Ps.22:27-31; Ps.72:17; 96:3,7-8).

But the kingdom was not beyond reproach. The dynasty which started in David's day came to full bloom in the Solomonic kingdom, where God's reign and protection of His people were gradually replaced with pompous rule and national alliances (1 Ki.3:1ff).

Solomon greatly increased his own and Israel's political power and wealth so that his kingdom impressed the nations. But the splendor did not come without breaking God's laws. Occasionally, Solomon confessed God's purposes for Israel, but more frequently he lived contrary to his own creed (1 Ki.8:22-61). Though a man of great wisdom, Solomon succumbed to the sensual. His alliances with the nations were sealed by taking foreign wives, disregarding the explicit instructions in the law of the king (Dt.17:14-20). He forced his own people to labor and lived indulgently at others' expense (1 Ki. 4:22-23; 27-28; 5:13-16; 9:14-23; 1 Ki.9:14-23; 10:14-22,25-29; 11:1-3; 2 Chron. 9:13-28). Sophistication and "culture" flourished in the courts of the palace. The king's residence and all state projects were noted for pomp and style (1 Ki.7:1-12; 10; 2 Chron.9). After Solomon the State supported religion to control it (2 Chron.8:14,15; cf. 18:5-27). A process of sacralization validated the divine authority of kings; God was still recognized, but only through ritual. Much of the nations' culture and values were introduced to consolidate the king's position. Theoretically, the state became God's kingdom with God's chosen people ruled by God's anointed son, the king. Practically, everything now centered on Israel the people and their king—the sovereign "greater than all the kings"—rather than God. The nations sought Solomon, but did they recognize God who gave him wisdom? (1 Ki. 4:34; 10:23-25). Solomon had disobeyed the divine law of the king and opted for the pagan law of the king (1 Ki.10:28-11:8). God's purposes in history became equated with maintaining the status quo favoring the privileged classes (1 Ki.11) while tolerating, even encouraging, the oppression of the less privileged (1 Ki.12:3-14).

Israel had forgotten God's purpose of declaring His glory to the nations and had no intention of sharing their blessings with the nations. The model God intended to be a blessing in the midst of the nations tragically degenerated. Although the process started long before Solomon, it was said:

> Solomon did what was evil in the sight of the LORD, and did not follow the LORD fully, as David his father had done. Then Solomon built a high place for Chemosh the detestable idol of Moab ... and for Molech the detestable idol of the sons of Ammon. Thus also he did for all his foreign wives, who burned incense and sacrificed to their gods. Now the LORD was angry with Solomon because his heart was turned away from the LORD ... who... had commanded him concerning this thing, that he should not go after other gods.... So the LORD said to Solomon "I will surely tear the kingdom from you, and will give it to your servant" (1 Ki.11:6-11).

Israel's declension accelerated with those who followed Solomon. She had rejected both her cultural and evangelistic mandates. The prophets became the irregulars in society, as they sought to call the people back to God. Israel compromised her religion, as she rejected the covenant. Out of this deliberate rejection of God's covenant came dehumanizing structures and practices that simply accelerated in a kingdom divided: "even the wicked women you have taught your ways. Also on your skirts is found the lifeblood of the innocent poor" (Jer.2:33-34). Social tension, a result of nepotism and favoritism at the royal court, plagued the nation. Taxation became burdensome (1 Ki.12:4-10,14). Forced labor became common practice, not only for aliens, but also for Israelites (2 Chron.10:18-19). Conscription into the military became accepted practice. Revolution was forced upon an oppressed people as the divine rights of kings were thought to supersede mercy, justice, and righteousness (1 Ki.11:26-40; 12:15-21; 2 Chron.10:12-19; 11:1ff.).

Israel had spurned God's mercy, rejecting the covenant. She forgot God's past dealings and deliverances (Jer.2:4-7; 3:19). Amos reminded the people that it was God who had acted in history:

> "It was I who brought you up from the land of Egypt, and I led you in the wilderness forty years that you might take possession of the land of the Amorite. Then I raised up some of your sons to be prophets and some of your young men to be Nazirites. Is this not so, O sons of Israel?" declares the LORD. "But you made the Nazirites drink wine, and you commanded the prophets saying, 'you shall not prophesy!' " (Amos 2:10-12)

Although there were significant revivals in response to the prophets, each renewal was short-lived. The people seemed to pursue their ways of depravity with demonic fervor:

> No man repented of his wickedness, saying, "What have I done?" Every one turned to his course, like a horse charging into the battle.... They have rejected the word of the LORD, and what kind of wisdom do they have? .... From the least even to the greatest every one is greedy for gain; from the prophet even to the priest every one practices deceit.... Were they ashamed because of the abomination they had done? They certainly were not ashamed, and they did not know how to blush (Jer.8:6,9,10,12).

God's purpose, however, was to work in grace and mercy through Israel to reach the nations.

> The story of Ruth underlines this earlier in the OT, and later the prophet Jonah furnishes a classic example.... The people of Ninevah repent, and much to Jonah's chagrin God spares the city. Here the great pity of God (4:11) is in full view and his desire that all should come to repentance is clear (Dyrness 1979:222).

Judgment on Israel was inevitable; God's character had to stand vindicated before the nations. The God of love, grace and mercy is also the God of wrath, righteousness and justice. Yet God's judgment is redemptive, and He desires man's restoration to fellowship.

Missiological Considerations
Whatever man gives himself to will either enslave him or liberate him.

God intended Israel to model His desire for the deliverance of man from all forms of slavery. The sociocultural patterns He structured for them were intended to show both Israel and the nations that true liberty is experienced when man operates within God's laws. Outside those parameters, man ends up as a slave either to his own sin-dominated appetites, or to the greed, cruelty, and self-centeredness of other sinful men.

Idolatry in its many forms, strongly appeals to man's sinful nature and is never far from any individual, community, or nation. There is idolatry of self, family, community, nation, things, ease, ambitions, even life itself. Life cannot be lived without making definite, deliberate choices between the good of God and the evil of idolatry. Man's choices bear their own consequence: "they do not say in their heart, `Let us now fear the LORD God, who gives rain ... who keeps for us the appointed weeks of the harvest.' Your iniquities have turned these away, and your sins have withheld good from you" (Jer.5:24-25). All these factors worked in Israel, first to divide the kingdom and then to bring exile.

God intended man to have a purposeful life, full of meaning for the individual, society, and all nations. Thus He commanded, "Obey My voice, and I will be your God, and you will be My people; and you will walk in all the way which I command you, that it may be well with you" (Jer.7:23). The only way Israel could live out her purpose, and fulfill her commission, was to abide in God's "statutes and judgments." Whenever she departed from them, she wound up in captivity of her own making. Whenever Israel cried to God in repentance, He readily restored her to the covenant relationship with its benefits and obligations. Israel's history reveals a close relationship between obedience to the cultural and evangelistic mandates and faithfulness to God's "statutes and judgments."

Throughout these chapters in Israel's history, the compassionate heart of God overshadowed even the tragic disobedience of His people. He desired only their welfare and alignment with His purposes for them and the nations. False prophets blatantly contradicted the laws of God, confirmed Israel in her sinful ways, affirmed her sensuality, and promised abundance. Thus God's people were effectively kept from fulfilling their commission.

Whenever Israel heeded God's message, repented of her sin and again knew the blessedness of walking with God, the nations stood in awe. They marveled at the greatness of Yahweh God, and a holy fear came upon them. Daniel, as a representative of Israel, elicited from Nebuchadnezzar the confession that "Surely your God is a God of gods and a Lord of kings and a revealer of mysteries" (Dan.2:47) Nebuchadnezzar further testified:

> I [Nebuchadnezzar] blessed the Most High and praised and honored Him who lives forever; for His dominion is an everlasting dominion, and His kingdom endures from generation to generation. And all the inhabitants of the earth are accounted as nothing, but He does according to His will in the host of heaven and among the inhabitants of earth; and no one can ward off His hand or say to Him, "What hast Thou done?" (Dan.4:34-35)

So too Darius was forced to confess:

> "I make a decree that in all the dominion of my kingdom men are to fear and tremble before the God of Daniel; for He is the living God and enduring forever, and His kingdom is one which will not be destroyed, and His dominion will be forever. He delivers and rescues and performs signs and wonders in heaven and on earth" (Dan.6:26-27).

Thus the glory due His name came from the lips of those nations which came to see God in action, both on behalf of and through His obedient people:

"The LORD will establish you as a holy people to Himself, as He swore to you, if you will keep the commandments of the LORD your God, and walk in His ways. *So all the peoples of the earth shall see that you are called by the name of the LORD*; and they shall be afraid of you" (Dt.28:9,10, emphasis added).

This was Israel's obligation and her glorious privilege. But if the obligation should be neglected:

"If you will not obey the LORD your God.... The LORD will cause you to be defeated before your enemies; you shall go out one way against them, but you shall flee seven ways before them, and *you shall be an example of terror to all the kingdoms of the earth*" (Dt.28:15,25, emphasis added).

History has recorded the awful consequences stemming from Israel's disobedience. And the same judgment would come to the disobedient churches in Asia Minor (Rev.2:1-7, 12-29; 3:1-6, 14-22).

CHAPTER 15

ENCOUNTER AND

VINDICATION

The fundamental issue the prophets addressed was the moral conflict between God and the forces of evil. The influence of the powers of darkness was seen in Israel's disregard of God's covenant and the blatant immorality and injustice characterizing both rebellious Israel and the nations.

Elijah's encounter with Baal (1 Ki. 17-18) was a call to Israel to remember that her own birth and life took place within the arena of conflict with powers (Exo. 4-15). In turn, she was to confront the nations and their gods to declare God's glory (cf. Is. 40:3-26). Israel was not delivered from captivity to be at ease in Zion, but to be fitted for battle. Her life would be one of conflict. It was therefore not surprising that whenever Israel warred against the gods of the nations, if she sought the help and intervention of God, she was less likely to forsake the God of covenant. On the other hand, when she trifled with God's covenant, made treaties, and avoided battle, she neglected and refused her mandates and followed the gods of the nations.

Yahweh God Versus Baal

Long before Elijah's encounter with Baal, Israel was warned:

"if you will not obey the LORD your God, to observe to do all His commandments and His statutes...that....The LORD will bring you and your king, whom you shall set over you, to a nation which neither you nor your fathers have known, and there you shall serve other gods, wood and stone" (Dt. 28:15,36).

179

Although the Mosaic curse related to exile, Israel's disobedience brought her to worship other gods, which were none other than demon spirits (Lev. 17:7; Dt. 32:17; cf. 1 Cor.10:20).

The Bible contends that there is only one valid religion; any other can only be ascribed to the powers of darkness. Biblically, it is safe to conclude that there are only two basic religions in the world: the worship of Yahweh God and the worship of Baal, the latter representing all religions other than biblical faith. Baalism is worshiping man-made divinities, fostered by demonic spirits, intent on keeping God from receiving the glory. Baalism (essentially animism—the recognition and worship of spirit beings) has been the religious preference of people ever since the Fall, and Israel was no exception.

The Baal worship Israel encountered was linked to the nature cycle. Religious ritual and activity focused on the seasons; fertility of field, beast and man; heavenly bodies; and nature in general; all to control forces hostile to man's welfare. Practices associated with Baalism were astrology, fertility rites, consultation with mediums, magic, witchcraft and sorcery, fire-walking, human sacrifice and other means to coerce the spirit world. When Israel compromised her faith, she too progressively tended toward these religious activities; she worshiped Baal. The very thing God had warned against—the detestable ways of the nations—became her way of life (Dt. 4:15-19; 5:6-10; 7:16,25; 18:9-14). Having rejected the God of the covenant, she adopted the "nature cycle" religion from the surrounding nations.

God had sought to protect Israel from the futile rituals, sensuality, and dehumanization of Baalism, warning her repeatedly, but she ignored her covenant relationship (Jer. 2:20-27).

The Composite of Biblical Faith

In contrast, biblical faith sought God to worship, trust and obey Him. What is commonly referred to as the Lord's Prayer (Mt. 6:9-13) is a composite of the characteristics of biblical faith. The reference point and focus of biblical faith is God alone.

It is He who will "teach us to pray." Biblical faith demonstrates and practices total dependence upon God, rejecting all attempts to manipulate God: "the awesome God who does not show partiality, nor take a bribe" (Dt. 10:17).

The specifics of biblical faith underscore a personal relationship with God: He is "Father" God, a loving, concerned father who responds to His children. But this father God is to be approached from within a family relationship. He is not only a particular person's father, He is corporately "our Father." Interpersonal relationships founded on interdependency and responsibility are mandatory.

He is not only the immanent God, known and experienced as Father; He is sovereign Lord over all peoples (2 Chron. 20:6). Thus the transcendency of God is always kept in focus: "Who art in heaven."

Biblical faith upholds God as alone worthy of honor: "hallowed be Thy name." In all spheres of life His name is to be celebrated and glorified.

God's agenda for creation takes priority over all else. He commissions man to a purposeful mission: "Thy kingdom come." He demands obedience to His laws: "Thy will be done." God's directives for life are imperative. Therefore, whatever is characteristic of life in God's heaven is to be reflected here on earth: "on earth as in heaven." Seeking God's kingdom and doing God's will lead to a godly and purposeful lifestyle before the watching world.

Total dependence on God for all life's needs is normative: "give us this day our daily bread." Life's provision comes from the hand of God and is so recognized.

Man's sinful nature and need of God's salvation are humbly acknowledged: "forgive us our debts." Claiming God as Father and then recognizing Him as the Father of fellow believers makes constant reconciliation imperative: "as we forgive our debtors." Knowing God's forgiveness is contingent on man's forgiveness of others.

As the God of redemption and enabling grace, He can enable man to triumph over all the temptations man encounters: "and lead us not into temptation." But He who controls all, and knows the heart of man, also has the power to shield man from the wanton attacks of Satan: "and deliver us from evil."

And then there is that all-encompassing acknowledgment that all kingdoms, in heaven and on earth, and all true power abide with Him alone, and that to Him belong all praise and adoration of men and heavenly hosts—"for Thine is the kingdom, and the power and the glory, forever. Amen." This composite statement, drawn together by Christ, reflected all that the prophets and apostles taught and demonstrated. Biblical faith is unlike anything known in the world religions.

The Composite of Baal Worship
What made Baal such an attraction to the nations and to the people of Israel? Baalism was a system of *sensuality and manipulation*, as were

all religious systems in the ancient world—and the modern world. They all sought to control God with rituals, magic, liturgies and words, to gain security, happiness, and success. Culture religion, or a religion of the status quo, of sensuality and self-indulgence, characterized Baalism. It was a religion of individualism and privatism, seeking to discover the secrets of reaching through to a god, a spirit, or even, they might have hoped, to God Almighty Himself.

Baalism was *a composite of complicated polytheisms.* The world was under the control of a pantheon of gods and goddesses. To these man had to relate appropriately lest the status quo be disrupted and all kinds of catastrophes befall. As a result, desperate efforts were made to bring man and society into harmony with the annual cycle of nature, because man saw himself as bound with nature. Believing that in the natural world all sorts of gods and goddesses interacted with one another harmoniously, man was obligated to subject himself to these lest he bring disruption to the processes within nature. Great pressure was exerted on all society to preserve the natural order in fear of demonic powers which constantly sought to disrupt the beneficent status quo.

It was imperative that man order his *life in harmony with the nature cycle.* Spring symbolized reincarnation—life recreated—the time of fertilization. Spring heralded the marriage rite when the rain and vegetation god copulated with the goddess of fertility, bringing about grains, vegetables, and fruits. But in order to relate to this symbolism and see its reality in the physical world, man had to show the gods what he desired them to do. Believing that whatever happened in the physical world had its coordinate in the spiritual, and vice versa, the worshipers practiced sacred prostitution to induce the gods to grant fertility to man, animals and fields. Summer symbolized the time of growth, but also of death because of the excessive heat. Various rites were used to protect crops, animals, and mankind. Fall, the time of harvest, brought the fall rains reviving the burned countryside. A rite of resurrection celebrated the god of rain and vegetation bringing renewal. Winter symbolized death and the expectationof reincarnation, followed by the cycle of nature starting again.

The many rituals for maintaining harmony were time-consuming. There was no historical memory or eschatalogical future. Man lived for the moment and sought to harmonize with the nature cycle as best he could. Redemption of time, nature, and man were totally incompatible with nature cycle religious practice. Time was going nowhere, nature was eternal, and man's place was to make the order of things workable.

Ritualistic re-enactments and sympathetic magic engaged the Baal worshiper in physical activities. These activities, by imitating the gods, aroused them to please man. They also demonstrated that man was siding with the gods against the demonic world of disorder and destruction. By taking part as a god, man temporarily became the god and his actions those of the god. In this way imitative magic—like produces like—came into operation.

The balance between fruitfulness and disaster was so tenuous that the religious system developed into an elaborate structure of rituals to *appease and manipulate the spirit world.* The annual revivals of nature in spring and fall would be attended by various ceremonial rituals, such as sacrifices, as well as sexual and intoxicating practices. The devotees' abandon would signal the gods to do likewise and look upon them with favor.

Baal and his pantheon were thought to uphold society so that all sociocultural structures could function properly. The status quo had to be upheld to prevent society's disruption. Man dare not pursue progress—unless it came naturally—or fight injustice and oppression, or help the less fortunate, because the gods had established the order of things. To interfere was tantamount to challenging the gods; such arrogant conduct would incur their disapproval, even their wrath.

In the time of Elijah, Baal's ascribed power controlled many areas of life. Baal, a chief god, and his company of minor gods and goddesses were considered the guardians of the "good" they had established for society, which translated into divine justification for a landed aristocracy. The wealthy had every right to live luxuriously and to exploit the less privileged. Had not the gods so ordered? An oppressive autocracy had the right to rule. The privileged enjoyed the good things of life, and the oppressed had to submit lest they upset the "beneficent" status quo. State-supported religion was both normative and essential: Baal worship was called upon to buttress the sociopolitical structures, and keep people in peaceful subjection. There was little or no concern for others, nor was there recognition of a stewardship mandate respecting people and resources.

At first Baal worship was associated with local fertility gods worshiped at village shrines giving or withholding fertility from man beast and field. Later the Baal pantheon was also thought to control the weather because Baal ruled in the heavens and became the equivalent of Yahweh God to many Israelites and devotees among the nations.

Contemporary Baalism

The parallels between the Baalism of antiquity and modern Baalism practiced by people and nations, both Christian and non-Christian, are obvious.

It is nothing but Baalism when civil authorities permit social, economic and political injustices and claim divine authority for the state. To justify the rich getting richer, the poor poorer, and tolerate growing economic disparity and sociopolitical alienation is totally contrary to biblical faith.

The person content with the riches and pleasures of life, justifying them as personal blessings from God, who does not ask, "Who am I?" and "What am I here for?" and "Why has God given me material means?" is caught up in Baalism. Such a person cannot even grapple with the real issues of life, having conveniently shut himself off from the hard realities of the less privileged. By seeing no need to help those alienated from God and oppressed by demonic structures, he has succumbed to Baalism. When his own private relationship with his god—his personal salvation—is all that he needs or wants and is the sum total of what his religion requires, he has succumbed to Baalism. When his concept of a right relationship with God does not include the evangelistic and cultural mandates and his responsibility ends with himself, he has succumbed to Baalism. When, in the final analysis, every man must look out for himself, his attitude is pure Baalism.

Epicureanism and Stoicism are forms of Baal worship that still exist today. Epicureanism is a "playboy" philosophy which justifies a life of pleasure and noninvolvement in the needs of others. Stoicism is a philosophy of false piety, self-righteousness, and "fatalism" so man can impress the deity with his self-abnegation. Furthermore, all of life has already been pre-ordained so man must bear the inevitable. There is not much man can do to change his (or his fellow man's) circumstances. The only proper response is to separate himself from all those who disagree with him, expect the worst, and await the end. If a god does rule and guide history it is only to make life hard and miserable; but if man can endure the misery, he will, by works of self-righteousness and self-abnegation, inherit the crown of life. Such a god is obligated to receive one who has made such sacrifices; the right to enter god's presence has been earned.

Tragically, Israel opted for Baalism. She rejected her covenant obligations, ignored her mandates, and lost her historical memory of God's redemptive acts. What festivals she still practiced had false rituals. She lusted for the luxury, ease, greed and eroticism of nature worship. Yet God still cared. He would still accomplish His good purposes for His people, Israel:

And it will come about that just as you were a curse among the nations...I will save you *that you may become a blessing*....Thus says the LORD of hosts, "The fast of the fourth, the fast of the fifth, the fast of the seventh, and the fast of the tenth months [Israel's historic celebrations] will become joy, gladness, and cheerful feasts...that peoples will come...saying, `Let us go at once to entreat the favor of the LORD, and to seek the LORD of hosts...' " (Zech. 8:13,19-21, emphasis added).

The Power Encounter

The Sovereign God, the One who stands at the beginning and the end of all—the Alpha and Omega (Rev. 1:17; Gen. 1,2; Rev. 21,22)—would not be thwarted. He still controlled history. His purposes were unchanged for all nations, including Israel. He would continue to work with man wherever he might be in terms of geography and ideology. The encounter would continue until every knee bowed before Him and confessed Him as Lord.

Elijah's encounter with Baal at Mount Carmel, focused the intensity and severity of the battle between God and evil powers and vindicated Elijah's confidence in God who ultimately controls all the universe and all powers: "The earth is the LORD'S, and all it contains, the world, and those who dwell in it...Who is the King of Glory? The LORD strong and mighty, the LORD mighty in battle" (Ps. 24:1,8). In this historic, paradigmatic encounter, Yahweh God sovereignly limited Himself to fallible human agency. His judgment upon declension was inevitable, because a holy and just God does not overlook man's rebellion. And so the God who is sovereign over all nature, through Elijah His servant, and in Israel's midst, turned off the cycle of rain for three years (1 Ki. 17:1; 18:1 cf. 2 Chron. 7:13-14).

God's confrontation with Baal and his priests provoked a power encounter with the demonic powers controlling Israel and tempting her to reject God. The public challenge of Baalism and the dramatic victory endorsed the prophetic ministry of God's servant and exposed the weakness of Baalism. Through a power encounter, Israel was called back to her fundamental objectives: presenting and representing God who is unlike any other among the nations. Baalism and the social structure upholding it were exposed for what they were—bankrupt, dehumanizing, no match for Israel's true God.

Two Views of History

The events surrounding the encounter revealed contrasting concepts of history. Polytheists looked at time as being cyclical: the sole purpose of life's events was to buttress the status quo, maintain the balance and harmony of custom and nature, and encourage man to live in his sensuality. The prophets, however, viewed history as linear. History was moving toward fulfillment, toward the coming kingdom of God — and thus to the Day of the Lord, which will bring judgment upon all nations. (Zeph. 2:11; 3:8-10) This God had no peer.

Missiological Considerations

In missions, encountering other religions is much like Elijah at Mount Carmel. Missions' encounter takes place within the context of "Baal worship," so a theology of encounter is an important part of a biblical theology of missions.

The Old Testament detailed encounters with paganism, exposing paganism for what it was and raising a bulwark against it. The Old Testament records of these encounters reminded God's people not to be preoccupied with the subjective—with religious feelings—but to live in obedience to a righteous and just God. The Old Testament warned believers to avoid mystical religious experiences—the extra-biblical which sought experiences to feed man's appetites and curiosity, but with no Scriptural foundation. It also emphasized the need to constantly reflect on God's mighty acts and submit to the God of true power. The Old Testament revealed the *God of all power* who directed and controlled history for His redemptive purposes for all nations. Therefore God's servants were to reflect on His past faithfulness, His repeated intervention in human affairs, and His deliverances of His people. They would then confidently resist the seducing and deceiving powers of darkness.

The Old Testament exposed the gods of the nations for what they truly were and taught that entrance into God's kingdom was through faith and obedience, not ritual acts.

> Biblical hope and pagan comfort are not the same thing....Biblical hope is based solely upon God, upon his promises, and upon His election. It is known only in the context of judgment and of the Cross, in the acceptance of severe ethical demand....Proper worship begins with the proper inner attitude toward God, with fear (holy reverence), faith trust and love (Wright 1969:26, 27).

By contrast all other religions are utilitarian hoping for success, happiness and security.

186

In the struggle for existence the function of religious worship was that of integration of personal and social life with the natural world...balancing opposing forces such as life and death, rain and draught.... All...worship is based essentially on the conception of the efficacy of an individual's works whether of magic, sacrifice (food for the Deity's need), reason, mystical exercise, or the giving of alms (Ibid.:19, 20, 27).

The Old Testament exposed all polytheism as religion of the status quo: "None of them has ever produced a thorough-going social revolution based upon a high concept of social justice" (Wright 1968:45). Revolution of any sort, especially that which restores man's dignity to live out the image of God, is abhorrent to all natural religion. Man is too self-centered to concern himself with the welfare of others. Polytheism encourages social injustice, and only the Word of God can effectively counter it.

Baal means "master" or "owner," and at first glance had nothing to do with the nature sequence. In time, though, those in power wanted religious sanction for their oppression. Baal was claimed as the author of success, security, authority, fertility, good crops—all the blessings of life for the already prosperous. "Baal" became synonymous with an aristocracy ordained to rule and servants ordained to work. Baal was responsible for social injustice. To challenge the establishment was tantamount to offending Baal. "Accept your lot in life; it has been decreed for you;" such fatalism is normative in Baalism and leads to all kinds of dehumanization. To challenge Baal worship, in whatever form, was to challenge the exploitative systems which Baalism justified. According to all Baalistic religions, fate had ordained the ruling class and prescribed serfdom to the less fortunate. This religion justified a "theology" of acquisition, completely spurning stewardship.

Biblical faith, by contrast, builds egalitarian structures because it is based on a completely different premise.

Other religions, Zoroastrianism and Mohammedanism for example, know of the Divine power, holiness and goodness. But a righteousness that loves the weak and the outcast, a mercy in righteousness directed toward those whom the world's justice passes by—that is phenomenal and unique. It arose in the peculiar nature of the covenant law of Israel, given by God to the Chosen People; and it was that quality in God which transformed holiness from the non-moral to the moral, from fickle power to redemptive energy (Wright 1968:60).

Yahweh God's social system was not one of ownership but of stewardship. To guard against exploitation, God established every 50th year as the Year of Jubilee—the year of new beginnings. It would give everyone a fresh start—a new "signing" of the lease with God. God's system was always egalitarian; everyone was guaranteed security regardless of ability or inheritance. Mutual care and concern were mandatory; they were inseparably at the heart of the cultural mandate.

Biblical faith evaluates and confronts all human systems and structures. So the biblical challenge is not only religious encounter, but social and economic encounter. God hated the Baal system, He still does, and He denounces those who perpetuate any exploitative and dehumanizing system: "Woe to those who add house to house and join field to field, until there is no more room, so that you have to live alone in the midst of the land" (Is. 5:8).

Biblical faith demands a power encounter which calls the powers of darkness, in whatever form they may appear, to account. God tolerates no other gods or systems. God declares Himself against a spirituality that consults, worships, or recognizes other powers as replacements for or additions to God. Yahweh God alone is Lord; all other powers must submit to Him. Biblical faith demands a power encounter with sociocultural structures which dehumanize, demoralize, or destroy man. Whatever robs man of dignity before God and fellow men is an abomination to God, as is any glorification of man.

Throughout the Old Testament the theme of conflict and confrontation is prominent. God was concerned for His glory, and in grace He entrusted His people with the responsibility and privilege to declare His glory by word and deed. God delegated to them all the authority needed to deal effectively with the powers of darkness. The biblical account is replete with illustrations of God's intervention on behalf of His people in their redemptive mission. Any biblical theology of missions which does not refer to this encounter with powers of darkness, and which makes no reference to the authority delegated to God's people, omits much of the biblical evidence. The Psalmist declared:

"Let the godly ones exult in glory; let them sing for joy on their beds. Let the high praises of God be in their mouth, and a two-edged sword in their hand, to execute vengeance on the nations...to bind their kings with chains, and their nobles with fetters of iron; to execute on them the judgment written; this is an honor for all His godly ones. Praise the LORD" (Ps. 149:5-9).

CHAPTER 16

REBELLION AND

JUDGMENT

Israel's philandering with Baal led to her rejecting both her evangelistic and cultural mandates. When Israel ignored her commission to tell the nations of the greatness of God (cf. Jonah), she also ignored the God-given sociocultural mandate which prescribed her modeling of righteousness, justice, and equity (2 Ki. 24-25; 2 Chron. 36;).

Ignoring the cultural mandate in turn bred rebellion among the people of Israel, and revolution broke out through Jeroboam, an administrator of the hated forced labor system. The oppressive and unjust structures initiated by Solomon and expanded upon by his son Rehoboam brought the division of a once-great Kingdom. Instead of being God's model nation for His purposes in the midst of the nations, Israel became a divided kingdom in rebellion against the God who had delivered her from slavery in Egypt.

The Deterioration Which Led To Division

The injustice, immorality, and idolatry planted by Solomon, at one time considered the wisest of all men, stemmed from disregarding the covenant. God had given Israel sufficient warning what would happen if she did so (Dt. 28). God is always impartial (Dt. 10:17); not even His own people escaped the consequences of disobedience. It was inevitable that the kingdom would fall, and Israel would never recover from this disaster of her own making.

The Northern Kingdom had set up a syncretistic state cult unabashedly merging the worship of Yahweh with Baalism, which introduced all the "detestable things of the nations" (Dt. 18:9-14). Not only did her religious life totally contradict biblical faith, but her socio-cultural milieu was wholly against God's mandates (Is. 58:1-10; 59:2-8). But God is a jealous God who will not tolerate divided allegiance. Those who are not with Him in unqualified allegiance are judged as being against Him. Jeremiah observed: "Thou art near to their lips but far from their mind" (Jer. 12:2); and, "this people has a stubborn and rebellious heart; they have turned aside and departed. They do not say in their heart, 'Let us now fear the LORD our God' " (Jer. 5:23-24). In New Testament phrasing: "holding to a form of godliness, although they have denied its power" (2 Tim. 3:5).

The Southern Kingdom also succumbed. Although complete declension came later, the same evil forces and practices that brought judgment to Israel also overtook Judah. The only apparent reason for God's patience with the Southern Kingdom was the times of renewal during the reigns of godly kings such as Josiah and Hezekiah. Though Solomon contradicted his own counsel, he knew that "righteousness exalts a nation" (Prov. 14:34). Judah had no excuse. In great kindness God had acted in mercy toward her:

"No eye looked with pity on you...to have compassion on you...Then I passed by you and saw you, and behold, you were at the time for love; so I spread My skirt over you and covered your nakedness. I also swore to you and entered into a covenant with you so that you became Mine....Then your fame went forth among the nations on account of your beauty, for it was perfect because of My splendor which I bestowed on you" (Ezek. 16:5,8,14).

Tragically, Israel (the Southern and Northern Kingdoms) trusted in herself and turned her back on her covenant God. Ezekiel described Judah's rebellion (Ezek. 16:15-52) with this dreadful assessment:

"As I live" declares the LORD God, "Sodom, your sister, and her daughters, have not done as you and your daughters have done. Behold, this was the guilt of your sister Sodom: she and her daughters had arrogance, abundant food, and careless ease, but she did not help the poor and needy. Thus they were haughty and committed abominations before Me. Therefore I removed them when I saw it. Furthermore, Samaria did not commit half of your sins, for you have multiplied your abominations more than they" (Ezek. 16:48-51).

When God's judgment came, it was catastrophic (Jer.39,44,52). True to His character, Yahweh God cast Israel out of the land, and sent her back into bondage:

"The LORD your God promised this calamity against this place; and the LORD has brought it on and done just as He promised. Because you people sinned against the LORD and did not listen to His voice, therefore this thing has happened to you" (Jer. 40:2-3).

God's patience with man's disobedience is not limitless. Although His name reflects His longsuffering and compassion, He is also the God of wrath and judgment:

"The LORD, the LORD God, compassionate and gracious, slow to anger, and abounding in lovingkindness and truth; who keeps lovingkindness for thousands, who forgives iniquity, transgression and sin; yet *He will by no means leave the guilty unpunished*" (Exo. 34:6,7, emphasis added).

But God had not forgotten His covenant. He would again speak His word to Israel: "Go, and proclaim these words toward the north and say, 'Return, faithless Israel,' declares the LORD; 'I will not look upon you in anger. For I am gracious...I will not be angry forever' " (Jer. 3:12).

And the LORD, the God of their fathers, sent word to them again and again by His messengers, because He had compassion on His people and on His dwelling place; but they continually mocked the messengers of God, despised His words and scoffed at His prophets, until the wrath of the LORD arose against His people, until there was no remedy (2 Chron. 36:15,16).

Thus is the nature of God. Through His merciful imploring of Israel and many interventions on her behalf, the depth of the human heart's evil can be more clearly seen, if not always understood. Nevertheless, God's purposes would be fully realized. He had not completely rejected Israel (Ezek. 16:60-63; 34:11-16; 23-31; 36:8-12; 17-38).

The Message of the Prophets

Throughout the kingdom era, the prophets continued to declare God's indignation against the state and its desecration of His worship (cf. Jer. 3:1-11). They consistently stated that God's mandates demand obedience. The people would know God's blessings as they obeyed His law and displayed His righteousness and justice. But if they did not obey, He would bring the rod of judgment on them. God's judgment was inescapable: "For thus says the LORD of hosts, Cut down her trees, and cast up a siege against Jerusalem. This is the city to be punished, in whose midst there is only oppression" (Jer.6:6).

In spite of being rejected, the prophets persisted in calling the people back to their reason for existence, being His light and His witness to all nations (Is.42:6; 43:10,12). The prophets were fearless in revealing the people's true motivation:

> For wicked men are found among My people...they set a trap, they catch men. Like a cage full of birds, so their houses are full of deceit; therefore they have become great and rich. They are fat, they are sleek, they also excel in deeds of wickedness; they do not plead the cause, the cause of the orphan, that they may prosper; and they do not defend the rights of the poor....Every one is greedy for gain, and from the prophet to the priest every one deals falsely (Jer.5:26-28; 6:13).

But should they repent and renew their obligations, Jeremiah reminded them:

> "If you will return, O Israel," declares the LORD, "Then you should return to Me. And if you will put away your detested things from My presence, and will not waver, and you will swear, 'As the LORD lives,' in truth, in justice, and in righteousness; *then the nations will bless themselves in Him, and in Him they will glory*" (Jer.4:1-2, emphasis added).

In the midst of God's dealing with Israel, the prophets made clear that God's people were not necessarily identifiable with political Israel:

> "Behold, the eyes of the LORD God are on the sinful kingdom, and I will destroy it from the face of the earth; nevertheless, I will not totally destroy the house of Jacob," declares the LORD. "For behold, I am commanding, and I will shake the house of Jacob among all nations as grain is shaken in a sieve, but not a kernel will fall to the ground. *All the sinners of My people will die by the sword*" (Amos 9:8-10, emphasis added).

Judah pursued perversion and dissolution despite the prophets' warnings, the courageous efforts of some godly kings, some remarkable national reforms, and amazing deliverances such as Judah's from Sennacherib (Is. 37:33-38). It was as if Judah wanted judgment to come.

Although the Southern Kingdom of Judah outlasted the Northern Kingdom of Israel, her heart was hardened toward God's voice. That judgment did not befall the Southern Kingdom sooner was due to the prophets and to God's loving concern. Through Judah, God would continue His purposes for all nations. When a pure remnant of God's people demonstrated their visible commitment to God's mandates, He said:

> "do justice and righteousness, and deliver the one who has been robbed from the power of his oppressor....Also do not mistreat or do violence to the stranger, the orphan, or the widow; and do not shed innocent blood in this place. For if you men will indeed perform this thing, then kings will enter the gates of this house" (Jer. 22:3,4).

Part of the pure remnant were Daniel, Meshach, Shadrach, and Abednego. They and others lived in the presence of God by modeling the life which honored Him. They sought to reflect His image on earth. They witnessed to His glory by proclaiming Him to the nations, even though it could cost them their lives. They demonstrated social concern by fulfilling their covenant obligations to their fellow men. They lived expecting that God would fulfill all His promises to His people, especially those predicting the Messiah (Lk.2:25-32).

The prophets railed against the compromise of Judah. Although she knew what had happened to her sister Samaria, she ignored all warnings. Instead of confronting paganism, she readily tolerated Baalism and adulterated her own faith. Just as Samaria became entrapped through treaties, so Judah's tributary relationship to Assyria brought her the Assyrian deities and detestable practices. She submitted herself to divination, magic, sacred prostitution so typical of Baal practice (1 Ki. 14:22-24; 15:11-12; 2 Ki. 23:1-7), human sacrifice (2 Chron. 28:3), and much more.

The prophets upheld God's righteous character, which remained impartial and unchanging. Just as He was patient with the people of Canaan (Gen. 15:16), so He was with Israel and Judah. But the day of His patience came to an end. His character stood vindicated. His purpose for Israel was not thwarted; clearly God still had those who, even in captivity, would model His character (Dan. 3:16-30; 6:10, 16, 20-22). From Judah's fate, the nations would learn that God does not tolerate sin, even among those claiming to be His special objects of grace.

The prophets made clear that because of sin, the worship of God and stewardship of His creation were very easily exchanged for appeasement of deities (idols) and exploitation of God's created world. As Israel gradually exchanged more and more of her biblical faith for paganism, her approach to God and His creation changed from worship and stewardship to appeasement and exploitation. As a result, both kingdoms reaped what they had sowed: the bitter fruit of judgment. Man thinks he can break God's laws with impunity. But the truth is, man breaks himself against the immutable laws of God—laws originally established for his well-being: "Oh that they had such a heart in them, that they would fear Me, and keep all my commandments always, that it may be well with them and their sons forever" (Dt. 5:29; cf. Ps. 81:13,14). In the words of the prophet: "For I know the plans that I have for you, declares the LORD, plans for welfare and not for calamity to give you a future and a hope " (Jer. 29:11).

As judgment approached, divergent, clashing theologies prevailed. On the one hand were the false prophets who declared: *God will never judge*—" The LORD will deal with us according to all His wonderful acts" (Jer. 21:2). On the other was the minority theology that *God does judge sin*, regardless of man's claimed relationship to Himself:

> "I Myself shall war against you with an outstretched hand and a mighty arm, even in anger and wrath and great indignation....He will strike them down with the edge of the sword. He will not spare them nor have pity nor compassion" (Jer. 21:5,7).

Thus the prophets not only had to contend with a wayward people, but with false prophets who spoke from their ignorance, not according to revelation knowledge:

> The prophets are prophesying falsehood in My name. I have neither sent them nor commanded them nor spoken to them; they are prophesying to you a false vision, divination, futility and the deception of their own minds (Jer. 14:14; cf. Ezek. 13).

The Judgment

The God of promise and fulfillment, however, would not be mocked, and His agent of judgment was Babylon. Widespread destruction overtook the land. Practically every fortified town, including Jerusalem and its temple, was in ruins. Thousands of people were killed and about 11,000 went into captivity (Tenney 1967:147). Israel's demise as a political and religious entity was complete. Because Israel forsook her God and went after other gods, the enemy had won the day. But in the end God would judge Babylon (Hab.2:4-17).

A New Beginning

God's judgment of Israel presupposed a new creation of Israel that would follow. As in the Flood, God sought to provide a context of righteousness and justice so that Israel could continue to be His model before the nations. In the midst of judgment, God still had plans of blessing for His people, plans to be realized through her suffering in exile. She would be blessed only as she accepted this judgment as one which God had sent and in which she was to be His model in message and conduct (Jer. 29:4-11). Israel's exile did not excuse her from fulfilling her evangelistic and cultural mandates.

God's model Israel was to bear a precious treasure, the message of God. She knew the God who alone delivers and desires all peoples to know His deliverance. She knew God who is always ready to do a new thing. Even amidst suffering, "Israel's mission is so like that of a prophet: an ear to hear, a mouth to speak and a message to bring to the nations, prophetic Torah to impart to the peoples of the earth" (Crenshaw and Willis 1974:126).

From God's people, renewed by God's new creative work and new covenant (Jer. 31; cf. Zech. 1:8-21; 2; 4; 6; 8), the nations will hear of the goodness of God: "Hear the Word of the LORD, O nations, and declare in the coastlands afar off...for the LORD has ransomed Jacob" (Jer.31:10-11); therefore:

> "all the nations of the earth, which shall hear of all the good that I do for them...shall fear and tremble....In those days and at that time I will cause a righteous Branch of David to spring forth; and He shall execute justice and righteousness on the earth" (Jer.33:9,15).

Missiological Considerations

God was, is, and always will be in control of history. He is the Maker of history, to accomplish His purposes for the nations. His purposes continue to move forward in spite of the failure of people. He will raise up prophets, Isaiahs, Jeremiahs, Daniels and Ezekiels. The God of history does not lack for people who are committed to Him and His cause, willing to give their lives to declare His glory.

Biblical faith is unlike pagan religion. Biblical faith is an individual encounter with a living God which inevitably issues in social responsibilities (Jer. 7:21-23; cf. Jer .9:1-9). Both of these elements belong together. This relationship with God is based on historical fact and involves a commitment to God's redemptive mission. By contrast, pagan religion is the appeasement of evil spirits through sympathetic magic. The purpose is to get their help to do man's will in his pursuit for personal success, security, and happiness if need be, at the expense of others. A biblical theology of missions must take into account the tragic effects of paganism on human society. When man is robbed of his dignity and forced into dehumanizing structures, it is an affront to God, who made man in His image. We must come to grips with the cultural mandate— but it can never be an end in itself. God wants man to be restored to fellowship with Himself, and this can be achieved only through God's redeeming man.

God is the God of new beginnings. A new covenant *will* certainly be established. Israel's unrealized hopes constrained devout men to look forward longingly to the new covenant predicted by Jeremiah (Jer. 31:31-34). They believed that the God who had promised would surely fulfill. They were committed to remain faithful to God who is always willing to start afresh.

God is still at work in and through all circumstances to bring about His purposes. Though the present frequently looks as if it will end in total defeat, God is at work and will still use Israel to bring about that "new covenant." In like manner, He has decreed that His Church complete its task; then He will usher in His glorious reign to bring blessing to all nations.

Disobedient mankind will continue to pursue false hopes of salvation. This whole period in Israel's history was characterized by all the false hopes of redemption which mankind pursues. Religious ritual and mystical experiences, centered in man's desire for fulfillment, lead to individualism and false pride.

There will never be salvation in the political arena. The state and its policies, at best, are a crude imitation of God's righteous and just kingdom. Wealth and prosperity can never meet the real need of man's longings, for true prosperity is not found in the material things of life. Human efforts at social reform are commendable but seldom altruistic enough to sustain ongoing progress for all. None of man's efforts can create the "kingdom of God" or "Utopia." Says Bright:

"The earthly order is at its best a pale approximation of God's order, at its worst a travesty of it. In no case can it be that order or create it. On the contrary, it lives, now as then, under history's judgment. But here also we learn of the true hope. It lies in the grace of God, who accords to men a New Covenant—its law written on human hearts....The Old Covenant thus points to a solution beyond itself—the creation of a new people" (1953:126).

God's New Covenant will introduce a people in whom He has created new and clean hearts, of flesh and not stone (Ezek. 36:26). The New Testament people of God, redeemed by the blood of Jesus Christ, regenerated and indwelt by the Holy Spirit, have been entrusted with the gospel of God's grace—the gospel that speaks of God's new creation (Rom. 1:16; 2 Cor. 5:17).

Israel could only anticipate the coming Messiah, the One who would make all things new. The Church looks back in joy and gratitude, because He for whom they waited has come. Now the steward's task of reconciling man to God must ever motivate all of life.

CHAPTER 17

DEATH AND

RESURRECTION

It was unthinkable to the Israelites that those whom God had ordained to bear His message should be so humiliated before the nations, but their presumption on God's grace would not save them from the consequences of rebellion. Their problem was deep-seated: "The heart is more deceitful than all else and is desperately sick; who can understand it?" (Jer. 17:9) Israel needed a heart change before she would align with God's purposes. Some of that change came during the exile, but only enough to motivate a remnant to live for God's purposes.

The Death of Israel

When Israel trifled with her God, her faith, and her commission, God brought judgment as promised (Dt. 29:17-28). This judgment was so significant that a great deal of Scripture covered this period in Israel's history. Ezra, Nehemiah, Lamentations, Ezekiel, Daniel, Haggai, and Zechariah all spoke of Israel's death in exile and subsequent resurrection from captivity and restoration to the Promised Land. When Israel lost Jerusalem (2 Ki. 25:1-26; 2 Chron. 36:17-21; Jer. 15:5-9), she died.

Israel's "burial" took place in a foreign land. Those whom God intended to be a blessing in the midst of the nations were only fit for a grave in a land distant from their God-promised home. The exile was tantamount to a "burial" with professional mourners told to weep over the corpse (Jer. 9:17-22). Politically, and in many ways socially, Israel had died. She was back in slavery under the domination of a foreign king, subjected to all kinds of indignities. The proud kingdom of Israel was under the curse of God: the glory had departed.

Yet even amidst the mourning, God continued to watch over Israel and did not wholly abandon her to her enemies. Although Jeremiah regarded Jerusalem's capture and the destruction of Israel as *the day of the LORD* (Lam. 1;12, 21-22), he pled with God not to cast Israel off forever.In spite of her death and burial in the land of pagan deities, among alien people, there would be a day of resurrection. Both Jeremiah and Malachi spoke of a future "day of the Lord" (Jer. 30:7; Mal. 4:5). God was not through with His covenant people—He would resurrect them from captivity and recommission them for their mission to the nations. Jeremiah exclaimed:

O LORD, my strength and my stronghold, and my refuge in the day of distress, *to Thee the nations will come from the ends of the earth* and say, "Our fathers have inherited nothing but falsehood, futility and things of no profit." Can man make gods for himself? Yet they are not gods! (Jer.16:19-20, emphasis added).

The Exile: Bane or Blessing?

The Exile resembled the scattering at Babel, where humanity's pride focused on building the tower to make contact with God. Similarly, Israel's pride focused on Jerusalem's beauty, power, and wealth, which the people believed gave them the right to approach God on their own terms. While God expected His people to be humble and pure in heart, living in obedience to His commands, they structured a religion of pomp and style, of custom and ritual, alien to all they had learned about the God of their deliverance. Israel's sins separated her from God, and all that remained was judgment—Israel reaped what she had sowed.

What Israel had not done as the free people of God she now did as a captive in foreign lands. The Jews had not lost all historical memory, and they knew that God had in times past heard their cry of distress. Those among them who had not turned to the worship of idols (Neh.1; Dan. 3:16-18; 9:3-19) were still available to God for His purposes. Thus in grace God turned Israel's rebellion into blessing for others. His sending Israel into exile among the nations was ultimately for the blessing of all. Nations were brought to acknowledge that Yahweh God alone reigned over all kingdoms (Dan. 4:34-35). In her scattering, in spite of her sordid past, Israel was a witness to the greatness and wholly otherness of the God of Abraham, Isaac, and Jacob. And in her regathering she also testified that God, who delivers and controls all of history, also desires the salvation of all nations (cf Is. 25:7-9). God had turned wrath into blessing.

The exile was such an unnecessary tragedy. If only Israel had kept her covenant obligations, she would have been a blessing in the midst of the nations and would have known the abundant blessings of God. But Israel was seduced by the gods (demons) of the nations and rejected all that was good for herself and others, so judgment had to follow. God's righteousness and justice had to stand vindicated before all nations. Thus when the prophets railed against her disobedience, they were willing to risk the very existence of Israel rather than betray her spiritual heritage. God's holy character demanded Israel's dissolution.

Amidst the declarations of judgment, the prophets also held out the hope of God's impending intervention on behalf of His people. They had confidence in God's power (Jer. 32:6-27; 33:3-17) and faithfulness to His covenant promises. He would not forget His promises to His ancient people. The prophets firmly believed that God would again prepare Israel to be His new creation; that she would again participate in a new exodus; and that she would be recommissioned for a renewed mission to the nations.

The Burden of Ezekiel

God intended His people to live all of life in the presence of His glory. Ezekiel described what God desired of His people and underscored repeatedly that God would accomplish those purposes for the sake of His name, upon which Israel had brought so much reproach (Ezek. 36). Ezekiel described how God intended Israel to be His river of blessing to the nations (Ezek. 47:1-12), and will yet be, and that anyone touching that river would know God's abundance in every way. With that kind of vision for the people of God, Ezekiel spoke God's heart to Israel.

The collapse highlighted in Ezekiel is the result of the horrible consequences of sin. Because of Israel's sin, God left the temple and the heart and life of Israel. The prophet described how progressively the glory of God departed from Israel. First was the gradual withdrawing from the holy place in the temple (Ezek. 8:6). Then God's glory hovered over the threshold of the temple door (Ezek. 9:3), as if to indicate His reluctance to leave (Ezek. 10:4,18). Finally, "the glory of the LORD went up from the midst of the city, and stood over the mountain which is east of the city" (Ezek. 11:23). The glory of Israel—the God of creation—had to withdraw because of the abominations committed by the people (Ezek. 8-11). Thus, "God was Himself in exile with His people" (Dyrness 1983:109). He, too, was enduring the tragedy of their sin. They could not disregard His covenant and think it did not affect Him. Their pain would be His pain, too. They deserved theirs; He did not deserve His. But He was inextricably bound up with His people.

Though Israel discarded the covenant, God had not discarded her. Of that certainty Ezekiel himself was the witness, and more significantly, the watchman (Ezek. 3:17-21; cf. 33:7-9). God would act on behalf of Israel "for My Holy Name" (Ezek. 36:22) which Israel had desecrated among the nations.

Although Israel had failed in her original mission, God would send her, yet again, on that mission, saying He would put His Spirit in her and give her a new heart (Ezek. 36:26,27) so that she would do God's bidding. The "dry bones" of Israel's nonexistence as a nation (Ezek. 37:1-10) would be raised from the "death" of her captivity. Thus resurrected, Israel would take up her commission once more.

Though the resurrection and new creation would be God's doing, they would be mediated through God's prophet. To Ezekiel had been committed the responsibility to speak God's creative word to bring about a new Israel (Ezek. 37:1-10). In acknowledging God's creative ability, and in speaking God's creative word, Ezekiel also confessed Israel's responsibility to the nations. Thus, Israel's second Exodus out of captivity was a clear reminder to her and the nations that God's commission demanded that His glory be declared. There would be deliverance for those who sat in the bondage of slavery, even a slavery of their own making.

God's renewed and righteous people would once again spread His blessing, His healing, and His provision, even as He had intended from the very beginning of their history. Thus Ezekiel not only exposed Israel's insurrection for what it was, but brought Israel to realize that apart from God recreating her heart, she would again pursue perversity. He also called Israel back to her mission. It was her privilege to mediate God's creative word for a new creation, to be God's blessing in the midst of the nations, and to dispense those blessings until all had come to know the benediction of being the people of God.

The Return: Resurrection

The re-establishment of the religious and political life of Israel was a result of God's gracious intervention in response to the earnest prayer of Daniel (Dan. 9,10). God desires to have His people forget the past and participate in new things (Is. 43:18-19; cf. 45:22-25). There is, however, a biblical principle not to be ignored. God will act on behalf of His people provided they ask Him to do so. Such asking presupposes repentance, confession of sin, and recognition of His holiness:

> "I am the LORD, your Holy One, the Creator of Israel, your King....Who makes a way through the sea and a path through the mighty waters....Behold, I will do something new....*Yet you have not called on Me, O Jacob; but you have become weary of Me, O Israel*" (Is.43:16,19,22, emphasis added).

God's call to rebuild the land and re-establish Israel's religious and political life fell on many deaf ears. Few sought to remove the reproach that they had brought upon God's name. Josephus observed that "they were not willing to leave their possessions." Is this not the attitude which characterizes much of Christendom? Many among exiled Israel had become satisfied with their new life in a foreign land and were not willing to commit themselves to God's cultural and evangelistic mandates. They had come to believe that life in exile was better than involvement in God's purposes. The forces at work in national Israel before her captivity were still keeping Israel from accepting God's renewed call to be His blessing in the midst of the nations.

God, however, is never limited by small numbers. He would work through a remnant. He does not lack for ways or means: He raised up a "messiah" in Cyrus, king of Persia, to encourage the people to return (Is. 45:1-4). God's selecting a pagan king was another confirmation of His control of all nations, so that the nations might know Him (Is. 45:5-6). Through Cyrus, a remnant returned and began rebuilding and re-establishing the worship of Yahweh God.

The Ambivalence of Israel

Those who returned were quickly opposed and easily discouraged. Pessimism prevailed, and the people no longer maintained their theology of recital of God's mighty acts of deliverance. They had forgotten God's redemptive purposes and His past mighty acts. Their religion had become vain and self-centered. Yes, they had become religious, but inwardly, not upwardly and outwardly. They had indeed turned from visible idols, only to serve idols of vain thinking, mystical experiences, and selfish aims which would justify life with minimum involvement in God's purposes (Mal. 1:2-14).

Attitudes of self-pity, self-centeredness, and selfishness characterized the returnees just the same as those still in exile. It took them 24 years to rebuild the temple, and although the walls were rebuilt, it took 75 years to rebuild the defenses. More time was spent on their own dwellings and interests than on God's (Hag. 1:3-7).

God's people realized only partial restoration, not because God intended it that way, but because they had lost their vision. The restoration to the land did not bring the restoration of the kingdom. Israel realized only a partial control of the land God had given her. It was apparent that persecution and judgment did not necessarily restore the people to involvement in their divine commission. On the contrary, their captivity seemed to have made them more introspective and self-serving, seeking to preserve their own identity and religious cult (Mal. 3:7-15).

There were indeed times of religious renewal through the ministry of God's word, but the results were short-lived (Neh. 8-10). The people's introspection only led to pessimism and discouragement (Neh. 4:10). They were easily deflected from their objectives (Neh. 4:12ff). They took advantage of each other, even abusing their own kinsmen (Neh. 5:1-13). Inconsequential political and religious issues surfaced frequently. Political upheaval prevailed (Neh. 6:1-19). The fall of the Persian Empire to Greece simply added to the unsettling climate of the day. Israel was weak, a has-been. All she could do was cling to her few verities—such as her glorious historical past—but her attitude called even these into question. The predicted universal kingdom seemed so distant, so unreal.

Nevertheless, a few sustained the hope of the coming Messiah and His kingdom which would encompass all nations. In part, Israel's task was to draw the nations to receive the blessing of Abraham. Thus the post-exilic prophets emphasized God's universal purposes:

> "Sing for joy and be glad, O daughter of Zion; for, behold I am coming and I will dwell in your midst declares the LORD. And many nations will join themselves to the LORD in that day and will become My people" (Zech.2:10-11).

The prophets maintained a worldwide perspective, because their hope was firmly anchored in the God of promise and fulfillment, always concerned for all peoples:

> Thus says the LORD of hosts, "It will yet be that peoples will come, even the inhabitants of many cities; and the inhabitants of one will go

to another saying, `Let us go at once to entreat the favor of the LORD, and to seek the LORD of hosts; I will also go.' So many peoples and mighty nations will come to seek the LORD of hosts in Jerusalem....In those days ten men from all the nations will grasp the garment of a Jew saying, `Let us go with you, for we have heard that God is with you'" (Zech.8:20-23; cf. Mal.1:11-14).

The Introversion of Israel

Israel's introversion kept her occupied with issues unrelated to God's purposes for the nations. Israel's preoccupation with herself and her status as God's people may be traced first to her *loss of purpose*. After the wall was rebuilt, Israel closed herself off from the rest of the world.

Second, she maintained an even *greater exclusivism* than during her previous days. Bright, Wright and others contend that the book of Jonah was written during this period, to rebuke Jewish introversion and exclusiveness. Even if this is a very late date for Jonah, the message— obey God no matter how unpopular the commission—was certainly needed by Israel. During the post-exilic period, reprimanded Israel apparently felt she had every right to turn within. The only way to face the future was, in self-pity, to re-establish and cultivate her religious life.

The religious parties of the intertestamental period found their roots during this era. A variety of schools of religious thought sprang up, all seeking to justify theologies of introversion. Jesus Christ's response to the Pharisees, Sadducees, and scribes dealt with Israel's preoccupation with the inconsequential. The people were committed to rules and regulations which had little to do with declaring God's glory.

Third, Israel had committed herself to *new ideological idols*. While the Exile appeared to have delivered Israel from worshiping Baal idols, she replaced them with other ideological idols—all kinds of cabalistic approaches to God. Malachi spoke forthrightly to Israel's introversion and obstinate refusal to carry out God's purposes:

"A son honors his father, and a servant his master. Then if I am a father, where is My honor? And if I am a master, where is My respect?...Oh that there were one among you who would shut the gates, that you might not uselessly kindle fire on My altar....For from the rising of the sun, even to its setting, My name will be great among the nations" (Mal.1:6,10-11).

205

Israel was to be a people rightly worshiping God as a witness to the nations; but instead she adopted new forms of paganism to manipulate God (Mal.1:6-10,12-14; 2:13-17; 3:8-10). She had more than enough religious practices to keep her from turning in true repentance to God. She so busied herself with these that she felt insulted when God dared to question her commitment to Him (Mal.2:17; 3:8). Few submitted in obedience to God's objectives in history (Mal.3:16-18).

The coming Deliverer, the challenger and destroyer of all false worship, would yet bring salvation to God's creation. Malachi, who spoke God's last message in the Old Testament, predicted that the Deliverer would come (Mal. 3:1), that all false worship would be fully exposed and judged (Mal. 3:3-6), and that the final crisis in God's mission will be ushered in. Malachi predicted that God would send Elijah as the forerunner of that day of judgment (Mal. 4:5-6), and four centuries later John the Baptist was so identified (Mt. 11:7-14). Though it seemed as if God's purposes for creation would falter, His program was right on schedule (Heb. 1:1). Not even a disillusioned introspective, trivial-minded people would delay His plan for all nations (cf. Mt. 16:18).

Missiological Considerations

Seven lessons arise from the death and resurrection of Israel. Each has a significant bearing on the involvement of God's people in missions today, for God's interaction with Israel during the restoration highlights some remarkable truths which apply to ministry anywhere.

First, misdirected priorities (Hag. 1:1-5) led to pessimism, which had a deadening effect on the spiritual life of God's people. Life became dull and barren. There was little evidence of God's blessing, little or no expectation that God would demonstrate His presence and power for His people. Selfishness and self-centeredness robbed God's people of spiritual vitality. As a hapless minority, they thought that they might as well limit themselves to maintaining their faith in a hostile world. Instead of pursuing God's mission (Is. 43:10; 49:6), they pursued the material things of life.

Second, the people's unwarranted self-confidence in their ability to reconstruct Jerusalem soon led to discouragement. They had forgotten that "unless the LORD builds the house, they labor in vain who build it" (Ps. 127:1). Discouragement is one of the most effective ways to stop God's people from confronting the powers determined to distract them from participation in God's mission. When discouragement overtakes, the future seems bleak. God's servants tend to think they have exhausted all their resources. The underlying reason for discouragement in this case was *lack of faith* (Hag. 2:1-9). Few in number, they thought they could not possibly accomplish the task. They had forgotten God's past mighty acts of deliverance.

Third, when God withholds anticipated blessings and does not appear to hear or meet needs, in desperation man resorts to manipulation. The focus on blessings, rather than on the Giver of the blessings, is bound to lead to unhealthy religious practice. The problem in Israel was that *they neglected the true worship of God* (Mal. 1:6-14). Through either sloth or excessive activism (the barrenness of a busy life), Israel ignored God's commands about how to approach Him. He was not even acknowledged as the Holy One deserving the worship and praise of His people. Instead, it was said of Israel "you have wearied the LORD with your words" (Mal. 2:17).

Fourth, when opposition becomes fierce and the adversaries are bold, fears multiply and cares increase. The problem in Israel was *a superficiality toward God and an indifference toward cultivating fellowship with Him.* As a result, she did not discern His heart and purposes (Mal. 3:13-14; cf. Mal. 1:11-13; 2:8-9, 17). God's people need to understand the message of 2 Chronicles 20 as a message and model for all times. Opposition and conflict are normal; dependence upon God is foundational; humility and recognition of weakness are essential; confidence in God is indispensable; obedience to God's commands is crucial; praise, boldness, and faith are irreplaceable in doing battle with God's enemies.

Fifth, when God's work languishes, progress will be minimal and problems will multiply. The problem in Israel was *lack of vision* on the part of leadership and therefore of the people (Zech. 1:7-2:13). The charter for faith and action was either ignored or forgotten. What was God's intention for Israel? Why did she not remember the God who called her and therefore would enable her?

Sixth, when workers are tempted to quit, they will find the work tiring and too demanding. The problem in Israel was *introspection and self-depreciation* (Zech. 3:1-10). When we forget our call and who it is that enables us for the task, there will be a tendency to question self-worth, leading to despondency and malaise.

Seventh, when leadership fails, followers become divided and demoralized. The problem in Israel was that *the leaders neglected and did not discern the work of the Holy Spirit in ministry* (Zech. 4:1-14). An indispensable ingredient in working with people is developing trust and then trusting the Holy Spirit to do His work in people's lives.

The restoration prophets had a message for those who had genuinely responded to God's call to return to the land, who had some understanding of what it meant to be the people of God and some knowledge of God's purposes. The prophets emphasized that God's program marches on to the realization of the New Covenant (Zech.12:10; 13:1-14:21). What the prophets declared has enormous significance for world missions today.

Haggai and Zechariah, the prophets of "work," preached to those who had a heart for God. Their message was not to those who remained in Babylon but to those who had, by returning, committed themselves to God and His purposes. Nevertheless, they, too, needed to be reminded of priorities which demanded their constant attention. The temple, a reminder of God's centrality, His presence and purpose, remained unfinished. Unfortunately Israel had other priorities of more immediate concern, and her way of life would know dissolution unless she aligned herself with God's mission. Through these prophets, God also reminds His Church that His objectives are still unrealized. The task of missions still waits while God's people trivialize His mandates.

CHAPTER 18

THE HOPE OF ISRAEL

The themes of the hope of Israel and the remnant are closely tied. Paul refers to this hope, claiming that his chains of imprisonment were due to "the hope of Israel" (Acts 28:20). But the two themes are not equal. Man is exhorted not to put his trust in man, remnant or not, but in God (Is. 2:20-22).

The Messianic Hope

The beginnings of the messianic hope—the Hope of Israel—are traced to God's earliest dealings with man. This was progressively revealed to Israel, in statement and in type, to inspire and motivate the people to persevere in God's mission to the nations. The pledge came through the seed promise to Eve, the Shiloh promise to Judah, Balaam's prophecy of star and scepter, the king promise to David, and numerous other promises (Gen. 3:15; 49:10; Num. 24:17; Ps. 2; 110:1-4; Is. 2:2-4; 4:2; 9:1-7; 11:1-5; 52:13-53:12; Jer. 23:5-6; 30:9; 33:14-18; Ezek. 34:22-31; 37:24-28; Hos. 3:5; Amos 9:11-15; Mic. 4:1-4; 5:1-5; Hag. 2:6-9; Zech. 6:12-15).

Associated with this hope was the hope of having dominion over the nations. This was not a vain hope, nor one in which political Israel would exercise dominion. Israel misunderstood this and so rejected the servant role to which she had been appointed. The messianic hope was at first associated with David, thought to be the one sent to deliver Israel from all her enemies. David indeed represented God's concern to save His people and bless the nations.

Isaiah translated the messianic hope into its larger dimension and spoke of One yet to come who would be of the seed of David. He would be the "Wonderful Counselor, Mighty God, Eternal Father, Prince of Peace. There will be no end to the increase of His government or of peace" (Is.9:6-7). His rule would include dominion over all nations.

This coming Messiah would destroy Israel's enemies and transform and rule the remnant (Is. 11:1-5; Mic. 5:2-4). He would be a new Adam, starting afresh, ruling in a new Eden over a new Israel and would bless all the nations of the world from Jerusalem (Is. 2:2-4; 11:6,7; Mic. 4:1-4). He would rule the world in righteousness with power, love, justice, and holiness (Is. 60:10-14).

God used the remnant's yearning for the Messiah to kindle the hope of Israel for His intervention in their history. Never did the hope shine brighter than when the people were under oppression or in exile. Times of oppression simply moved the remnant to focus more on this "Hope." As God purified His people in the exile, He also rid them of their outward idolatry and encouraged them to focus their loyalty on Yahweh God and His purposes (cf. 2 Pet. 3:9-13).

The post-exilic prophets, reflecting on the David of history, introduced other aspects of this coming Messiah. The Hope of Israel would be a servant king. Although this was contrary to what Israel expected, it had been predicted by the prophets even before the exile. He would not come as a soldier-king like David, but rather upon the colt of a donkey. He would be righteous and victorious, lowly and peaceful, but by the power of God strong to deliver, to help and to save (Zech.9:9). He would conquer through the powerlessness of the servant and further expose the weakness of the gods and kings of the nations.

Apocalyptic Obsession

There were both positive and negative ramifications of the future Hope of Israel. Positively, apocalyptic literature—focusing on this Hope—kept God's remnant thinking eschatalogically. The present was not all there was to life. Apocalyptic literature kept alive the flame of hope of God's triumph in history. It made men strong in their confession of God before a hostile, pagan world. Focusing on the Hope of Israel made people concerned to know and obey God's law (especially the Mosaic law) and kept them interacting with it. The book of Daniel served that positive purpose, while also stimulating further apocalyptic speculation and literature which proliferated after Malachi.

There were negative results as well. *First*, the focus on the judgment of the nations and the elevation of the kingdom of Israel, rather than the deliverance of all nations, captured the attention of God's people. The remnant longed for God to judge their enemies (the Gentile nations) and establish a kingdom with themselves at the center, not as God's redemptive agents, but as recipients of God's special blessing.

Second, the Israelites thought of themselves as superior to all others. Nationalism was condoned, if not encouraged. Furthermore, the conservatives within Israel considered themselves the restoration arm. They became active in the interest of the coming kingdom, and although Judaism spread rapidly it carried a very mixed agenda of ethnocentrism, cabalism, and legalism. At best its thrust was sectarian. So the spread of Judaism was with little or no concern for the nations' salvation.

Third, preoccupation with the future kept Israel from taking responsibility for the nations. This apocalyptic obsession captured the imagination of the people, and as before, God's mandates became unimportant. The Pharisees, Essenes, Herodians, and Sadducees illustrated this rejection of God's pursuits. The disregard and contemptuous treatment of others and mistreatment of the poor and less privileged contradicted their claimed commitment to the covenant. The legalism of the Pharisees, the added religious burdens placed upon people and the haggling over petty matters kept Israel introverted and busy with inconsequential concerns. Tragically, most Israelites were far from knowing and obeying God as their Father, the Lord of all nations and Savior of the world. Regarding this shortsighted approach to life and history, Bright correctly observed that Israel was

> Forever scanning the times for signs of the coming end, drawing diagrams, as it were, of how that end should come. They moved in a dream world where the coming of the Kingdom was momentarily expected in clouds and glory....When men seize upon the things of the end, fix their interest upon these things well-nigh to the exclusion of all else, there issues a disease of faith (Bright 1970:168).

The prevailing apocalyptic emphasis also encouraged a very pessimistic approach to the world. It issued in legalistic forms and casuistry as religious life became the sole focus. Formalism became an imperative as dynamic interaction with a living God went into the background. People searched Scripture for further guidelines to support formal correspondence to religious conventions supposedly God's design for life—a life apart from God's evangelistic and cultural mandates.

Because the evangelistic and cultural commissions were not considered important, religious instruction and leadership focused only on the conservative remnant who were becoming more and more legalistic. They set aside the historical perspective of God's redemptive acts in favor of an allegorical (spiritualized) interpretation of Scripture. Some claimed that any given passage might have many equally valid interpretations (Terrey 1976:168-174), an approach which led to a self-centered, ethnocentric interpretation of the Bible. The conservatives' interpretation of Scripture which led them to believe they alone would enjoy the Messianic era finally contributed to the demise of the prophetic movement.

When God stopped speaking, fanciful prophecy and the apocalyptic emerged even more. Speculation became more important while the true prophetic perspective was lost. Only the apocalyptic was thought worthy of study. George Ladd observed that "this sense of God's acting redemptively in history the apocalypses lost....History has not been abandoned to evil." And speaking to God's people today, Ladd adds, "In fact, the powers of evil which the apocalyptists felt dominated history have been defeated [in Jesus Christ]" (Ladd 1964:322). A messianism divorced from God's redemptive activity became current. The misunderstanding of Scripture, negative attitudes toward other peoples and the misdirected religious enthusiasm of the conservatives proved destructive for the Jews. Misinterpreted messianic expectations led to the tragic Maccabean Revolt of 167 B.C., the destruction of the Temple in 70 A.D., and Bar Kochba's failure in 135 A.D. at Masada.

The same consequences still hold true for the Church today. Should God's people ignore the historical and prophetic perspectives of Scripture and neglect God's commission for involvement in the world, they will inevitably turn inward and destroy themselves. Many a struggling or empty church stands as a monument to man's disobedience.

The Suffering Servant

The messianic hope apart from the suffering servant theme was not biblical because the Messiah, the Hope of Israel, was the Suffering Servant (Is. 53). From the very beginning, suffering was to characterize the coming Deliverer: "And I will put enmity between you and the woman, and between your seed and her seed; He shall bruise you on the head, and you shall bruise Him on the heel" (Gen. 3:15).

The theme of conflict and confrontation cannot be without suffering. This will inevitably characterize the battle with the kingdom of darkness for man's deliverance. The principle is later reviewed by Paul:

we are afflicted in every way, but not crushed; perplexed, but not despairing; persecuted, but not forsaken; struck down, but not destroyed; always carrying about in the body the dying of Jesus, that the life of Jesus also may be manifested in our body. For we who live are constantly being delivered over to death for Jesus' sake, that the life of Jesus also may be manifested in our mortal flesh. So death works in us, but life in you (2 Cor. 4:10- 12).

The Suffering Servant theme takes on meaning within the context of encounter with the kingdom of darkness.

This motif appears in several key passages, but especially in Isaiah (Is. 52-53). Suffering to accomplish redemption is inherent in the concept of the Messiah. He would come to give His life a ransom for others (Is.53; cf. Mt. 20:28). The view of the Suffering Servant is further supported by New Testament statements such as, "Behold, this Child is appointed for the fall and rise of many in Israel, and for a sign to be opposed—and a sword will pierce even your own soul—to the end that thoughts from many hearts may be revealed" (Lk. 2:34-35). There was also the incarnational model for mission: "And being found in appearance as a man, He humbled Himself by becoming obedient to the point of death, even death on a cross" (Phil. 2:8). Therefore, to exclude suffering is to reduce Israel's mission (and by extension, the Church's) and to subvert her best interests.

Israel's mission was to parallel that of God's Suffering Servant. She, too, should have been willing to give her life a ransom for other nations (see Isaiah's servant songs, chapters 40-55). She, too, should have walked a pathway of suffering if necessary to bring people into a relationship with her covenant God. Her agenda was to be that of the Suffering Servant, longing that the nations would know her God. Such is now the mission of the Church, emulating her Lord (Jn. 17:18; 20:21).

As the Suffering Servant, the Messiah was destined for death to fulfill His mission (Is. 53; cf. Lk. 24:13-27). He was commissioned to carry the light to all nations (Is. 49:5). He was "the true light which...enlightens every man" (Jn. 1:9; cf. Jn. 8:12). He was a willing sacrifice (Is. 53:10), dying by choice, but not for himself. Nobody took His life from Him; He gave it to remove the sins of others. He Himself was sinless (Is. 53:9). He was also the universal Savior (cf. Jn. 3:16). His suffering was of the widest efficacy. The time would come when the nations would confess that they, too, deserved what He vicariously endured for them:

It will yet be that peoples will come, even the inhabitants of many cities; and the inhabitants of one will go to another saying, "Let us go at once to entreat the favor of the LORD, and to seek the LORD of hosts; I will also go." So many peoples and mighty nations will come to seek the LORD of hosts in Jerusalem and to entreat the favor of the LORD (Zech. 8:20-22).

Israel questioned and rejected the Suffering Servant role. When Isaiah reminded Israel of her mission as the servant of God, he introduced a model which was unattractive and laden with offense. To this day most Jews consider it a mystery and cannot reconcile this concept with their Messiah. But Israel does not stand alone. The Church questions the extent of such loyalty and subtly rejects suffering as part of the sacrifice to be made for the salvation of the nations. Of course, neither Israel's nor the Church's suffering could ever bring reconciliation with God; only God's Messiah could do that. But in carrying out the evangelistic and cultural mandates, suffering cannot be avoided.

God's servant would know redemptive suffering, and through it, the people and kingdom of God would come to triumph and eschatalogical fullness. He would have a purposeful, worldwide mission. Isaiah speaks of the servant's election, preservation, divine anointing, universal mission and certain triumph; but he would know this exaltation only through rejection. Yes, he would be despised, rejected, and slain, but afterward there would be exaltation and the establishment of a lasting Kingdom (Is. 53:10,11; 60:1-22).

Isaiah spoke of God's Servant in varying ways. The Servant was *a corporate group*—Israel, blind and deaf to God's purposes (Is. 42:19). He was representative of *a righteous remnant* within Israel (Is. 44:1,2,8; 51:6,7). He was thought of as *another Moses* who would lead a new exodus out of the captivity of sin (Is.48). He was *the great Servant* who would lead a servant people out to the nations in mission:

Awake, awake, clothe yourself in your strength, O Zion...How lovely on the mountains are the feet of him who brings good news...who announces salvation....The LORD has bared His holy arm in the sight of all the nations, that all the ends of the earth may see the salvation of our God (Is. 52:1,7,10)

He was *the sinless Servant*, which qualified Him to take to His innocency the sins of His people and thus achieve the victory of the kingdom of God (Is. 53:4-6,10-12).

The New Testament applied the role and theme of the Suffering Servant to none other than Jesus Christ, and the Church has believed and taught this from the beginning. In some measure, the Church must know the same suffering if she is to bring the nations to faith in her Lord. Thus the Church is reminded: "Now I rejoice in my sufferings for your sake, and in my flesh I do my share on behalf of His body (which is th e church) in filling up that which is lacking in Christ's afflictions" (Col. 1:24; cf. 2 Cor. 1:5; 1 Pet. 4:13).

Missiological Considerations

When Israel focused on just one aspect of biblical truth— eschatalogy— she not only became introverted and self-centered, she also ignored her obligation to declare the glory of God (Mal. 1:11-14; 3:8; 8-12). Emphasizing certain biblical truths to the exclusion of others is counterproductive to the missions task of God's people. It is bound to produce an abundance of inconsequential, cabalistic ideologies.

When God's people wanted only to preserve themselves, they became introverted. They no longer felt obligated to confront others with the message of redemptive grace. They no longer acted in faith. They refrained from taking risks and believing God to vindicate and validate their dependence on Him (Mal; cf,. Acts 3,4,5).

Suffering is the price of identification and participation in declaring salvation to the nations. Only a bond-servant would be willing to endure suffering (cf. Rom. 1:5; 2 Cor. 4:8-12). Jesus Christ offered His disciples the role of servant which would lead to a cross (Mt. 16:24). Suffering is certainly part of the cost involved in making Jesus Christ known to the nations. There will be opposition and conflict— sometimes even loss of life.

Rejecting the role of Suffering Servant, Israel kept its faith to itself, thereby losing the true dimensions of biblical faith. However, Israel was still missionary, making proselytes throughout the Mediterranean basin and forming them into believing and practising communities. These synagogues, in fact, later became centers for Paul's evangelistic strategy. But rather than produce converts with a singular purpose to declare the glory of God, Israel drew these converts to her own intro-version (Mt. 23:15). Preferring her own ideological pursuits, she was set aside by God (Rom. 9:30-33; 10:1-3; 11:7, 15-26).

Even today it is quite possible to convert people to ideologies and even "evangelical" theologies destructive of the God-given commission to make disciples of all nations. These ideologies and theologies may actually keep converts from knowing that Jesus Christ's servants cannot avoid the fellowship of His sufferings (Acts 14:22; 20:24; 1 Pet. 4:1-2, 12-19). The role of Suffering Servant is imperative for identification and involvement in mission. His followers are to be servants to others for His Name's sake (Rom.1:1,5). They will have the *motivation of the servant*—to respond in obedience to the Lord of the Church. They will have the *mindset of the servant* —to please the Lord of the Church and be conformed to His pattern (Phil. 2:1-8). And they will eagerly await His return to hear His commendation: "Well done, good and faithful slave;... enter into the joy of your master" (Mt. 25:21).

The certainty of the return of Jesus Christ should cause God's people to live in obedience "to observe all that I commanded you" (Mt. 28:20). It should motivate believers to implement the Great Commission. Answering the critics who questioned the return of Jesus Christ, Peter pointed out that Christ was delaying out of His concern for the nations. Peter stressed that believers could hasten the Second Coming through obedience to the Lord of the Church, including their commitment to be His servant people on mission to all nations:

> I am stirring up your sincere mind by way of reminder, that you should remember the words spoken beforehand by the holy prophets and the commandment of the Lord and Savior spoken by your apostles....The Lord is not slow about His promise, as some count slowness, but is patient toward you, *not wishing for any to perish but for all to come to repentance.* But the day of the Lord will come like a thief, in which the heavens will pass away....Since all these things are to be destroyed in this way, what sort of people ought you to be in holy conduct and godliness, looking for and *hastening* the coming of the day of God....Therefore, beloved, since you look for these things, be diligent to be found by Him in peace, spotless and blameless, and regard the patience of our Lord to be salvation (2 Pet. 3:1,2,9-12,14,15, emphasis added).

The ever-present danger is that believers so involve themselves in the *good* of biblical studies that they ignore the *best*, namely obedience to God's commission. Our Lord commanded "that repentance for forgiveness of sins should be proclaimed in His name to all the nations" (Lk. 24:47). That responsibility can only be ignored at our peril, even as it was by Israel (Rom. 11:11-32).

CHAPTER 19

THE

INCOMPLETENESS

OF THE OLD

TESTAMENT

Israel was to be God's means to recover His Lordship over the whole earth. God would not coerce her; she must choose to obey Him and perform His will. God specifically called her to confront the nations (and their gods) so that they would know God and His claims on them. With this understanding, the nations would choose between their gods and the God of revelation knowledge.

The purpose of Israel's election was, therefore, very specific.

> The election of Israel was not one of special privilege alone, and the story of Israel as told by her own writers is utterly different from that of overweening nationalisms....With a dynamic, persistent and independent energy, he [God] set his course and that of his people for his own name's sake (Wright 1968:48).

Israel was elected to be a divine possession for service to God and the nations. "Israel was only elected in order to serve God in the task of leading [the] other nations to God. In Israel God seeks the world. Israel is God's point of attack on the world" (Vriezen 1960:76).

Israel's corporate salvation had meaning only in relationship to God's purposes for creation. Israel's own salvation was not primary; she was to be an agent of blessing (salvation) to all nations. "The people does not exist for its own sake and God did not give it a special place in order that Israel might keep this for itself, but only to prepare the way for Him and His kingdom" (Vriezen 1960:230). *Election has no goal in itself, but only for the kingdom of God*—"the kingdom God would reveal in Israel for the sake of the whole world" (Vriezen 1960:371). Election conveyed responsibility, not primarily privilege. Israel was to be God's mirror of His grace and mercy.

In God's unfolding purpose, Israel was to be a model of a true theocracy, her first responsibility being an example of God's gracious rule and an obedient people. She was also to preach to the nations of the God who "is slow to anger and abundant in lovingkindness, forgiving iniquity and transgression; but...visiting the iniquities of the fathers on the children to the third and the fourth generations" (Num. 14:18; cf. Exo. 34:6-7). She was to be a priest standing before God on behalf of the nations, seeking to bring them into a relationship with Him. And she was to be a prophet speaking for God, calling the nations to live by His law.

We see the conflict between universalism (God's concern for all nations) and particularism (Israel retaining God for herself) throughout the Scriptures. The Old Testament consistently stresses God's concern for the nations. But His saving intent is particular in the heart of the individual, a matter Israel tended to forget (cf. Jer. 24:7). The Bible, however, never descends to Israel's distortion that the blessings were hers alone.

The Great Commission in the Old Testament

Although the implicit Old Testament commission to "go" to the nations is not as clear as in Matthew 28:18-20, it must have been well known, being repeatedly emphasized in different ways (Num.14:21; Ps. 66:4; 72:17; 86:9; Mal. 1:11). One cannot fail to sense the commission to confront the nations with the greatness, and yet the compassion, of God.

The commission was delivered in several ways. Israel sang about declaring His glory among all nations; Psalm 67, Psalm 96:1-10, and other passages charged the people to tell of God and His mighty acts among the nations (cf. 1 Chron. 16:8-36). The commission was also declared in prayer (1 Ki. 8:41-43). The commission to go, even if not explicit, was certainly implicit in God's dealings with Israel. An example is clearly seen in Jonah and his mission to Nineveh.

Israel's "presence" in the midst of the nations attested that their evangelization would in part be accomplished by Israel modeling what it meant to be God's people. The nations would hear of her reputation and be drawn to investigate (cf. Rahab, the queen of Sheba). Her first priority, then, was to be a distinct people in the land. Her goal was the Law going out and the nations flowing in to Jerusalem. Israel should have reflected not only God's righteousness, justice, and, holiness, but also His compassion, lovingkindness, and mercy, to show the nations that there is a God different from their own.

But Israel failed to carry out her mission, and God had to raise up another people: "The time is coming to gather all nations and tongues. And they shall come and see My glory" (Is. 66:18). How will this take place? Jesus Christ tells us in the parable of the wicked tenant farmers: "Therefore I say to you, the kingdom of God will be taken away from you, and be given to a nation producing the fruit of it" (Mt. 21:33-43). Both in "presence" and "proclamation" Israel practically ceased to be God's servant. Legalism replaced her living relationship with God. God's revelatory words came less and less often and finally ceased. There was no need to hear from God. Israel had already decided what she would accept of God's revelation, and the rest simply did not apply. Israel fell into sectarian interests, as various sects sought to resolve her spiritual dilemma. This problem soon absorbed Israel, and she became victim to further rabbinic legalism. None could (or would) identify the "Son of Man" of Daniel or the "Suffering Servant" of Isaiah as the long-awaited Messiah.

The Old Testament was a forceful presentation of biblical faith. It exposed the weakness of the gods of the nations, and the appeal they had to man's sinful nature. (Throughout Israel's history there was a marked absence of moral strength, contrasted with the strength of sin and the temptation to evil, a fact that can only be ascribed to the innate sin principle and the activity of demonic powers.) The Old Testament, clearly opposed all forms of false worship and their dehumanizing practices. It also presented a purposeful mission. To be with God in His redemptive mission was not only Israel's duty but also her privilege. The Old Testament predicted the Messiah, who would bring deliverance to all people, and also pointed to the enabling He would provide to fulfill God's mission:

"And I will give them a heart to know Me, for I am the LORD; and they will be My people, and I will be their God, for they will return to Me with their whole heart" (Jer.24:7);

"I will give you a new heart and put a new spirit within you and I will remove the heart of stone from your flesh and give you a heart of flesh. And I will put my Spirit within you and cause you to walk in My statutes, and you will be careful to observe My ordinances" (Ezek. 36:26-27).

Throughout the Old Testament were those "whose heart[s] [were] completely His" (2 Chron. 16:9). Paul affirmed that God did not leave Himself without a witness (Rom. 11:4). In the New Testament we are introduced to men and women who eagerly anticipated the coming Messiah, but who were also involved in carrying out His mandates for all peoples.

The Organic Agreement between the Old and New Testaments

There is an organic agreement between the Old and New Testaments. The purpose for both God's Old Testament people and God's New Testament people remains exactly the same: "to declare His glory", and "to be to the praise of His glory."

We need to see that the Old Testament is more than preparation for the New Testament. It records God's interaction with His people in history on behalf of all mankind, and that interaction continues to the present. Although the *Word of Truth is foundational, the Work of Truth continues*. The God who spoke in revelation is the God who continues to act in history.

The discontinuity between the testaments comes in the realized redemption in and through Jesus Christ by His death on the cross. In His completed work of atonement, He not only reconciled man to God and God to man, He also "disarmed" the powers of darkness and "made a public display of them" (Col. 2:14-15; 1 Jn. 3:8). Furthermore, although the Holy Spirit was working among the Old Testament people of God to launch them into the same mission that Jesus came to perform, ("preach[ing] the Gospel to the poor...proclaim[ing] release to the captives, [bringing] sight to the blind; [setting] free those who are downtrodden...[and proclaiming] the favorable year of the Lord" [Lk. 4:18; cf Is. 61:1-3]), He was not resident *in* them exactly as described in Acts 2. Now God has been reconciled to man, and His people are called to proclaim the completed work of the cross to mankind everywhere.

Now the Holy Spirit gives Christians the knowledge of Jesus Christ's presence with them as Savior and Lord, as they carry out the task (Acts 1:8).

The early Christians recognized and accepted their organic continuity with the Old Testament people of God. To them, the Old Testament was their charter for faith and mission. The way God acted on behalf of His Old Testament people was foundational to their own faith and mission (Heb. 11,12). The same great themes which characterized Israel as God's model before the nations were true of Jesus Christ and the Church. Therefore, God's calling of Israel is exceedingly relevant to the mission of His people in all ages. We must remember, however, that God dealt with His people, whether Abraham, Isaac, Jacob, Joseph, or all who followed, in and through historical circumstances. God's bottom line in dealing with His people in all of their history was always, as so earnestly expressed in the words of Joseph, that "God meant it for good in order to...preserve many people alive" (Gen. 50:20).

PART III

THE CHURCH

GOD'S NEW

TESTAMENT PEOPLE

ON MISSION

CHAPTER 20

GOD'S MODELS

IN THE

MIDST OF THE

NATIONS

The Bible essentially presents three models which were to reveal the heart of God to the watching world. None stood apart from the others. They were interrelated and interdependent, but each in its own right testified who the Lord God of the Bible was:

> "The LORD, the LORD God, compassionate and gracious, slow to anger, and abounding in lovingkindness and truth; who keeps lovingkindness for thousands, who forgives iniquity, transgression and sin; yet He will by no means leave the guilty unpunished, visiting the iniquity of fathers on the children and on the grandchildren to the third and fourth generations" (Exo. 34:6-7).

The three groups were the Old Testament people of God, Israel; Jesus Christ, the Son of God; and the Church, the Body of Christ.

Israel was called God's son (Exo. 4:22), and through that son, God sought to bring the nations to Himself. As Kaiser observed in explaining Psalm 67:

Israel was to be a maturing, proclaiming, and evangelizing nation. The Gentiles had to be brought to the light. This purpose for Israel is seen even more clearly in...the "Servant of the LORD" passages of Isaiah 42 and 49 which reflect that Israel is that Servant of the LORD....As such, Israel was to be "a light to the nations," just as Abraham had been told....(Winter and Hawthorne 1982:33).

Jesus Christ, in His high priestly prayer, captured God's purpose for His first coming (Jn. 17:6,26): to glorify the Father and show the watching world who God is. "He who has seen me has seen the Father" (Jn.14:9). However, Christ was more than God's model; He was God in human flesh, who reconciled, in His own body, man to God and embraced within Himself both God's grace and judgment. He did not "come to judge the world, but that the world should be saved through Him" (Jn. 3:17).

Through the third model, the Church, God would make known His manifold wisdom "to the rulers and the authorities in the heavenly places" (Eph. 3:10). What is commonly called the Lord's Prayer is in essence the description of God's New Testament people (see chapter 15).

God's models were characterized by certain themes, each of which were evidenced through God's interaction with Israel. What were those themes, and what conformity is reflected in Jesus Christ and the Church?

The Distinctives of God's Models

Begotten of God

God *begot* Israel out of the anguish of Egyptian oppression. At one point in history, the people of Israel were "no people," but the Lord called them into being as His son and gave them life: "Then you shall say to Pharaoh, 'Thus says the LORD, "Israel is My Son, My firstborn" (Exo. 4:22). Jeremiah 31:9 states: "For I am a Father to Israel, and Ephraim is My firstborn." Hosea 11:1 points out, "when Israel was a youth I loved him, and out of Egypt I called My son." Moses reminds the people: "My father was a wandering Aramean, and he went down to Egypt and sojourned there, few in number; but there he became a great, mighty and populous nation" (Dt. 26:5). In His grace and mercy, God set His love on Israel, not "because you were more in number than any of the peoples, for you were the fewest of all peoples, but because the LORD loved you...and brought you out by a mighty hand, and redeemed you from the house of slavery...." (Dt. 7:7-8) The purpose was to know "that the LORD your God, He is God, the faithful God" (Dt. 7:9).

This pattern can be readily applied to both Jesus Christ (Heb.1:5) and His Church. God's Son was sent for an express purpose, and so was His Church. Of the Church Peter noted, "For you once were not a people, but now you are the people of God" (1 Pet.2:10). Jesus came to show man the Father (Jn. 14:9-11; 17:6,26), and the Church is to manifest "the excellencies of Him who has called [her] out of darkness into His marvelous light" (1 Pet . 2:9).

A Public Confession

Soon after Israel was begotten, she was "baptized" in a public confession at the Red Sea into a trusting relationship with God. This was done openly before the nations, to prove both Israel's commitment to God and God's commitment to Israel. Israel needed to know beyond the shadow of a doubt that the God who had called her was the God who would prove faithful: "I am the LORD your God, who brought you out of the land of Egypt, out of the house of slavery" (Exo. 20:2), and "the LORD your God has chosen you to be a people for His own possession [purpose]" (Dt. 7:6). This "baptism" established Israel's unique relationship to God and initiated her into an irreversible role in God's mission. Paul applied the same figure to the Church (1 Cor. 9: 25-10:5), pointing out that although Israel accepted God's mission in her "baptism," she later wanted to abdicate her public commitment to Him and His purposes. However, in spite of her disobedience, Israel continued to be a witness before the nations of either God's blessing or His judgment. She could not escape her responsibility to be His witness, even when she sought to do so.

Immediately after our Lord was baptized, the Holy Spirit pressed Him into battle with Satan (Mk. 1:9-12). In His temptation, Christ demonstrated that there was a new presence among men, and that He would overcome Satan through the Word of God. As the Son of Man, He would be a witness of the only true God.

Even as God called Israel for an explicit purpose, so He has raised up the Church. Paul exclaimed: "I run in such a way, as not without aim" (1 Cor.9:26). That aim is equally true for the Church, which is to testify to "One Lord" (Eph.4:5) to whose authority it submits, and whom it represents. The Church accepts "one faith," exclusive in its demands and yet universal in its application—as the gospel says,

"Whosoever will may come." The Church submits to "one baptism," an initiation into a mission to declare God's glory among the nations. The initiatory rite of baptism, therefore, begins an irreversible role in God's ongoing purposes.

A Stewardsip of Servanthood

Another great moment in Israel's history was God's calling her into *a stewardship of servanthood*. At Sinai, God entered a covenant with Israel by which He established the obligations of her stewardship, which related to her fellow man, her environment, and the nations and their environment. Her servanthood involved priestly activity, both in serving before God and in bringing people to God. Israel was given specific instructions through Gods laws about how to be God's model people. She was also given the prophets' ministry to keep her on task, because God is a jealous God, and His reputation is at stake (Exo. 20:1-5). One thing must be clear: God's laws were not given to *establish* a relationship with Him; they simply *defined* that relationship. Israel had already entered into a relationship through a suzerainty-vassal treaty made when God begot her in Egypt (and even earlier when He made a covenant with Abraham and reconfirmed it with Isaac and Jacob). The excellence of God's laws (Is. 42:21) and Israel's obligation to maintain them were results of a relationship already established. Israel was constantly reminded of God's past mighty acts, both on her behalf and in God's dealing with other gods. On that basis she was called to a stewardship of relationship issuing in servanthood:

> "You yourselves have seen what I did to the Egyptians, and how I bore you on eagle's wings, and brought you to Myself. Now then, if you will indeed obey My voice and keep My covenant, then you shall be My own possession among all the peoples, for all the earth is Mine; and you shall be to Me a Kingdom of priests and a holy nation...." And all the people answered together and said, "All that the LORD has spoken we will do!" (Exo. 19:4-6,8)

Isaiah selected the same theme in the Servant Songs, reminding Israel that she had agreed to be God's servant people. However, she had conveniently set that obligation aside: "Who is blind but My servant, or so deaf as My messenger whom I send? Who is so blind as he that is at peace with Me, or so blind as the servant of the LORD? You have seen many things, but you do not observe them ..." (Is. 42:19-20). To what had they been blind and deaf? Isaiah tells us:

"I am the LORD, I have called you in righteousness, I will also hold you by the hand and watch over you, and I will appoint you as a covenant to the people, as a light to the nations, to open blind eyes, to bring out prisoners from the dungeon, and those who dwell in darkness from the prison. I am the LORD, that is My name; I will not give My glory to another, nor My praise to graven images" (Is. 42:6-8).

Israel was to see that praise was directed to God and not to graven images. As God's servant people they were "the people whom I formed for Myself, [who] will declare My praise" (Is.43:21). Thus God would confirm "the word of His servant, and [perform] the purpose of His messengers" (Is. 44:26).

Supremely in Jesus Christ we see God's Servant doing exactly what God intended for Israel as His people on a redemptive mission (Is.61:1-3; Lk.4:16-21). Although there was a sense in which Israel could never have made such a supreme sacrifice, Isaiah described the Servant's role as the one "pierced through for our transgressions...crushed for our iniquities...[chastened] for our well-being...and by His scourging we are healed" (Is.53:5).

To this task the Church, too, has been called. To His servant the Church our Lord said:

"Truly, truly, I say to you, unless a grain of wheat falls into the earth and dies, it remains by itself alone; but if it dies, it bears much fruit. He who loves his life loses it; and he who hates his life in this world shall keep it to life eternal. If any one serves Me, let him follow Me; and where I am, there shall My servant also be; if anyone serves Me, the Father will honor him" (Jn. 12:24-26).

The Church must follow Christ into "the fellowship of His sufferings" (Phil. 3:10). In consequence:

You also became imitators of us and of the Lord, having received the word in much tribulation with joy of the Holy Spirit, so that you became an example to all the believers in Macedonia and Achaia... also in every place your faith toward God has gone forth, so that we have no need to say anything. For they themselves report about us what kind of a reception we had with you, and how you turned to God from idols to serve a living and true God, and to wait for His Son from heaven, whom He raised from the dead, that is Jesus, who delivers us from the wrath to come (1 Thess.1:6-10).

The role of God's servant people remains unchanged. The truth of this stewardship of servanthood is emphasized throughout the Old and the New Testaments.

An Inheritance

A recurring theme in Israel's history is the *inheritance of the promised land*. This was God's gift to Israel. She was to enter and possess what God had already given to her: "arise, cross this Jordan, you and all this people, to the land which I am giving to them, to the sons of Israel" (Josh.1:2); and "go in to possess the land which the LORD your God is giving you, to possess it" (Josh.1:11). This promise of the land as a gift from God is the theme of many portions of the Bible, for example, "See, I have placed the land before you; go in and possess the land which the LORD swore to give to your fathers, to Abraham, to Isaac, and to Jacob ...and their descendants..." (Dt.1:8;cf. Ps. 78:54-69).

Despite the desperate and massive opposition of the Canaanites, Israel possessed the land. Success came not through her military vigor, but through the irresistible power of the LORD of hosts (Josh. 5:13-15; 21:44-45). In a very real sense God showed His power through Israel's powerlessness, and the people recognized that fact. What God gave was beyond expectation,"an exceedingly good land....A land which flows with milk and honey" (Num. 14:7-8).

> "I gave you a land on which you had not labored, and cities which you had not built...vineyards and oliveyards which you did not plant. Now, therefore, fear the LORD and serve Him in sincerity and faithfulness; and put away the gods which your fathers served beyond the Euphrates and Egypt, and serve the LORD" (Josh.24:13- 14).

Obviously, our Lord's kingdom overarches all other kingdoms. Though His kingdom is not materialistic or worldly, it will invade the hearts of men. His inheritance is His people, redeemed by His blood and set free to be to the praise of His glory. In turn, Christian believers have their inheritance in Jesus Christ (Eph.1:11,14), being co-heirs with Him and partners in a heavenly calling. We take as our example the mission of our Savior and Lord (Heb.3:1-3) and enter the land of salvation's rest (Heb.3,4).

A Kingdom Stewardship

Israel also was *established as a kingdom*. The Davidic dynasty was to be the model of God's authorized presence with His people. God was

King and Shepherd, and David was his vice-regent and under-shepherd. Though David was no paragon of virtue, his humility and openness before God and His people earned him the title of "a man after God's own heart." David well understood why God had called Israel. The kingdom was not an end in itself, but God's means to make His Name glorious among the nations (1 Chron.16:8,24,28; Ps. 67;86:8-10; 96:3-10). Through the righteous rule of an earthly king, God would not only draw nations to Himself, but the message of His glory would be carried to the nations by His people through trade, state business, and ordinary encounters with peoples.

The kingdom was so significant that our Lord made it the theme of His earthly ministry. He compared Israel's stewardship of the kingdom to a vineyard which was to be kept for God's purposes, describing how, by default, the kingdom was taken away from those who had originally received it, and given to another who would return to Him its yield (Mt.21:33-41). Immediately before His ascension, the kingdom was still the topic of discourse (Acts 1:6-7).

The Church has been entrusted with the same kingdom steward-ship. Christians, too, are to live so that the watching world will see their good works and glorify the Father (Mt.5:16). The charter of the king-dom was given in the Old Testament, the standards were spelled out more clearly in the Gospels, and the directions for maintaining that Kingdom to "the praise of His glory" in the Epistles.

Although the kingdom now is not earthly, but spiritual, its norms and values are to be practiced universally by all of God's people. The Church is to present a true alternative to man's self-centered economic, social, and political systems. Part of the genius of this kingdom is that it transcends all language groupings (tongues), tribes, and nations. It breaks down walls of partition, making of all nations one body in Christ, through the cross (Eph. 2:13-16). Israel was *called* for such a mission to the nations, and the Church is *sent* on such a mission to the nations.

A Tested People

Moses spoke of God *testing the people's loyalty* (Exo. 15:25;Ps. 105:19). Following the Egyptian slavery, times of testing were allowed "that He might humble you, testing you, to know what was in your heart...." (Dt. 8:2). Later, Israel was reminded, "Do not be afraid; for God has come in order to test you, and in order that the fear of Him may remain with you, so that you may not sin" (Exo. 20:20). On Mount Carmel God pressed home the antithesis between the LORD God and the gods of the nations (I Ki. 17, 18), in order to test Israel's fidelity. He alone is the Lord; He has no equal, nor will He tolerate divided allegiance (Exo. 20:2-6).

Testing was for two purposes. On the one hand, the nations had to know that "the earth is the LORD's" (Exo. 9:29), and also to confess, "Surely your God is a God of gods and a Lord of kings...." (Dan. 2:47; cf. Dan. 3:28-29). On the other hand, testing was to build faith and commitment in the lives of God's people: "And when Israel saw the great power which the LORD had used against the Egyptians, the people feared the LORD, and they believed in the LORD and in His servant Moses" (Exo. 14:31). Israel could confidently face any circumstance, knowing that "the earth will be filled the glory of the LORD" (Num.14:21). Omnipotence was pledged to fulfill the promise. She could thus walk and work in faith, facing her Jordans, Jerichos, and even her Ais, to be God's redemptive people.

Jesus Christ was thrust out to be tested (Mk. 1:12-13) and to declare to Satan the power of a new Presence. The Lord of all the earth had come to be with man—"Immanuel...God with us" (Mt. 1:23)—and to redeem man—"you shall call His name Jesus, for it is He who will save His people from their sins" (Mt.1:21).

The Church will not be spared testing. Who could better express and demonstrate this than Paul?

> We have this treasure in earthen vessels, that the surpassing greatness of the power may be of God and not from ourselves; we are afflicted...perplexed...persecuted...struck down...always carrying about in the body the dying of Jesus, that the life of Jesus also may be manifested in our body (2 Cor.4:7-10).

And the purpose of it all was "that the grace which is spreading to more and more people may cause the giving of thanks to abound to the glory of God" (2 Cor.4:15). All testing helps us to witness to God's sufficient grace and thus declare His glory. Wherever the Church submits to the ministry of the Holy Spirit, she will know that being filled with the Holy Spirit does not remove the believer's problems. Rather, it is the signal for problems and attacks to begin in earnest, so that the Christian may testify to the glory and greatness of God (Jas. 1:2-10; cf. Rom. 8:28-39). God's strength triumphs through our weakness.

A Judged People

Israel also *knew God's judgment*. Indeed, Israel was slain for her sins. She refused to heed God's repeated correction and persisted in living a life characteristic of the nations (Dt.18:14; 32:15-18). God's judgment came upon Israel through Assyria in the Northern Kingdom, and later through Babylon in Judah. This led to "burial" in which she "descended into Sheol" in the lands of captivity. Jeremiah picked up the lament for God's Old Testament people:

> Is it nothing to all you who pass this way? Look and see if there is any pain like my pain which was severely dealt out to me, which the LORD inflicted on the day of His fierce anger. From on high He sent fire into my bones...He has made me desolate.... In fierce anger He has cut off the strength of Israel....He has burned in Jacob like a flaming fire (Lam. 1:12-13;2:3).

It was Israel's just desert.

God had planned blessing in order that Israel might be a blessing, but when she abdicated her commission, God made her *a spectacle* (Dt. 32:21-27). However, even in God's indignation against Israel, the nations saw that He was a God of justice, holiness, and righteousness, impartial in judging rebellion (Dt. 10:17). Ezekiel compares God's judgment to being in a grave: "Thus says the LORD God, `Behold, I will open your graves and cause you to come up out of your graves, My people'" (Ezek. 37:12). As God's priestly servant, Israel would not have been spared suffering, but it would have been, and should have been, redemptive suffering. Righteous ones, such as Daniel and his three friends, carried away with the rebellion knew this redemptive suffering (Dan.3:12-29; 6:12-26).

Isaiah 53 well described the suffering and the slaying of our Lord, not because of personal sins, but for sinful man. In the words of Paul, "He made Him who knew no sin to be sin on our behalf, that we might become the righteousness of God in Him" (2 Cor. 5:21). He took in His own body the wrath of God which sinful mankind rightly deserved. Our Lord's suffering was redemptive, but it also disarmed the powers of darkness arrayed against man (Col.2:14-15; 1 Jn.3:8).

The Church will encounter the same powers Israel faced . She will know spiritual warfare in her mission when by faith she conquers kingdoms, performs acts of righteousness, obtains promises, shuts the mouths of lions, quenches the power of fire, escapes the edge of the sword, from weakness is made strong, becomess mighty in war, put foreign armies to flight, and sees women receive back their dead by resurrection. But she will also know misfortune, maulings, scourgings, chains, imprisonment, stoning, being sawed in two, and being put to death (Heb.11:33-37). But amidst victories and apparent defeats, as David Livingstone said many decades ago:

> What we greatly need is more missionaries to sow the seed of spiritual truth. The fields are white unto harvest. Glorious is the prospect of the outpouring of the Holy Spirit on all the ends of the earth (Sedgewick and Monk 1858:36).

Livingstone also reportedly said that although missionaries in the midst of masses of the unconverted seem like voices crying in the wilderness, future missionaries will see conversions after every sermon. "Missionaries do not live before their time. Their great idea of converting the world to Christ is no chimera: it is divine. It is equal to all it has to perform." Comparing the missionaries with the Reformers, he added:

> Those who now go forth as missionaries, and endeavour to advance the knowledge of Christ and His Gospel, are pre-eminently their representatives. Like the morning star before the dawn, they entered into the thick darkness, and began the glorious task of making known the promises of Christ, for which posterity will bless their name. Indeed to be a missionary is a great privilege and honour. The work is great and glorious, that it has this promise of Him who "is the same yesterday, today, and forever:"— "I will never leave thee, nor forsake thee," encouraging both itself and its promoters (Sedgewick and Monk 1858:36).

The battle to make God's name glorious among all nations is both essential and unavoidable. The Church may be slain, but the blood of the martyrs is the seed of the Church. The Church committed to the glory of God knows all too well that:

> to the degree that you share the sufferings of Christ, keep on rejoicing; so that also at the revelation of His glory, you may rejoice with exultation. If you are reviled for the name of Christ, you are blessed, because the Spirit of glory and of God rests upon you (1 Pet. 4:13-14).

A redemptive ministry takes up the cross, follows, and never counts life dear to itself in order to testify to the Gospel of the grace of

God (Acts 20:24). The Church is confident that "the earth will be filled with the knowledge of the glory of the LORD, as waters cover the sea" (Hab. 2:14; cf. Num. 14:21), and that is reward enough. Therefore she can afford to walk in faith, for Omnipotence is pledged to fulfill the promise that "Jesus shall reign where'er the sun does his successive journeys run, His kingdom stretch from shore to shore, till moons shall wax and wane no more" (Isaac Watts, 1674-1748).

A Resurrected People

God deals with His people for time and eternity. What He set out to do He will do. He is not a man that He should lie. Through Cyrus of Persia and others, Israel was *resurrected* from the grave of exile and sent back to the land of inheritance. Some went back with Zerubbabel, with Ezra, and with Nehemiah. Ezra recorded the king's decree:

> Now in the first year of Cyrus king of Persia, in order to fulfill the word of the LORD by the mouth of Jeremiah, the LORD stirred up the spirit of Cyrus king of Persia, so that he sent a proclamation throughout all his kingdom, and also put it in writing, saying, "Thus says Cyrus king of Persia, The LORD, the God of heaven has given me all the kingdoms of the earth, and He has appointed me to build Him a house in Jerusalem, which is in Judah. Whoever there is among you of all His people, may his God be with him! Let him go up to Jerusalem which is in Judah, and rebuild the house of the LORD, the God of Israel; He is the God who is in Jerusalem. And every survivor, at whatever place he may live, let the men of that place support him with silver and gold, with goods and cattle, together with a freewill offering for the house of God which is in Jerusalem" (Ezra 1:1-4).

Although all seemed lost, the just and faithful God of Israel brought Israel into a new life. Israel's calling, her commission, her tenure in the land, her rebellion, her judgment, and her resurrection all happened in the sight of the nations. Not only was God proving Himself to be a mighty, holy, and everlasting God, He was also the covenant-keeping God whose concern included all nations (Is. 25:7). Israel's resurrection was to demonstrate that

> "from the rising of the sun, even to its setting, My name will be great among the nations, and in every place incense is going to be offered to My Name, and a grain offering that is pure; for My name will be great among the nations," says the LORD of Hosts (Mal. 1:11).

The resurrection of our Lord is an unquestioned, foundational truth: "If Christ has not been raised, your faith is worthless ....But now Christ has been raised from the dead, the first fruits of those who are asleep" (1 Cor.15:17,20). Hebrews attests that there is now a new life for whoever will respond to the claims of Christ:

> Since then the children share in flesh and blood, He Himself likewise also partook of the same, that through death He might render powerless him who had the power of death, that is, the devil; and might deliver those who through fear of death were subject to slavery all their lives (Heb. 2:14-15).

In Revelation our Lord categorically states His Lordship over life and death: "I am the first and the last, and the Living One; and I was dead, and behold, I am alive forevermore, and I have the keys of death and of Hades" (Rev. 1:17,18). Therefore "He is able to come to the aid of those who are tempted" (Heb. 2:18), enabling His model people to manifest "the excellencies of Him who has called you out of darkness into His marvelous light" (1 Pet. 2:9).

The Church is now God's resurrected people (Rom.6; Col.3:1), God's new humanity, His new creation, lifted from the pit of sin to walk in newness of life with Him. We are to exercise our delegated authority, to use the weapons of warfare to pull down all strongholds of the enemy, and to declare God's victory over all His enemies.

Beyond all these great moments in Israel's history is an eschatalogical day of the Lord. Peter spoke of it as "the great and glorious day of the Lord" (Acts 2:20). Isaiah described it as a day of restoration when "I create Jerusalem for rejoicing and her people for gladness" (Is.65:18; cf. Is. 65:19-25). Ezekiel pointed out that the nations would take note of what God had done in Israel: "Then the nations that are left round about you will know that I, the LORD, have rebuilt the ruined places and planted that which was desolate; I, the LORD, have spoken and will do it" (Ezek. 36:36). The focus is always that the God of the Bible is the only God of Glory, the sole claimant to all His creation.

Through the Lord Jesus Christ, what Adam lost was reclaimed and restored (Rom. 5:17-19; Eph. 1:21-23; 2:5-10; 3:9-12). Paul pointed out that even our mortal bodies are revitalized by the Holy Spirit (Rom.8:11). He maintained that the Church has always been led in triumph (2 Cor. 2:14) in declaring His glory. These themes look forward to the day when all creation will be redeemed, and the Creator and His creation will rejoice together in an environment without the possibility of sin.

CHAPTER 21

FROM

PARTICULARISM

TO UNIVERSALISM

The Old Testament concluded with a message to an introverted and self-centered people. God, through Malachi, chided Israel for her half-hearted commitment to Him and for deliberately ignoring His commission to the nations. He reminded the people, "from the rising of the sun, even to its setting, My name will be great among the nations, and in every place incense is going to be offered to My name...for My name will be great among the nations...but you are profaning it" (Mal. 1:11,12). And again, "If you do not take it to heart to give honor to My name...then I will send the curse upon you, and I will curse your blessings" (Mal. 2:2).

God's purpose for the nations never changed, but the Old Testament's focus steadily narrowed until there were just a few ready to welcome the Messiah. The Old Testament began with nations, as God in judgment scattered the peoples across the face of the earth. Out of all the nations, God selected one family to be a model of His purposes in their midst. Although greatly blessed, only a pure remnant of Israel consistently maintained His cause, but through them His suffering Servant, the Messiah, came to make atonement and bring reconciliation through His death and resurrection.

By contrast, the New Testament focus was outward. It began with the coming of the Messiah and His mission. It featured the selection of the 12 apostles whose ministry, by the Holy Spirit, produced the Church. It then reviewed the Church carrying the Gospel to the "uttermost parts" of the earth, entrusting the mission to all members of the Church.

Not surprisingly, therefore, all the Old Testament themes converge in the person and work of Christ. He did more than simply bring together and fulfill in His person the Old Testament. He announced and demonstrated that God has a continuing concern for the world (Jn.3:16; cf. Mt. 28:18-20; Acts 1:8). He maintained that God's program from the beginning of time was unchanged. What He designed creation to be and purposed for Israel to discharge, He intended the New Testament people of God to carry out. He came specifically to complete the work of redemption and enable God's mission to all nations to continue. Christ's death was not something that might have been prevented; it was the very reason He came. It was not a martyr's death, but a conqueror's victory. The Gospels affirmed that Jesus Christ, the Suffering Servant, was the Savior of the world and Lord of all creation.

The Transition from The Old to The New Testament

John the Baptist, the herald of the coming King, connected the two epochs. Jesus confirmed John's role: "Behold, I am going to send My messenger, and he will clear the way before Me." (Mal. 3:1; cf. Mal. 4:5-6; Mt. 11:12; Mk. 1:2).

The Wilderness Motif

John the Baptist's entrance to herald the coming Messiah was a re-enactment of the wilderness theme which figured so significantly in the history of God's people. In the wilderness of Sinai God commissioned His people as a priest nation. In the wilderness He demonstrated His requirement for undivided allegiance and taught His people to rely totally upon Him. The wilderness became the place for the consolidation of a people of God commissioned for service to the nations, the place of judgment, renewal, re-commissioning, and preparation for encounter with the powers controlling and motivating rebellion against God. The call to renewal and preparation for encounter came in the absence of all visible resources and came to represent the place of "nothingness." In such a place God displayed His power on behalf of and through the weak. He, and He alone, did the delivering. And yet He did it with and through His people:

> Now Moses was pasturing the flock...[on] the west side of the wilderness....And the angel of the LORD appeared to him....And the LORD said, "I have surely seen the affliction of My people...and have given heed to their cry...I am aware of their sufferings. So I have come down to deliver them from the power of the Egyptians....Therefore come now, and *I will send you* to Pharaoh, *so that you may bring My people, the sons of Israel, out of Egypt*" (Exo.3:1,2,7,8,10, emphasis added).

John also appeared in the wilderness to announce another Exodus, this one led by the Messiah Himself. The preparation for this Exodus started in the wilderness with a baptism of repentance, renewal for involvement and commitment to God's purposes.

The wilderness was a recurring theme in God's redemptive activity. Abraham was found in the wilderness: "My father was a wandering Aramean" (Dt. 26:5). Jacob met God in the wilderness (Gen. 32:24-30) before his encounter with Esau, and also in preparation to be God's redemptive agent in the midst of the nations. His name change from Jacob to Israel signified his standing in relationship to God and the nations (Gen. 32:28). The people of Israel came to know their covenant-making God in the wilderness while preparing to face their enemies in the promised land. John the Baptist came as a voice crying in the wilderness, preparing the Israel of his day for encounter with their Messiah. Christ spent 40 days in the wilderness preparing for His ministry. When He was most vulnerable, without any resources, without food and weak, He faced the enemy, letting him know there was a *new presence* among men—Emmanuel, God with us. As a new Israel, the Lord Jesus Christ succeeded where the old Israel had failed. In His weakness Christ demonstrated His power, exposing the devil for what he is—in comparison with God—a powerless spirit (Col.2:15; Rev.20:1-3,10,14).

The Announcement of the Coming Deliverer

John's appearance heralded impending judgment and the coming of "Another," who would lead a new humanity in a worldwide thrust to the nations. He would lead an Exodus of deliverance never before equalled (Is.61:1-3; Lk.4:18-19), a deliverance that would include all nations (Is. 66:18-23; Mt. 3:11-17). John, however, did not recognize Christ until the Holy Spirit descended on Him:

The next day he saw Jesus coming to him, and said, "Behold the Lamb of God who takes way the sin of the world!... And I did not recognize Him...." And John bore witness saying, "I have beheld the Spirit descending as a dove out of heaven; and He remained upon Him. And I did not recognize Him, but He who sent me to baptize in water said to me, `He upon whom you see the Spirit descending and remaining upon Him, this is the one who baptizes in the Holy Spirit' " (Jn.1:29,31-33).

This coming One would be known for His identification with humanity. Jesus did not have a "call" such as the Old Testament prophets or even John had. He simply submitted to John's baptism, thereby identifying Himself with sinners who needed to repent. John had emphasized that only those broken about their sin and its horrible consequences could repent and align themselves with God's mission. The sinless Son of God announced His "brokenness" by submitting to a baptism of repentance. Identifying himself and becoming one with man, He also became a model for God's new humanity, broken and repentant, walking in obedience before God. The baptism of Christ confirmed that His identification with man was preparation for God's redemptive activity. He was acknowledged as the obedient One— God's Beloved Son, the one who would deliver mankind.

Christ's entry into ministry was like that of the prophets, and yet different. The prophets claimed a commission from God, but Jesus spoke in His own right, claiming God as His Father. He engaged in the pursuits of ordinary men who had to make their living by soiling their hands—an affront to the Greeks. Although there was a strong work tradition in Judaism, it was less than desirable to the religious Jews. Jesus came from plebeian stock and not from the contemporary leaders in Israel (i.e., priests, scribes and Levites). He did not demand the right to be heard, but rather earned the right to be called the Savior of mankind (Mt. 27:54; Lk. 23:47-48; Jn. 7:46).

John's appearance in the wilderness and his message also heralded God's call to a new lifestyle which would more nearly reflect what it meant to be God's new humanity. Being a part of this new humanity demanded repentance and identification with God and His purposes. He called people to participate in another Exodus, one in which they were to be a pilgrim people on God's mission, following the Lamb of God, who takes away the sin of the world.

John's ministry was brief, but it bore significance for all times and all peoples. He stood on the threshold of a new kingdom, pointing the way to a new age, announcing the presence of a new power. This power would supersede all others and bring restoration and reconciliation to all who would submit to His Lordship. Of John, Jesus said, "Truly, I say to you, among those born of women there has not arisen anyone greater than John the Baptist; yet he who is least in the kingdom of heaven is greater than he" (Mt.11:11).

The Ministry to Israel

Jesus' focus was at first directed to lost Israel, "God's son." In keeping with the covenant promise (Gen. 12:1-3), He continued to remind Israel, His model people, to impress the nations with the Father's glory (cf. Jn. 8:50,54-56; 12:20-23; 13:31-32). In His own ministry and in assigning work to the disciples, Christ concentrated on the house of Israel and commanded His disciples to go to the lost sheep of Israel (Mt. 10:5-6; Mt. 15:24).

Unreservedly He identified Himself with Israel's particularism. By entering her frame of reference, Jesus demonstrated how she as a nation had rejected His mandate to be His model and witness to the nations (Is. 43:10-13). However, Israel's particularism was not without basis. Had God not especially selected this nation to be the apple of His eye? (Zech. 2:8) Her particularism had caused her to turn in on herself rather than to be a blessing (Ps. 67:1-2). In essence, Israel had come to believe that her God was a national deity who was there for her sake only. How contrary to the plans and purposes of God! The nations had been and are evermore on His heart.

Christ, however, did share Israel's perspective on the Gentiles. He taught that they were materialistic and merely sought the things of the world. They were not only contrary to God, they were anti-God, given to all forms of idolatry and the worship of demon spirits. The Gentiles were ready for judgment. They were the oppressors of the Jews. Jerusalem, the city of God, would be trodden down by them. But God would not forget—their judgment was sure. Like some in Israel, He, too, was concerned for the name of God, a name reproached by Israel and the nations alike.

Christ maintained the continuity between the Old and the New Testaments. He used Jonah's ministry as an indication of His own. The sign of Jonah, which enabled him to bring a Gentile city to repentance, would parallel His own in His bringing even more into the kingdom of God (Mt. 12:40-41). By appearing with Moses and Elijah on the Mount of Transfiguration, Jesus tied together the Old and New Testaments in their emphases on deliverance from and confrontation with the powers of evil. He frequently referred to Old Testament characters and their

241

ongoing relevance to the present day. Jesus affirmed that He did not come to destroy the message of the Old Testament but to bring it to fulfillment.

The Ministry to the Gentiles

Jesus Christ showed impartiality to all—Jew and Gentile alike—making it clear that judgment awaits all sin-loving people. Belonging to Israel conveyed no particular guarantee that one would escape judgment. Being a Gentile brought no particular liability either (Mt. 12:50; Jn. 10:16). While concerning Himself with Israel, Jesus also deliberately responded to Gentile needs, using the issues of His day to transcend prejudice and demonstrate His concern to bring all peoples into His Kingdom. Examples included the encounter with the Samaritan woman at the well, the account of the Good Samaritan, Christ's response to the disciples upon being refused hospitality in a Samaritan village, and the healing of the Canaanite woman's daughter (Mt. 15:22-28).

Christ demonstrated a constant concern for all nations, a concern which disturbed the Jews. They were convinced that they, God's chosen people, would not know judgment again, but the Olivet discourse shattered their optimism (Mt. 24). His universal concern for all nations (Mt. 24:14) would be maintained when the vineyard would be given to others (Mt. 21:33-45).

A Forceful Reminder

The parable of the prodigal was a forceful reminder to Israel of the lostness of people. It served also as a reminder that the nations were indeed God's business (Lk. 15:11-32). God, the loving Father, was greatly concerned and longing for the day of the return of the lost son (the Gentile nations). Centuries ago that father-son relationship was severed by choice (Rom. 1:18ff; cf. Gen. 11), and Jesus Christ reminded Israel, the older brother, of the Father's longing to see that relationship restored. But the older brother Israel was committed to his own concerns and quite unmoved by the longing of the Father's heart.

Israel's selfishness made her insensitive to the Father's concern for the younger brother's restoration. As far as the older brother was concerned, the younger brother had, by choice, severed himself from the Father, and therefore his conversation never concerned the "lost son." The nations fully deserved what they had coming to them. According to Israel, the lost son deserved the judgment of idolatry for deliberately turning from God (Rom. 1:18-32).

Israel was indifferent to the fate of those who did not know God; she never volunteered to go after them. Instead, she basked in the goodness of the Father, absorbing all the blessings and expending them on herself. Israel's sole motivation for association with Him was the guarantee of an inheritance which she could expend on herself. That the nations might know Him as the only true God and Savior seemed foreign to Israel.

Jesus' coming to Israel was consistent with God's covenant promise (Gen. 12:3). As Abraham was raised up in order to reach all nations, so Christ's coming in and through the Israel of His day was for the sake of the nations (Mt. 28:18-20). Just as Abraham was not to be the sole bearer of the "gospel" (Gen. 18:18-19; Gal. 3:8), so Jesus exhorted Israel to carry out her evangelistic and cultural mandates.

The New Era

Jesus Christ commenced His ministry by announcing His purpose for coming, bringing incalculable hope to many:

> "The Spirit of the LORD is upon Me, because He anointed Me to preach the gospel to the poor. He has sent Me to proclaim release to the captives, and recovery of sight to the blind, to set free those who are downtrodden, to proclaim the favorable year of the LORD" (Lk.4:18; cf. Is.61:1-3).

His coming also augured deep offense to those who rejected Him. He affirmed John the Baptist's declaration:

> "He will baptize you with the Holy Spirit and fire. And His winnowing fork is in His hand, and He will thoroughly clear His threshing floor; and He will gather His wheat into the barn, but He will burn up the chaff with unquenchable fire" (Mt. 3:11-12).

Jesus identified Himself as the one who would be the Deliverer, but also the final judge:

> "I have come to cast fire upon the earth; and how I wish it were already kindled! But I have a baptism to undergo, and how distressed I am until it is accomplished! Do you supposes that I came to grant peace on the earth? I tell you, no, but rather division" (Lk. 12:49-51). "Now judgment is upon this world; now the ruler of this world shall be cast out. And I, if I be lifted up from the earth, will draw all men to Myself....He who rejects Me, and does not receive My sayings, has one

who judges him; the word I spoke is what will judge him at the last day" (Jn.12:31- 32,48).

In Jesus Christ, God did a new thing. His Presence sounded victory over Satan. At the victorious confrontation in the wilderness, driven by God's Spirit, in His weakness Christ demonstrated that He was the Victor, God's new Presence in human flesh. He did what He did by God's power as He acted in His full humanity (Jn.5:19,30). He rejected all options by which man usually sought to display his own ingenuity and power: economic endeavors—"turn these stones into bread"—providing people what would feed their appetites; political conquest—"bow down and worship me and I will give you all these kingdoms"—kingdom building for personal glorification; religious showmanship—"cast yourself down from the temple pinnacle and He will give His angels charge concerning you"—avoid the suffering servant pilgrim-way by using attention-getting religious gimmicks. Jesus rejected all these options as unworthy of God's mission. Jesus Christ proved Himself to be the Power over all powers, including death (Mk. 10:38-45; Lk. 12:50). As God's Son and yet true man, He mediated God's power in confronting all the forces destroying man. He died as God's man, flesh of our flesh, and rose again as the conquering Lord (Acts 2:22-24).

The Inauguration of a New Kingdom

In the process of ministry and through His victorious death and resurrection, Christ inaugurated a new age for God's rule over His people. The Lord brought a new people into being who would demonstrate His righteous and just rule, modeling on earth what God does in heaven (Mt. 5-7). His kingdom was to be a present reality, already having been initiated in this age, but not fully here until He returns with His saints to reign on earth (Mt. 14:62; Jn. 18:36-37).

The citizens of His kingdom were to rejoice, whereas John's disciples fasted (Mk. 2:18-20). His kingdom people were given the marks of belonging and delegated authority because of their intimate relationship with the King (Lk. 9:1-6; 10:1-16; 22:29,30). It was their privilege "to act and to judge" on behalf of the King. His citizens were to live under a "kingly rule" with an understanding of community (Mt.8:9-11). In the fellowship of true community they had all things in common, their faith as well as their means. They were to be concerned not only for the common good, but also for the needs of each individual (Acts 2:42-47). His kingdom would exercise influence through its citizens upon lives and structures. His kingdom possessed men. It came upon them and delivered them from alien powers (Mt. 12:28; Lk. 11:20) resulting in a different perspective on life .

His kingdom not only would be in their midst (Lk. 17:20-21); it would also be universal. The kingdom was not political but redemptive. It was not national, but universal—including Jews, Romans, and Greeks (Gal. 3:8; Eph. 2:14-16). It was a present reality, but it had an eschatalogical future at the consummation of God's redemptive purposes and worldwide blessing, when the twelve apostles would judge the twelve tribes (Lk. 22:30).

The parables about the seed, fishnet, harvest, mustard seed, and leaven told how the kingdom's message would reach all nations during the interim between Christ's ascension and return. Taking the message of His kingdom to all nations is now the privileged responsibility of all God's people.

The Final Redemptive Act

In His coming Jesus Christ ushered in God's final redemptive act (Heb. 1:1-2; cf. Acts 4:12). He was God's spectacle, the root out of parched ground with no appearance that we should be attracted to Him (Is. 53:2,3). He was the sign of Jonah (Mt.16:4) taking God's judgment, not for His own sin but for others'. He was also the sign of God's resurrection power which all those who have died in Him would realize (Jn. 11:25-26). He was the desire of all nations (Lk.10:23,24; cf. Hag. 2:7 see margin) even though they did not recognize Him as such. As God's final redemptive act, the Messiah was to bring salvation for all peoples. He would bring into being a liberated people who would know His resurrection power to demonstrate His praises before the nations (Eph. 1:19,20; 1 Pet. 2:9; cf. Is. 43:21).

A Kingdom Suffering Violence

Throughout this new era, His kingdom will suffer violence (Mt.11:12) and struggle to announce itself. There are powers aligned working for its destruction (Ps. 2:1-2; Eph. 2:1-2; 6:12; 1 Thess. 2:18), seeking to prevent others from hearing its good news (2 Cor. 4:4; 1 Tim.4:1; 2 Tim.2:26). Spiritual encounter and conflict are normative as the powers seek to prevent the good news from penetrating people's understanding, but conquest is assured because the Lord of the kingdom promised th at all of Satan's hosts would not withstand its triumphant march (Mt.16:18; cf. Rom. 8:32-39; 2 Cor. 2:14,15).

The Intent of the Gospels

Although the Gospels affirm that Jesus Christ is the Savior of the world, they do not fully describe His life, (Jn.20:30-31), nor do they explain fully how He may be experienced. However, they call readers to a historical record, and also to a living Lord. In the words of the Apostle John,

> And the Word became flesh, and dwelt among us, and we beheld His glory, glory as of the only begotten from the Father, full of grace and truth (Jn. 1:14).

> What was from the beginning, what we have heard, what we have seen with our eyes, what we beheld and our hands handled, concerning the Word of Life—and the life was manifested, and we have seen and bear witness and proclaim to you the eternal life, which was with the Father and was manifested to us—what we have seen and heard we proclaim to you (1 Jn.1:1-3).

Materials later seen in the Gospels formed the basis of early apostolic preaching and were quoted to communicate the Good News. The church accepted them as God's record of His Son and understood them to present the final historical act of God on behalf of man's redemption—God's decisive saving act. The author of Hebrews spoke of "a sacrifice once for all" (Heb. 7:27). In their preaching they did not reflect on a plan of salvation as much as they presented a person, the Savior Jesus Christ (Heb. 1:1-2). They understood the Mount of Transfiguration episode to have brought together the universal, the Messianic, and the missionary emphases of the Old Testament in the person of Christ. The Good News which Jesus proclaimed told how to enter a kingdom of power and liberation which had both *already come* and was *yet coming.* His appearance with Moses (the deliverer) and Elijah (the prophet who called the powers of darkness to account) testified to God's central focus for all ages: to deal decisively with all opposing powers and deliver mankind (Col. 2:13-15; cf. 1 Jn. 3:8). Salvation in its full measure had arrived, available in an intimate and indispensable relationship with God through Jesus Christ. His life and ministry underscored the offer not only of forgiveness of sins, but of deliverance from all that enslaves. A faith-motivated, vital relationship with the Messiah results in a liberating fellowship and a joyful stewardship (Jn. 20:31; Jn. 8:32; 2 Cor. 3:17; 2 Cor. 8:1-5).

The Gospels presented Jesus Christ as God's Suffering Servant of Isaiah 53 who came to save all peoples (Jn. 3:16). The writers understood that the servant role gave unity to the New Testament and the whole redemptive activity of God. Christ was no martyr. His death was a historical performance of the very mind of God, the very heart of God's redemptive activity.

Missiological Considerations

The above should have a profound effect on both the message and method of mission, because it brings the missionary face to face with the challenge of the task and the message undergirding world mission.

The question we must face is this: when we reflect on God's redemptive activity as we fellowship at the Lord's table, what thoughts concern us? Are they thoughts of compassion and urgency concerning those who are missing from His table? *That* is His concern.

Jesus Christ announced and demonstrated that God has a continuing concern for the whole world (Mt. 28:18-20; Acts 1:8). He maintained that God's program from the beginning of time was unchanged. To be allied with Him demands involvement with world evangelization. Anything less contradicts, even rejects, His life and ministry.

The wilderness motif helps us prepare for and engage in world evangelization. In the wilderness experiences of life, God's people may be renewed, re-commissioned, and prepared to meet the powers motivating rebellion against God. In the absence of all visible resources, God's servants learn to depend upon Him who has said that the battle is His, and that His servants are to demonstrate His glory and not their own. Wilderness experiences teach God's servants to declare that the *new Presence* among men is *God with us*. It is through what onlookers term weakness that the kingdom of God is realized (1 Cor. 1:23-29).

As Jesus Christ fully identified with sinful man, God's servants also are to identify humbly with "sinners" who need to repent (cf. Neh. 1; Dan. 9). It is an identification in which one sinner reaches another with the message of deliverance through Christ's death and resurrection. Only those broken-hearted about their sin and its horrible consequences repent and are able to align themselves with God's mission. God's people are to be a model of His new humanity—broken and repentant, walking in obedience before Him. They do not demand the right to be heard, but earn the right to declare that Jesus Christ is the Savior of man. Their lives are consistent with their message; they model on earth what God does in heaven (Mt. 5-7).

As their Lord announced His purpose for coming, God's people commit to the same ministry: "to preach the gospel to the poor...to proclaim release to the captives, and recovery of sight to the blind, to set free those who are downtrodden, to proclaim the favorable year of the Lord" (Lk. 4:18). But they also proclaim the impending judgment awaiting disobedient and rebellious man. Their going out with the Gospel is thus "a fragrance of Christ to God among those who are being saved and among those who are perishing; to the one an aroma from death to death, to the other an aroma from life to life" (2 Cor. 2: 15-16).

God's people are to reject all human options and willingly submit to the Suffering Servant's pilgrim-way. They realize that man will not be liberated by economic pursuits, by political power or by religious deceptions. Salvation is only through God's Suffering Servant.

Although Christ emphasized man's continued responsibility for the cultural mandate, this must not take precedence over man's spiritual regeneration, "for as he thinks within himself, so he is" (Prov. 23:7). The cultural mandate flows out of the proper understanding of the spiritual mandate. Only regenerated man can have God's perspective on man's true needs, whether physical or spiritual.

Since Jesus proved Himself to be the Power over all powers, including death (Heb. 2:14-15), God's servants should expect His intervention in all events in life, although not to the exclusion of suffering (Rom. 8:35-36). They are aware that the kingdom will suffer violence (Mt. 11:12); that it will struggle to announce itself; that there are "powers" aligned against it (Ps. 2:1-2; Mt. 16:18); and that powerful forces are seeking to prevent others from hearing the Good News (2 Cor. 4:4; 1 Tim. 4:1). Spiritual encounter and conflict are normative. We must fight on with the confidence that conquest is assured because the Lord of the Church has promised that Satan's hosts will not be able to withstand the march of triumph.

CHAPTER 22

THE MISSION

OF THE SERVANT

Jesus Christ's life and ministry imparted the raw materials from which His hearers had to draw their own conclusions. "Are You the Expected One, or shall we look for someone else?" Jesus' answer: "*Go and report* to John *what you hear and see*: the blind receive sight and the lame walk, the lepers are cleansed and the deaf hear, and the dead are raised up, and the poor have the gospel preached to them" (Mt. 11:3-5, emphasis added). Jesus Christ was unlike the religious leaders of His day. In His uniqueness, unpredictability, practicality, and commitment to fulfill His mission (Lk. 4:18), He earned the right to be heard.

Christ's Summons to Servanthood

In the context of giving "His life a ransom for many" (Mk. 10:45), Jesus issued a radical, decisive and authoritative summons: "Follow Me, and I will make you become fishers of men" (Mk. 1:17); "If anyone wishes to come after Me, let him deny himself, and take up his cross daily, and follow Me" (Lk. 9:23). All other priorities must give way before His summons. The Messiah—the King of kings and Lord of lords—is here. No excuse will discharge a person from obeying His call. Christ demands total homage and obedience:

"For I tell you that none of those men who were invited shall taste of my dinner....If anyone comes to Me, and does not hate [compared to his love for Me] his own father and mother and wife and children and brothers and sisters, yes, and even his own life, he cannot be My disciple. Whoever does not carry his own cross and come after Me

249

cannot be My disciple....So therefore, no one of you can be My disciple who does not give up all his own possessions" (Lk. 14:24,26-27,33).

Christ declared that God was about to act redemptively and eschatalogically once for all through Him:

"This generation is a wicked generation; it seeks for a sign and yet no sign shall be given it but the sign of Jonah. For just as Jonah became a sign to the Ninevites, so shall the Son of Man be to this generation" (Lk.11:29,30);

and

"For just as the Father raises the dead and gives them life, even so the Son also gives life to whom He wishes....He who hears My word, and believes Him who sent Me, has eternal life, and does not come into judgment, but has passed out of death into life" (Jn. 5:21,24);

and again "I am the door; if anyone enters through Me, he shall be saved, and shall go in and out, and find pasture....I came that they might have life, and might have it abundantly" (Jn.10:9-10).

His summons to engage in His mission could not allow any equivocation. He demanded repentance: dislodge yourself from the center of your being and move in God's direction (Lk. 5:32; 24:47). He expected renunciation: turn from all other loyalties and priorities and unconditionally accept the will of God for your life (Mt. 5:29,30; Lk. 14:15-35). Renounce the cares of the world, the deceitfulness of riches, the pleasures of life, and follow Me alone (Mt. 16:24-27).

He demanded the rejection of all other solutions to life: deny all human options, such as the political maneuvering of the Saducees, the withdrawal of the Essenes, the revolution of the Zealots, the orthodoxy (without orthopraxis) of the Pharisees, the fatalistic "status quo" of the Herodians. None of these could ever bring mankind to utopia. Each in its own way sought to supersede commitment to the Person and truth of Christ Himself. For example, the Pharisees' "commitment" to orthodoxy with its "we have the truth and God desires nothing but the truth" attitude allowed proud satisfaction. As contenders for truth, the Pharisees simply prescribed in the Talmud the rules for life. These rabbinic teachings touched on every area of life, but unfortunately gave the impression that a man could please God by busy orthodoxy done in his own strength. To accomplish this they strained at exegeting the text. Beyond "laying burdens upon people," however, the religious leaders felt they had no responsibility to implement the evangelistic and cultural mandates.

On the contrary, association with Christ meant participation in His mission of servanthood: He "did not come to be served, but to serve, and to give His life a ransom for many" (Mt. 20:28) and "to seek and to save that which was lost" (Lk. 19:10). The task was urgent; the presence of the King must be announced; there could be no postponement. Those who yielded to His summons were to proclaim the message of the kingdom in both word and deed (Mt. 5-7; 9:36-38; 28:18-20; Jn. 20:21). Association with Him meant calling others to faith in Him and in His redemption. Life began with Jesus Christ and issued in responsible political, economic, social, and religious activity. Human attempts at establishing utopias are parodies of paradise because man's truth has pride and polarizes human behavior.

Jesus' summons implied a commitment to death: "Keep on *denying yourself*...keep on *taking up the Cross* [a one-way path to death]...keep on *following* [obey] Me...and *I will make you fishers of men*" (Mt. 16:24 [free translation], emphasis added). In other words, be willing to accept *the pathway of the Suffering Servant* and you will be more than conqueror in life. His followers were to reject the pattern of the Gentiles and follow His example:

> But Jesus *called them to Himself*, and said, "You know that the rulers of the Gentiles lord it over them, and their great men exercise authority over them. It is not so among you, but whoever wishes to become great among you shall be your servant, and whoever wishes to be first among you shall be your slave" (Mt. 20:25-27, emphasis added).

The Model Servant

Christ not only took the form of a servant but indeed was a servant:

> who, although He existed in the form of God, did not regard equality with God a thing to be grasped, but emptied Himself, taking the form of a bond-servant, and being made in the likeness of men. And being found in appearance as a man, He humbled Himself by becoming obedient to the point of death, even death on a cross (Phil.2:6-8).

Jesus personally and formally declared His servanthood and commenced His public ministry as a servant. The role Israel rejected, He would take. As the Servant, He began His work (Lk. 4:18) and exerted the irresistible power before which all knees would bow.

The servant character described every aspect of His life and ministry. He was more aware of others' needs than His own. He knew who He was and where He belonged in the society of His day. Humility was one of His prime distinctives. He was totally dependent on His Father for survival, even for the most basic needs. He accepted the office of stewardship, knowing He did not own but only handled His Father's assets; Christ's concern was His Father's interests, not His own. He was unafraid of total involvement in whatever was required of Him; He had nothing to lose—reputation, possessions, or life itself. Whatever He had was due to His Father's benevolence. His Father's desires were the Servant's duty. The Father's choice was the Servant's obligation. He performed what was commanded, regardless of the nature of the work. He was available for whatever had to be done without expecting any consideration. He accepted suffering as part of His working conditions, expecting nothing else. He was totally loyal to His Father. Christ lived a disciplined life in which His time and talents were accounted for and were called upon anywhere, at any time, for anything.

In revealing Himself as Servant He caused both offense and acknowledgment. Those who refused Him stumbled over His lack of majesty and social status, His humility, message of repentance, and renunciation. Those who accepted Him recognized Him as God's sent One, the Messiah, the Savior of mankind. They gladly responded to the apparent powerlessness of Jesus. Although they did not understand that His kingdom would come by a "power" other than political or military means (Lk. 24:13-21), they saw Him as "the Holy One of God" who had "words of eternal life" (Jn. 6:68-69). His was the power of the Servant, the Lamb, the One who takes away the sin of the world.

The Signs of the Kingdom

God's new Adam would not resort to His own power. He set it aside (Jn. 5:19,20,30; Phil. 2:7-8), displaying what happens when a man denies himself, takes up his cross, and follows God in total obedience. When one is fully committed to God there is an unexplainable new Presence within and an anointing power (2 Cor. 1:21; 1 Jn. 2:20,27) upon his life. That Presence is none other than God's Presence, mediated through a human instrument. By delegated authority, God's people would call powers of darkness to account (Lk. 9:1-2; 10:1,17-20; Acts 13:4-12; 19:13-20).

The signs (Mt. 11:4-5; Lk. 11:20; cf. Exo. 8:19; Is. 35:5-6) of the Servant were assaults on the enemy of man, but Christ's miracles, signs, wonders, and exorcisms were just the preliminary attacks, "sparring" encounters with the powers. Later came the mortal combat on the cross, where He assuaged the wrath of God and reconciled man to the Father (Col. 2:10-14) and in the process destroy the works of the enemy (1 Jn. 3:8). He would disarm the enemies—render them powerless, and make a public display of their powerlessness (Col. 2:15). In His own "powerlessness," Christ would subdue all other powers and declare victory over all of man's enemies.

The signs of the Servant were not to show God's power; His resources were limitless and His power supreme. He worked miracles not to vindicate Himself but to identify Himself. The miracles were evidence of the King and His Kingdom in the people's midst. He, the Creator, was indeed Lord of *all*: He revealed His power over defilement ("I am willing; be cleansed" Mt. 8:3), geographical distance ("say a word and my servant will be healed" Mt. 8:8), the deep ("cast the net on the right-hand side" Jn. 21:6), disease, demons, death, darkness, and every dilemma man faces.

Signs revealed the presence of His kingdom, which would expose whatever sought to deceive, dehumanize, or destroy man. God's kingdom became exceptionally clear in the person, words, and works of the Messiah; therefore, the miracles and parables help us understand how God's kingdom is to be revealed in every age. His kingdom is to address every human need: poverty, sickness, hunger, sin, demonic temptation, and even death. How unlike the life and work of other religious leaders or systems, which encourage man to care only for himself, or at best, his own group. Each miracle proclaimed that in God's name wherever and whenever human needs and problems were addressed, cared for and overcome, there God's kingdom would be shining through.

The signs of the kingdom were not merely humanitarian acts of compassion. If they were, Christ would have healed all afflicted people. However, whenever God's glory was at stake, signs and wonders declared that there was a new Presence ready to confront, expose and deal with all evil forces. Power encounters simply demonstrated the presence of the King and His sovereign kingdom, that He had power over *all* crises and circumstances.

The signs were simply archetypes of the coming kingdom. In both Isaiah 35 and 65 signs were vivid descriptions of what would precede the decisive act of God's full restoration of all things. God revealed His kingdom in such dramatic ways because of His desire to deliver man from all of sin's bondage. Thus both the evangelistic and cultural mandates were to be the application of kingdom principles, demonstrating the difference between submission to the gods and submission to the true God.

The signs of the Servant announced something new on earth: God's kingdom was in the midst of men. In Jesus Christ God did a new thing for all those who elected to believe Him and walk by faith. Sin no longer exerted dominion over them (Rom. 6:11-14). He set them free to be involved in His mission (Rom. 6:7,22; Gal. 5:1; Eph. 2:8-10; Tit. 2:11-14; 3:8; cf. Rom. 1:5). He, by the Holy Spirit, would give them gifts for effective ministry (Rom. 12:3-8; 1 Cor. 12; Eph. 4:7-13) to bring deliverance to all nations.

Christ was no "miracle worker." He came to usher in a kingdom of justice and righteousness which would reflect on earth what God does in heaven (Mt. 6:10). For this reason Jesus' healing ministry was subordinated to His preaching and teaching ministry. First in priority would be a Holy Spirit-engendered regeneration. Then through "teaching them to observe all that I have commanded you" a Church would arise to declare His glory in both word and deed. It would ascribe Him the glory through word of witness, through service to others and through worship and praise, all in response to His majesty and mighty acts on behalf of redeemed mankind.

The Death of the Suffering Servant

For a short time Christ worked, but from the inception of His earthly ministry, Jesus deliberately moved toward Golgotha (Lk. 9:51). Each prophecy He made concerning Himself reflected an aspect of Isaiah 53. As the Suffering Servant He had to perform the decisive events to inaugurate the kingdom: demons were exorcised, cures were performed and the third day He finished His course, dying in Jerusalem (Lk. 13:32-33). In His death on the cross, the Servant atoned for man's sin (Is. 53:6,11-12), in accordance with the Scriptures (Lk. 24:25-27; 1 Cor. 15:1-3). In His powerlessness, Christ conquered all powers by the power of God working through Him. Death, the last enemy, was defeated on its own ground (Heb. 2:14).

To the disciples, however, Christ's death was a mystery. In spite of all the instruction He gave His followers, they so firmly believed the Judaistic concept of a politically conquering Messiah that they could not reconcile the Suffering Servant with the Messiah, and His death brought only an anguished response: "We were hoping that it was He who was going to redeem Israel" (Lk. 24:21). They did not understand that God's new Adam needed to conquer *all* man's foes, including death, before setting up a kingdom of total superiority. God was not interested in just one land, but all lands. Redemption was to come to *all* peoples. He earned the right to be Lord of all nations and Conqueror of death!

Man's rebellion, sin and moral turpitude barred his re-entry into God's presence, but all other powers preventing such a reconciliation were dealt with in Jesus Christ's death. The veil was torn (Mt. 27:50-51; Heb. 6:19-20); the way into the presence of God was re-opened. Christ's death had a God-ward dimension: God accomplished a propitiatory sacrifice (1 Jn. 2:2). His sacrifice assuaged God's anger. It satisfied the justice of God (Col. 2:14); and God's love toward man was released. This is the "good news" of man's reconciliation to God. But His death also had a Satan-ward dimension: He came to destroy the works of the devil (1 Jn. 3:8), in spite of the powers of darkness attempting to demean, confuse, contain, deflect, destroy, and discourage the proclamation of the Good News. His death also had a man-ward dimension in that the effects of the Curse were removed. Man could now know total forgiveness for all his sin. There is no sin too unspeakable for God to forgive (1 Cor. 6:9-11; 1 Jn.1:9-2:2).

The Resurrection of the Servant

Christ's resurrection vindicated His mission: He is the only way of salvation (Jn. 14:6; Acts 4:12). He was "declared the Son of God with power by the resurrection" (Rom. 1:4-5), a statement of right to rule. God's new Adam—a new Presence, a Victor—had successfully championed man's cause against Satan. He passed through death into life and opened the way for man to be restored to full fellowship in God's presence.

The affirmation of the resurrection was more than a confession of faith. It was more than a simple proclamation of fact on the part of His followers. They not only believed it to be an indispensable verity, they had individual, experiential knowledge of the resurrected Jesus Christ (Acts 2:32; 1 Cor. 15:1-4). Although Christ's death was primarily the climax of redemption history, in it He also released resurrection power to His followers for continuing His mission to the nations (Mt. 28:18-20; Acts 1:8).

In His death and resurrection Jesus triumphed over the powers of darkness. But fear of death still keeps man enslaved to sin and hinders the mission of making disciples of all nations: "That through death He might render powerless him who had the power of death, that is, the devil; and might deliver those who through fear of death were subject to slavery all their lives" (Heb. 2:14-15). The guarantee came through

255

His own words: "I am...the living One; I was dead, and behold I am alive forevermore, and I have the keys of death and of Hades" (Rev. 1:17-18). Fear of death no longer need keep His disciples (Mk.14:50-54,66-71) from identifying with Him and engaging in His mission. The Conqueror of death had triumphed gloriously and promised that He would never leave them (Mt. 28:20), and that they need fear no man (1 Pet. 3:14-15).

In His resurrection, Christ provided them with a confident expectation of a victorious mission and an assured kingdom. There would be the full realization of "the hope of the Glory of God" (Rom. 5:2). Every knee *will* bow and every tongue *will* confess that He is Lord (Phil. 2:10-11). He alone is indeed "the resurrection and the life." There is no other.

On the cross the Lord Jesus vicariously endured God's judgment due all mankind. His cross and resurrection brought liberation from all powers. *The hour for decision had arrived.* The Lord of all had powerfully subdued the powers of darkness which were destroying the souls and bodies of men. He had come to renew those who were the victims of these forces. Therefore, man dare not put off accepting Jesus Christ's redemptive work on his behalf. God's gracious and saving work had already appeared for all people. It is at the peril of life itself, both now and in the age to come, that anyone disregards Jesus Christ's offer of salvation (Acts 4:12; 17:30-31; Gal. 4:4-5; Tit. 2:11-13; 1 Jn. 5:12). "Today if you hear His voice, do not harden your hearts" (Heb. 4:7).

The Evangelistic Mandate

Prior to His death and resurrection, Christ repeatedly communicated God's concern for people, a concern that men might know and be reconciled to God.

Christ stressed submission to His *Lordship* for those who reject Him as well as for those who claim to follow Him (Mt. 7:21-23; Lk. 10:16). Obedience is not optional: the New Testament mentions His Lordship 660 times.

Jesus spoke often of the *lostness* of man (Lk. 15:4,8). Man needs to be found because he is lost, alienated from the Father. Man must be sought, found and restored to his rightful owner. Israel, God's elected priest-nation, in her misguided particularism had rejected this mandate (see Jonah).

Jesus introduced the theme of the *sower* and *seed* (Mt. 13:3-9). There must be sowers for the seed to be sown. The "seed," God's revelation knowledge, will be acted upon differently in different "soils" (hearts).

In those who respond to God's word, the word produces a crop. Those who believe and produce fruit (growth in grace and obedience) are true believers, producing fruit 30-, 60-, and 100-fold (Mt. 13:18-23). The incontrovertible evidence of being in Christ is producing fruit (Jn. 15:1-8). First, there will be the fruit of the Spirit, which produces a model of God's grace, growth in Christian virtue. Second, the fruit refers to reproducing what is already there: namely, bringing others to faith in Jesus Christ (world evangelization). In turn, those who produce fruit sow the seed. This metaphor had in view the evangelistic mandate Israel had rejected in spite of God's repeated call. Thus, if Israel were to be God's witness, she also had to be God's model, reflecting His gracious rule over her and in her. The message and the model are inseparable.

Jesus Christ highlighted His provision of gifts (Mt. 25:14-30; Lk. 19:12-27). Each man is accountable for his gifts, for every disciple of Christ has been charged with the stewardship of the evangelistic mandate (2 Cor. 5:10-20). God has entrusted everyone with an ability—a spiritual gift—for the edification of His disciples, and for the evangelization of the world (Eph. 4:7-12; cf. Mt. 9:35-38).

The theme of *conflict* stressed encounter with evil forces (Mt. 13:24-30; Mt. 24:2-14). Christ's disciples were not to be ignorant of Satan's devices (cf. 2 Cor.2:11). They knew that there was an enemy who would seek to prevent, hinder, imitate, deflect, destroy and confuse the gospel. This enemy would also tempt man to disregard the Savior. But, in the face of these challenges, God, by His Holy Spirit would provide authority, power, and strength for confrontation (Lk. 9:1-2; 10:2-20; cf. Phil. 4:13). Hindrances, trials and temptations can be turned into opportunities to demonstrate God's presence with His people (1 Cor. 10:13; 2 Cor. 4:7-18).

The theme of *feast and celebration* kept in view the blessedness of those in fellowship with God. To know God, to live in His presence, to submit to His just rule brought blessing, issuing in feasting and celebration. But these blessings were not only for the celebrants. God has full provision for everyone, and He wants a full house of regenerated people (Lk. 14:16-24). He "desires all men to be saved and to come to the knowledge of the truth" (1 Tim. 2:4), to know Him as the Great Deliverer (Lk. 4:18). The theme of feasting and celebration indicates that He does not send His servants on a fruitless quest to the harvest fields. He planned and expected a harvest for the sake of His name. "Thou hast made them to be a kingdom and priests to our God; and they will reign upon the earth" because the harvest will be gathered "from every tribe and tongue and people and nation" (Rev. 5:9-10).

In both His pre-crucifixion and His post-resurrection ministry,

Jesus Christ concerned Himself with *"the kingdom of God"* (Mt. 4:17,23; Acts 1:3). His kingdom was to demonstrate the righteous rule and blessedness He intended for all creation from the beginning of time. It would reveal to the nations the vast difference between man's kingdoms and the one He came to institute. His kingdom was one of peace, justice, blessedness, and righteous authority. It was set against the powers of darkness. His kingdom was a community (*koinonia*) of the King in the midst of the "principalities and powers." But in the age to come, His kingdom will do away with the principalities and powers (Rev. 20:7-10).

Throughout His ministry, Jesus gave His followers the mandate to disciple the nations. Everything He did was to encourage and motivate them to carry out that mandate. Even when He discussed character, He had in sight the making of disciples (Mt. 5:13-16). So His disciples were to "teach everything" that He commanded, because God desired all people to be saved.

Jesus exhorted His followers to forsake all and engage in His mission to the nations, for His name's sake (cf. Rom. 1:5). The primary bearers of His gospel were Peter (Acts 15:7) and Paul (Acts 9:15-16; Gal. 2:7), who received that command directly (Gal.1:15-16). All the apostles carried the Gospel to various nations; according to strong tradition all but one suffered martyrdom. Of each it could be said,

> "But I do not consider my life of any account as dear to myself, in order that I may finish my course, and the ministry which I received from the Lord Jesus, to testify solemnly of the gospel of the grace of God" (Acts 20:24).

The evangelistic mandate was committed to all believers (Mt. 28:18-20; Mk. 16:15; Lk. 24:47; Jn. 17:18; 20:21; Acts 1:8). Should His followers, however, not obey the Great Commission, then God would arrange circumstances to get the message out. As a result of persecution (Acts 8:1,4) the Christian believers went everywhere with the Gospel. As to persecution, Paul responded: "I am ready not only to be bound, but even to die at Jerusalem for the name of the Lord Jesus" (Acts 21:13).

Missiological Considerations

No one claiming to be a follower of Christ dare excuse himself from the obligation to disciple the nations. Participation will keep in focus the following essentials. First, the message Jesus modeled kept in view the whole man:

And Jesus was going about all the cities and villages, teaching in their synagogues, and proclaiming the gospel of the kingdom, and healing every kind of disease and every kind of sickness. And seeing the multitudes, He felt compassion for them, because they were distressed and downcast (Mt. 9:35,36).

And again,

"Go and report to John what you hear and see: the blind receive sight and the lame walk, the lepers are cleansed and the deaf hear, and the dead are raised up, and the poor have the Gospel preached to them" (Mt. 11:4-5).

The evangelistic mandate was to take place in the context of the cultural mandate. Although both mandates are inseparable, the evangelistic always takes precedence. Man is alienated from God and must be restored to fellowship with Him. From that relationship will flow the cultural mandate, not vice versa.

All human priorities must yield before His summons to follow. If Jesus Christ is the King of kings and the Lord of lords, then no excuse can be tolerated. His agenda takes precedence (Mt.6:33). He demands total homage and swift obedience. All His followers are obligated to submit to His Lordship in all of life.

All other options must yield to the evangelistic mandate—options such as political ideologies, systems, and revolutions (which contend for the truth at the expense of obedience to the truth); the tendency to maintain the status quo at the expense of applying the Gospel. Jesus Christ came to seek and to save the lost. That must remain the chief concern of His disciples.

But involvement with Jesus Christ in His mission will always involve suffering. His followers must be willing to accept *the pathway of the Suffering Servant*. It is through suffering that they will bring "sons to glory" (Heb. 2:10) and be more than conquerors in life and in death (Jn. 12:24; Rom. 8:35-39).

As every detail in Christ's life related to the servant theme, so should every detail in the life of His disciples: knowing the role of the servant, being aware of others' needs, demonstrating humility, depending totally on God, understanding that God alone is owner of all, committing to stewardship of His resources, not fearing total involvement in whatever is required, even to the point of death, and being ready to respond to the Master's command at anytime, anywhere, and for anything. In no other way will the task of world evangelization be completed.

Experiential awareness of God's presence and anointing power (2 Cor. 1:21; 1 Jn. 2:20,27) is fundamental to participation in God's mission. *Without this awareness the task will not be accomplished.* Only as they mediate God's Presence will His followers be able to call all powers to account, expose them as no match for God, and see people delivered from the kingdom of darkness (Lk. 8:28-56; 9:1-2; 10:17-24).

A confident expectation that all things are possible with God should characterize His disciples. Whenever God's glory is at stake, signs and wonders will declare that there is a God ready to confront, expose, and deal with all evil forces. Power encounters simply demonstrate the Presence of the King and His kingdom (Acts 16:16-40).

Jesus' death and resurrection are the bases and imperatives for worldwide mission. Through His death the way into the presence of God was re-opened. The threefold message of the Cross is at the heart of the evangelistic mandate. It has a God-ward dimension: God's anger was turned away from man. It has a man-ward dimension: man can now receive forgiveness for all his sin, total release from all bondage, and re-entry into the presence of God. It has a Satan-ward dimension: Satan was dealt a decisive defeat (Col. 2:15) and his works were destroyed (1 Jn. 3:8). Without the cross there would be no salvation for man.

In His resurrection, Christ laid the groundwork for real hope. Without it our "faith is worthless; you are still in your sins....we are of all men most to be pitied" (1 Cor. 15:17,19). But Christ is risen (1 Cor. 15:20). Death *is* defeated. There *is* life awaiting man (1 Cor. 15:21- 24). His resurrection also declared a victorious mission and an assured coming kingdom. Every knee *will* bow and every tongue *will* confess that He is Lord (Phil. 2:10-11). He, and He alone, is indeed "the resurrection and the life." There is *no* other.

Announcing the kingdom and living according to its principles are not optional. True, His kingdom is not of this world, but we are to do on earth what God is doing in heaven (Mt. 6:10). We are ambassadors of the King and His kingdom and must order our lives by His standards.

The evangelistic mandate belongs to *all* God's people. Wherever they are, His followers are obligated to engage in the Great Commission. Only disobedience will keep us from such involvement. To be missionary-minded and involved is simply to be a member of Christ's Church.

CHAPTER 23

THE MISSIONARY

MANDATES OF THE

GOSPELS AND ACTS

The Gospels and the Acts of the Apostles state the same missionary mandate. In each, the command is given by the risen Lord Jesus Christ. Each states that the disciples are to continue a mission begun by Christ which would know no boundaries or limits. Each connects the missionary mandate with the coming of the Holy Spirit, who would enable obedience and provide the necessary power to carry out the task. Each provides ample illustration and motivation for involvement in world evangelization. Each is a missions textbook, directed to a specific people, to encourage involvement in the missionary task. Each accepts the Old Testament mission of Israel as foundational for the mission of Christ and the continuing mission of His disciples. Each portrays how the Gospel came to be, how it is to be communicated, and what it will cost to reach the "remotest part of the earth." Each underscores that missions is not one among many aspects of discipleship; it is central.

The Missionary Mandate in the Gospel of Matthew
Matthew is primarily a missions handbook. Matthew's objective was to instruct recent converts about the person, work, and coming kingdom of Jesus Christ. Such an instructional record would assist them in spreading the message to others. It is therefore both an apol-

261

ogetic for the person and ministry of Jesus Christ and a missionary manual. This book connects implementing the Gospel to the promise of Christ's presence with His people to the end of the age.

Matthew selected much of his material to remind Israel of both her God-given mission and her miserable failure (Mt. 21:33-43; 23:1-39; 25:14-46). Not only did Matthew review Israel's evangelistic responsibility, but he frequently reminded the nation of the cultural mandate, covering such topics as the poor, the alien, and the widow. Although the Sermon on the Mount was specifically directed to Christ's disciples (Mt.5:1), it also reminded Israel of the lifestyle she had to exemplify before the nations in representing God as His priest-nation (Mt. 5:19-21,27,31,33,38,43).

Matthew sought to bring Israel to accept her mandates, issuing a strong call to communicate the faith to both Jewish (Mt. 10:5) and non-Jewish peoples (Mt. 28:18-20). Because of Israel's role in God's mission, Matthew affirmed the priority of mission to Israel as well as permanent obligation toward her from all Christian believers. Thus recognizing Israel's unique relationship to God, Matthew still stressed that the commission to evangelize is universal—the Gospel must be taken to all nations. All peoples are to be discipled and taught all that Jesus commanded.

Matthew left no doubt that the task would be demanding, complex and enormous, but he included the assurance that although all hell be loosed against the task, victory is certain. God will enable His disciples (Mt. 16:18).

Matthew asserted that Christ's death on the cross and the resurrection are the basis for worldwide evangelization. The key to understanding Matthew's selection of material is given in the Great Commission passage.

> And Jesus came up and spoke to them, saying, "All authority has been given to Me in heaven and on earth. Go therefore and make disciples of all the nations, baptizing them in the name of the Father and the Son and the Holy Spirit, teaching them to observe all that I commanded you; and lo, I am with you always, even to the end of the age" (Mt. 28:18-20).

The Threefold Pronouncement

The threefold pronouncement in the Great Commission affirmed Jesus Christ's indisputable authority, His unquestionable command,

and His unfailing promise, each of which were also emphasized in His earthly ministry. Their application to the task of missions provides both confidence and assurance in making Christ known to the nations.

Christ's Indisputable Authority

The carrying out of the mission's mandate is not the basis for Jesus Christ's enthronement over all; rather it follows from the fact of His indisputable authority. "All authority has been given to Me in heaven and on earth." Throughout the Gospel record, Matthew refers to Jesus Christ's exalted authority over all creation. No area—physical, spiritual, interpersonal, or cultural—lies outside his power and authority. "All rule and authority and power and dominion, and every name that is named, not only in this age, but also in the one to come" (Eph. 1:21) has been put in subjection to Him (Eph. 1:22). "There are therefore not such things as natural law, natural power, asserting their own domain over against Jesus, deserving homage, trust, fear and obedience in their own right" (Barth, 1961:61). *All power has been given to Jesus Christ.* He alone has such power.

He who was the crucified Savior now rules as the resurrected Lord, using His power not as a despot bent on destruction, but for the total welfare of man and for liberation from all that oppresses. A saving and liberating authority proceeds from Him; therefore the work of judging and liberating is His.

To His disciples Christ delegated His authority to accomplish the task. Thus to Peter He said, "I will give you the keys of the kingdom of heaven; and whatever you shall bind on earth shall be bound in heaven, and whatever you shall loose on earth shall be loosed in heaven" (Mt. 16:19). Again:

> "Truly I say to you, whatever you shall bind on earth shall be bound in heaven; and whatever you loose on earth shall be loosed in heaven. Again I say to you, that if two of you agree on earth about anything that they may ask, it shall be done for them by My Father who is in heaven" (Mt. 18:18-19).

In the words of Paul:

> And He put all things in subjection under His feet, and gave Him as head over all things to the church, which is His body, the fulness of Him who fills all in all...and raised us up with Him, and seated us with Him in the heavenly places, in Christ Jesus (Eph. 1:22-23; 2:6).

Having commissioned His Church to take the Gospel to all nations, He also has given her authority to finish the task in spite of all circumstances.

Christ's Unquestionable Command

Matthew progressively reveals how Jesus, Himself, did all that He required of His disciples (perhaps with the exception of baptizing).

As Jesus continually crossed boundaries to announce the kingdom, so his disciples must be ready to cross boundaries. They were to "Go therefore" to make His Gospel known to all people groups. Before giving this command, He had commissioned the disciples to "go to the lost sheep of the house of Israel" (Mt. 10:6). Now there was an added dimension, as He commanded them to go to all people everywhere, to cross all barriers, whether racial, sociological, political, cultural, or geographic. World evangelization is an urgent task; the spiritual need is great, the days are uncertain, the time is short. The day of salvation is here, a day of judgment is coming; no boundary can be allowed to stop world evangelization.

The Lord's command continued with the words "make disciples," a specific task involving encounter with people in meaningful relationships. Jesus modeled these kinds of relationships not only with the disciples, but with others, covering a wide cross-section of humanity. Highlighting the importance of such relationships, Jesus reserved His harshest judgments for the religious leaders of His day who rejected His model.

Making disciples takes commitment and perserverance. To make a disciple is to move a person "to surrender to Jesus Christ's liberating authority" (Verkuyl 1978:107) and to involve him in the new order. It is to mold a person into a functioning member of Christ's kingdom. Becoming a disciple involves sharing with Christ in His death and resurrection and joining Him in disclosing His kingdom among all nations. It takes a disciple to make a disciple, who in turn will make other disciples to participate in His mission. Until such commitment is evident, discipling is incomplete.

The task of going and making disciples is to extend to all peoples. The term "all the nations" (panta ta ethne) refers to all humanity. The Gospel is to transcend every limit of family, clan, tribe, ethnic background, nation, society, culture, politics and religion. People must be sought out wherever they are, in whatever state they are. No people group can be overlooked. Only when the Gospel has been proclaimed in the whole world—to all people groups—will the end come (Mt. 24:14).

The command further requires that there be a public declaration of a change of allegiance. "Baptizing them" signifies a changed status; the disciple testifies that he is no longer held captive to sin, death and demonic powers. The rite signifies a new relationship, allegiance to a new Master—the Lord Jesus Christ. But it is not only a rite of renunciation of the former life, it is also a rite of incorporation into the kingdom of God. There is now identification with formal social relationships and practices of the people of God. Baptism visibly demonstrates entry into a new kingdom—a transfer from "the domain of darkness...to the kingdom of His beloved Son" (Col. 1:13; cf. Acts 26:18). Baptism followed an understanding of what it meant to be a follower of Jesus Christ. Baptism is the volitional affirmation and visible demonstration that the convert is now a citizen of the kingdom of God. This is no small honor, but it also brings great responsibility and accountability.

The baptismal rite of renunciation and incorporation is done "in the name of the Father and the Son and the Holy Spirit." The trinitarian form emphasizes the power and authority conferred by Jesus Christ, in which the believer now stands. The trinitarian form emphasizes that the faith and message of Jesus Christ's followers are not from a rootless Christianity. Rather, Christianity is lived out within, and undergirded by, the love of the Father, the grace of the Son, and the fellowship of the Holy Spirit. Matthew had already revealed these explicit truths to his readers and had shown how disciples cannot preach liberation without mentioning the Liberator. They cannot speak of peace without speaking of the Prince of Peace. They cannot speak of salvation without speaking of the Savior. The Gospel has content, focus and authority. The triune God Himself is central to the Christian faith.

The Great Commission further commands instruction of converts, "teaching them to observe." Teaching involves initiation, a thorough introduction and practical participation in what the life, cross and resurrection of Jesus Christ mean. Teaching is not merely the transfer and absorption of information; it produces change, and change issues in visible results. Teaching is training and giving guidance, pointing out the ways by which discipleship is expressed and then giving opportunity for it to be expressed. Disciples are to imitate Jesus Christ's life and mission. "The real aim is to get disciples walking along Jesus' way and then to nourish them...from the Law and the Gospel" (Verkuyl 1975:108). Teaching is to facilitate obedience to Christ's commands to "clear a path through the wilderness" (ibid.), so the disciple may freely move forward to fulfill his responsibility as a follower of Jesus Christ.

The content to be taught is all-encompassing: "all that I commanded you." The converts are to be taught everything: all the commands and the promises. They are to place themselves under the authority of Jesus Christ, seek out His commands, and make them part and parcel of their own life. Thus, as disciples, they assume the responsibilities commanded by their Lord. They do not question His authority. They simply submit in humble obedience to all His instruction.

Christ's Unfailing Promise

The capstone of the Great Commission is Jesus Christ's unfailing promise: *"Lo, I am with you always."* He, the omniscient, omnipresent and omnipotent Lord, will Himself be with them in the task of world evangelization. In John's Gospel we learn that He will be present among them and in them in a new way (Jn. 14:16-23). The Holy Spirit is the risen Lord resident in and among His disciples. "The presence of the hidden and exalted Lord within the Church is her richest gift" (Verkuyl 1978:108) and her enablement for effective ministry. He is present with His Church in all His authority and power. By the Holy Spirit, Christ is with His Church on every continent, in every imaginable circumstance, in all kinds of alluring temptations, in both her decline and growth. That assurance will continue to sustain His Church to complete the task of world evangelization.

His promised Presence will not cease until time is no more: *"even to the end of the age."* Although circumstances may change in countries and nations, and His Church may endure all kinds of trouble, His presence is both a guarantee of success and an urging on to complete the missionary task.

The Missionary Mandate in the Gospel of Mark

Mark presents Jesus Christ as the incontestable Lord. All circumstances, people, and powers (physical or spiritual) are subject to Him; for this reason Mark highlights Jesus' miracles. If Christ is Lord over all, then all men need to know Him as Savior and Lord.

Mark's objective was twofold: to make known the Gospel of Christ and to provide a manual for winning people to faith and involvement in His Kingdom. Mark progressively presented Jesus Christ in a way that called the reader to a verdict, even as acknowledged by the centurion: "Truly this man was the Son of God" (Mk. 15:39).

Mark's writing was patently missionary; he intended his written Gospel to do what itinerant missionaries were doing orally. Mark was convinced that the Gospel was for sharing, and he upheld the Great Commission as imperative and urgent. To be a disciple of Jesus Christ required journeying the world over to make disciples. The Gospel is a decisive issue which involves salvation or condemnation.

> And afterward He appeared to the eleven themselves as they were reclining at the table; and He reproached them for their unbelief and hardness of heart, because they had not believed those who had seen Him after He had risen. And He said to them, "Go into all the world and preach the gospel to all creation. He who has believed and has been baptized shall be saved; but he who has disbelieved shall be condemned" (Mk. 16:14-16).

To make this Gospel known worldwide requires supernatural ability—an ability conferred by the risen Lord Jesus Christ on His disciples. Thus, Mark adds a dimension to the Great Commission not mentioned as explicitly by the other writers.

> "And these signs will accompany those who have believed: in My name they will cast out demons, they will speak with new tongues; They will pick up serpents, and if they drink any deadly poison, it shall not hurt them; they will lay hands on the sick, and they will recover" (Mk. 16:17-18).

Although this section may be a later textual insertion, and some of the miracles may be figurative, Acts records these events as literally accompanying the expansion of the Church (Acts 2:1-8; 3:1-8; 5:14-16; 9:32-35; 28:3-6).

Many scholars believe that miracles were not limited to the first century (see Ramsey MacMullen, *Christianizing the Roman Empire AD 100- 400*, Yale University Press, 1984). If the Holy Spirit is present with God's people, then we should expect Him to act in a way consistent with God's purposes and for Christ's glory. Significantly, Mark associates the miraculous with world evangelization. Mark has already shown that Jesus was no mere miracle worker seeking human applause; He was Lord over all powers. Thus when Christ commissioned His disciples, He assured them that He whom they had known in ministry would accompany them in their task of discipling the nations. Their association with Him would make the disciples equal to any challenge.

The Missionary Mandate in Luke and Acts

Luke emphasizes that the Gospel is based on the suffering, death, and resurrection of Christ, connecting the mandate for missions to the risen Lord (Lk.24:46-47). Luke ties the call to missions not only to the completed work of Christ on the cross, but also to the promise of the Holy Spirit.

Luke wanted to make the Gospel known to foreigners (especially the Greeks) and to the powerless of his day (including women), so his materials especially focus on subjects of interest to the less privileged. Luke wanted them to know that Jesus Christ had come to be their Savior and Lord, and that He was vitally interested in their circumstances.

Like Mark, Luke wanted to reflect in a literary form what missionaries were doing orally. Wanting people to believe and submit to Christ as Lord, Luke showed how Jesus Christ involved Himself in every area of human need. He detailed Christ's Lordship over every area of life—even when He delegated His authority to the disciples to confront the powers. Luke graphically described the conflict in making the Gospel known. He wanted his readers to understand there are forces keeping man enslaved but that Jesus Christ had come to set men free (Lk. 4:18).

Luke emphasized the lostness of man: people stand in mortal peril if Jesus Christ is not their Lord and Savior. The task is urgent, "repentance for forgiveness of sins should be proclaimed in His name to all the nations" (Lk. 24:47).

In Acts, Luke continued describing how the risen Lord was concerned about the ongoing work of His kingdom. To accomplish the task, He renewed the commission to His disciples: "you shall receive power when the Holy Spirit has come upon you; and you shall be My witnesses both in Jerusalem, and in all Judea and Samaria, and even to the remotest part of the earth" (Acts 1:8). Pentecost validated Christ's victory and boldly declared that the end time had begun. The outpouring of the Holy Spirit as spoken by Joel had taken place (Joel 2:28-32; Acts 2:16-21; 2 Cor. 1: 22; Ephes. 1:13-14).

After the Holy Spirit's coming, Luke described how the disciples received power to carry the Gospel to the remotest parts of the world. He detailed the problems encountered—religious, economic, racial, social and political. In spite of deception, persecution, imprisonments and much suffering, the Church grew to encompass the world of his day. The indwelling Holy Spirit fit believers to the task. Luke wanted readers to know that the Holy Spirit was and available to those who joined His movement to change the world (Acts 4:8-12,31; 6:5,8-10; 10:44-45; 11:22-24; 20:28).

The specifics of the missionary mandate in Acts 1:6-8 detail essential factors inherent in world evangelization. First, *the Gospel is to be proclaimed to all mankind.* The Holy Spirit indwells, empowers, enlightens, and propels His disciples into worldwide service until every tongue, tribe, and nation acknowledges that Jesus Christ is Lord. Wherever the Gospel has not been preached Christ's disciples have an obligation to go. Second, *the specific message to be proclaimed embraces the life, death, and resurrection of Jesus Christ.* Apart from Him there is no Gospel. Faith in Him is decisive for every person. Third, *world evangelization is a witness to the majesty and glory of Christ.* Witnesses are not to fabricate information, but to be caught up in every detail of the life of Jesus Christ. We are expected to simply tell what we know of Him. Fourth, *the geographical order is spelled out.* The Gospel's impact on these respective areas is then reported in the succeeding chapters: Jerusalem (1-7); Judea and Samaria (8-9); and the rest of the world (10-28). Fifth, though there is a prophetic calendar in Scripture, *God the King holds the timetable.* It is idle to speculate about times and seasons. Sixth, *the Holy Spirit is the agent of missions.* His purpose is to help men respond to the Gospel and to enable the disciples to discharge the missionary mandate. Before Him all other powers must yield. Seventh, Christ's return is certain. At a definite point in time He will again break into this world—out of eternity into time and history. Triumph is assured. Judgment will not be delayed indefinitely (cf. 2 Cor. 5:10; Jude 14-15).

The Missionary Mandate in the Gospel and Epistles of John

John's material, too, is missions-oriented (Jn. 4:35-38; 13:20; 17:18; 20:21). He wanted to bring people to faith in Jesus Christ (Jn. 20:31) and tied the missionary mandate to the completed work of Christ and the giving of the Holy Spirit (Jn. 14:12-20; 16:7-15; 20:22-23).

Having come to know Christ, and having heard, seen, and touched Him, John wanted all people (especially Greeks) to know that Jesus was indeed the Lord and Savior. Like the other Gospel writers, John presented Jesus Christ as Lord over all powers, as the One who broke in on the human scene to deliver man.

John's aim was fivefold. First, he presented his material to reach the Good Shepherd's other sheep (Jn. 10:16). Second, John sought to keep believers steadfast in their confession that Jesus Christ "has come in the flesh" (1 Jn. 4:2-3): his writings were apologetic, answering the heresies of his day. Third, John encouraged believers to maintain fellowship, regardless of ethnic or other differences (Jn. 13:34-35; 1 Jn. 1:3; 3:14-17). Fourth, he wanted believers to learn from Jesus' ministry that submission to the Father is the key to success in the Christian life and in carrying out the missionary mandate (Jn. 5:19-20,30; 14:12). Fifth, John sought to remind Israel of her failure to reach other nations (Jn. 4:5-42). Sixth, he emphasized that apart from the Holy Spirit neither messenger nor target audience would know the truth (Jn. 16:7-15). Seventh, John maintained that God Himself is involved in missions, standing behind Jesus and doing the sending (Jn. 13:20). The Father sends the Son, the Son sends the Holy Spirit who enables the disciples to gather from all peoples a people for God (Jn. 10:16; 12:32; 17:18-21).

Missiological Considerations

God's concern for the nations, communicated to Israel in the Old Testament, is unchanged in the New, but in Jesus Christ especially God revealed His heart's compassion (Jn.3:16). Indeed, He "desires all men to be saved" (1 Tim. 2:4).

Without the Old Testament's missions thrust, the Gospels and Acts would appear to be mere interjections, not necessarily normative for the Church today. And without a thorough knowledge of the Old Testament, the epistles become the focus of edification only, rather than edification with a view to mission. The blessing of Abraham, justification by faith, was to come to all nations (Acts 3:25; Gal. 3:8). The emphasis, therefore, in both Old and New Testaments is a people for other peoples (Dt. 9:26-29; Is. 42,43,44; 1 Pet. 2:9; cf. Exo. 9:16).

CHAPTER 24

THE MISSIONS

THEOLOGY OF THE

APOSTLE PAUL

Nowhere do either Paul or Peter explicitly remind the churches of their missionary mandate. Their letters were already witnesses to their own missionary activity. The missionary mandate was not only a given, it was beyond dispute. It was a responsibility the Church readily accepted: "She [the Church] was not an army whose leader had to repeatedly issue His command; she did it voluntarily because this call to mission had become part of her very flesh and blood" (Van Swigchem 1955:35).

The Called Missionary

Paul did mention the missionary mandate, but primarily to remind himself of the obligation to proclaim the Gospel to the nations. He knew God had saved and called him for a definite purpose (Acts 9:15-16; Rom.1:5). He was entrusted with a mission (1 Cor. 1:17; 2 Cor. 5:18-20); necessity rested upon him to proclaim the Gospel (Acts 13:47; Rom. 1:14-16; 1 Cor. 9:16); and because he had come to know the power of the Gospel personally, he was unashamed and ready to proclaim it to all people. Thus he began his Roman epistle by stating that his commission was "to bring about the obedience of faith among all the Gentiles, for His name sake" (Rom. 1:5).

271

The Missions Strategist

Paul was first and foremost a missionary, so his systematic theology was framed within the context of God's purposes for the nations. Fluent in Greek and Hebrew, Paul was well-trained in the Scriptures, having studied them for 20 or more years before God placed him in ministry. Much of Paul's writing reflects his thorough knowledge of God's purposes for Israel. He understood the Church's purpose to be totally tied in with the Great Commission. All his epistles seek to keep the churches walking worthy of this calling (2 Cor. 4:1-6; Phil. 1:12-18; Col. 1:25-29).

Paul modeled a sensitivity to the Holy Spirit and was willing to make any sacrifice for the missionary mandate (Acts 20:24). So confident was Paul of his understanding of God's purposes for the Church, that he could say, "Brethren, join in following my example, and observe those who walk according to the pattern you have in us" (Phil. 3:17; cf. 1 Cor. 4:16; 11:1; 1 Thess. 1:6).

Paul was also culturally sensitive, a keen observer of culture and its effect on people's understanding of the Gospel. In his writing he included Palestinian Jewish, Hellenistic Jewish, and Hellenistic Gentile concepts. In his journeys he targeted the vital urban areas of trade and culture, because from there the Gospel would radiate to all surrounding areas. He constantly sought to take the Gospel to the unreached places of his day (Rom. 15:20-24).

The Literary Missionary

Paul's letters were intended to keep churches spiritually healthy in order to represent and proclaim the Gospel worthily. Each letter is practical dealing with problems and issues reflective of new converts in growing churches. True Christians must know correct doctrine and how to live a godly life (2 Tim. 4:2-4; cf. 1 Tim. 1:10).

Paul's epistles are missionary letters in that they unlock the secret of God's revelation in Jesus Christ—God in Christ reconciling the world. Paul's sole interest was to spread the Gospel and encourage others to press on to the same goal.

Seven Basic Assumptions

Paul's teaching centered around six basic assumptions: God is self-revealing; God is the Lord of all; the Gospel is for all peoples; there are opposing powers; the Church is God's new humanity; Jesus Christ truly liberates from all bondage; and salvation brings wholeness of life (cf. Gilliland 1983:49-64).

God is Self-revealing

Reflecting on God's creative activity and subsequent revelation to the patriarchs, Moses and the prophets, Paul presented God as always taking the initiative in His overtures to man (Rom. 1:19,20). The Old Testament clearly showed that God revealed Himself directly in history as well as through the Scriptures (cf. 2 Tim. 3:16). Paul maintained that God has never left Himself without a witness:

> And in the generations gone by He permitted all the nations to go their own ways; and yet He did not leave Himself without witness, in that He did good and gave you rains from heaven and fruitful seasons, satisfying your hearts with food and gladness (Acts 14:16-17).

The apostle may have been thinking of Psalm 19, which describes how natural revelation gave witness to God. Paul believed that the God of creation, the One who revealed Himself in the Old Covenant, was Jesus Christ of the New Covenant (Col. 1:15-19).

God is the Lord of All

Paul firmly believed that God has no equal. All other gods are simply opposing demonic spirits seeking to alienate man from God (1 Cor. 10:20-21; 2 Cor .4:4). Therefore, God must be proclaimed as the God for all peoples, who alone has the right to rule and who alone can secure their salvation.

Everything exists to serve only God's purposes. He alone is Lord over all spiritual powers, lords, rulers, and authorities and holds the destiny of all. To him every knee will bow, and every tongue will confess His Lordship (Phil. 2:10-11). Therefore, allegiance to Him is of paramount importance and the ground for new life.

The Gospel is for All People

If God is self-revealing, and if He is the only God, then His Gospel must apply to all. God has no favorite people: all are subjects of His saving intent. Christ died for *everyone in every place* (Rom. 5:18; 1 Tim. 2:4). Therefore, the Gospel is God's power to *all* who believe (Rom.1:16). *Everyone* who calls out to the Lord will be saved (Rom.10:13). God has revealed His grace for the salvation of *all* mankind (Tit.2:11). Concerning the Great Commission, Paul could say that the Gospel "was proclaimed in all creation under heaven" (Col. 1:23; cf. Rom. 16:26). The Gospel was being applied to all universally.

Paul maintained that just as God had shown His reconciling grace through Christ and had taken the initiative in man's redemption, so those who experience reconciliation through this grace must, in turn, become messengers of grace to the unreconciled (2 Cor. 5:18-20). Preaching the Gospel to all is an absolute necessity (Rom. 15:8-12; 2 Cor. 5:11; cf. 1 Cor. 9:16,19). Even as did the apostle, the Church stood under obligation "to bring about the obedience of faith among all the Gentiles for His name's sake, among whom you also are the called of Jesus Christ" (Rom. 1:5-6).

There are Opposing Powers

Although the Gospel is for all, not all will come to salvation. Paul had observed that throughout the Old Testament man had encountered opposing powers, "demons who were not God" (Dt. 32:17), and taught that messengers of the Gospel would experience the same conflict. Principalities, authorities, dominions, and powers have established a measure of control over human life (2 Cor. 4:4; Eph.2 :2; 6:12). The struggle with demonic powers is severe, but the outcome is never in doubt (Rom. 8:31-39; 2 Cor. 2:14). Echoing the apostle, John Bright maintained:

> the battle has already been won at Calvary by Him who in His sacrifice had taken men out of every nation and made them into the true people of God...The powers of evil simply cannot win, they have already been broken (Bright 1953:241).

The Church is God's New Humanity

The apostle taught that the regenerating work of the Holy Spirit produced a life set "free from the law of sin and of death" (Rom. 8:2). The Gospel makes man a new creation. God has caused light to shine in darkness. Something dramatic has happened. The believer is not only positionally righteous before God; he is "possessionally" so: "if any man is in Christ, he is a new creature; the old things passed away; behold, new things have come. Now all these things are from God, who reconciled us to Himself" (2 Cor. 5:17-18; cf. Rom. 6). "The total remaking of people is the way the Gospel works" (Gilliland 1983:64).

God's new humanity is a new creation, not only by omnipotence but also by grace, in opposition to what man became because of the Fall. God restores man to his pre-Fall potential by instilling in him the enabling power of the Holy Spirit (Eph. 3:14-21; cf. Ezek. 36:26-27; Jn. 15:4-5,26). The believer therefore knows a spiritual change touching every area of life: the ethical (1 Cor. 13:5-6); the moral (Rom. 13:12-14; Gal. 5:18-23); the aesthetic (Phil. 4:8); the physical (Rom. 8:11); the material (2 Cor. 8:2; 9:6-12); and the social (Rom. 12:3-21; 13:1-10). God gives His people a new perspective on life, with a focus upon His purposes and a release from the previous life's carnality (Eph. 4:17-24).

Jesus Christ Truly Liberates

Paul's commitment to freedom has been discussed by various authors such as F. F. Bruce (*The Apostle of the Free Spirit*) and Richard N. Longenecker (*Paul, Apostle of Liberty*). Paul understood that the regenerate person knows a freedom which brings a supernatural quality to life. This literal freedom arises from man's relationship with a living and holy God, a relationship which makes a man legally free. The believer in Christ has a personal liberty: freedom from personal sin and from the compulsion to sin (Rom. 6:1-2,18; 8:2). This personal liberty is experienced as freedom from self, from the law, from all spiritual forces of evil (cf. Gal. 4:3,8; 5:13). There is freedom from condemnation (Rom.8:1); from sin and death (Rom. 8:2); from idols (1 Thess. 1:9); from the law (Rom. 10:14); freedom in the Spirit of Christ (2 Cor.3:17); and freedom for the purpose of freedom (Gal. 5:1). This freedom touches every area of life, but never issues in licence to do as one pleases (cf. Jn. 8:36; 14:21; Rom. 15:3; 1 Cor. 6:12; 10:23). Freedom is the birthright of God's new creation.

To be set free from sin and all other bondage is to experience the beginning of life in Christ (Col. 3:1-4) that leads to sanctification (Col. 3:5-25) and continues into eternity (Rom.6:22). "On the question of liberty, the whole substance of Christianity was at stake" (Gal. 2:4) (Gilliland 1983:62).Only as God's free people can the Church execute her task with confidence, boldness and conviction.

Salvation Brings Wholeness of Life

Paul taught people to regard their bodies with reverence as the temple of God, the dwelling place of God's Spirit (1 Cor. 3:16). The body must be kept pure to serve God and bring Him glory (1 Cor. 6:13,19,20; 2 Tim. 2:19-22). When Paul used the term "new creation," he spoke of radical change which issued in a new order. This change was not only experienced and demonstrated by the individual, but it affected all of the person's surroundings. Christian believers had to note that what affected the mind affected the body and so affected all of the social environment (Eph. 4:17-6:9; Phil.4:4-9). The believer was not an island; each one had an effect on society (cf. 1 Cor. 13; 2 Cor. 10:5; 1 Thess. 5:11-18; and Philemon).

The renewed person was to become fully developed (mature), wholesome, and well-balanced (Eph 4:13;. Col. 1:28-29; 3:10-11). The "new creation" touched all of life and integrated its various components—the spiritual, psychological, physical, material, and social (1 Thess.5:23): all to be lived out under the Lordship of Jesus Christ.

The Missionary Task

Paul claimed that his task involved encounter with the powers and principalities. He saw man in bondage and under the control of these powers (2 Cor. 4:4; Eph. 2:2) who need to be rescued from the domain of darkness (Col. 1:13) as Paul himself had been (Acts 9:1-17). Paul was totally confident that the Gospel had the power to deliver from Satan, yet a man redeemed from Satan's domain might need to be brought into the realization of his freedom in Jesus Christ.

Romans 10:11-15 describes so aptly all that the missionary task encompasses:

> "Whoever believes in Him will not be disappointed." For there is no distinction between Jew and Greek; for the same Lord is Lord of all, abounding in riches for all who call upon Him; for "Whoever will call upon the name of the Lord will be saved." How then shall they call upon Him in whom they have not believed? And how shall they believe in Him whom they have not heard? And how shall they hear without a preacher? And how shall they preach unless they are sent? Just as it is written, "How beautiful are the feet of those who bring glad tidings of good things!"

Specifics of the Missionary Commission

The specifics of the commission to which Paul committed himself are in Acts 26:18:

> "to open their eyes so that they may turn from darkness to light and from the dominion of Satan to God, in order that they may receive forgiveness of sins and an inheritance among those who have been sanctified by faith in Me."

Although this commission came later than the other Great Commission passages, they all shared some of the same emphases (Mt. 28:18-20; Mk. 16:15; Lk. 24:46-48; Acts 1:8).

Paul's commission concerned the nations alienated from God. It was especially significant in light of his understanding that the demonic powers exercised control over people (Eph. 2:2), but he also spelled out the specific issues involved in evangelism anywhere.

His task was, first, *to open eyes*: People need to be able to see the Gospel (cf. 2 Cor. 4:4). Their eyes are blinded to the person and work of Jesus Christ on the cross and in His resurrection. They need to see who the God of the Bible is, what He has purposed and how He accomplishes His objectives. Second, Paul had *to turn people from darkness to light*. People are in the wrong place and need to be returned to the correct one. They need to realize what darkness has done to them, and what will happen if they come into the light. They need to understand that there is a vast difference between their darkness and Jesus Christ's light. Third, Paul had *to remove them from the dominion of Satan to the kingdom of God.* People are under the control of Satan. If a man is not in Christ, then he is in darkness. Fourth, people needed to be *forgiven of their sin*. God works man's redemption, leading to forgiveness. Only the Lord can release man from the guilt of sin. Fifth, Paul had to *introduce converts into their inheritance in Christ* and His Church. New Christians were to be incorporated into a fellowship of believers.

From this approach came numerous churches, which in turn evangelized others: "For the word of the Lord has sounded forth from you, not only in Macedonia and Achaia, but also in every place your faith toward God has gone forth" (1 Thess.1:8).

To Paul, life in all its fulness was available for the Christian. The mature Christian was to have the mind of Christ and be committed to the task of the Lord of the Church. Both the model of Christian living and the message of the Gospel made Christians debtors to all peoples everywhere; they were to take this message and set the captives free. To Paul, it was beyond question that every knee would bow and every tongue confess Jesus Christ as Lord, to the glory of God the Father. And thus Paul affirmed:

> Now to Him who is able to establish you according to my gospel and the preaching of Jesus Christ, according to the revelation of the mystery which has been kept secret for long ages past, but now is manifested, and by the Scriptures of the prophets, according to the commandment of the eternal God, *has been made known to all nations, leading to obedience of faith;* to the only wise God, through Jesus Christ, be glory forever. Amen. (Rom. 16:25-27).

CHAPTER 25

THE CHURCH IN STEP

WITH GOD

The Church came into existence because of the will and activity of God alone (Mt. 16:18). She was God-initiated and set apart for His purposes. Paul prayed:

> that you may know what is the hope of His calling, what are the riches of the glory of His inheritance in the saints, and what is the surpassing greatness of His power toward us who believe. ...And He put all things in subjection under His feet, and gave Him as head over all things to the church which is His body, the fulness of Him who fills all in all (Eph. 1:18-19,22-23).

Later Paul added,

> To me, the very least of all saints, this grace was given, to preach to the Gentiles the unfathomable riches of Christ...*in order that the manifold wisdom of God might now be made known through the church to the rulers and the authorities in the heavenly places*....to Him be the glory in the church (Eph. 3:8,10,21, emphasis added).

The Church is God's agent to reconcile the world to Himself (2 Cor. 5:18-20).

The Epistles and the Church
Each of the epistles dealt with the effectiveness of the Church's life and ministry. Each assumed the relevance of the Old Testament for the Church and built upon the oral Gospel accounts. Each sought to further

explain more fully the Christian's relationship to and position in Christ, and to detail a practical outworking in life and ministry. Further, each sought to keep the Church effective in mission theologically, structurally, corporately, and personally. To be the Church of Jesus Christ on mission required her to be robust in her faith, intimate in her relationship, and unswerving in her obedience.

The names of most of the epistles—Galatians, Ephesians, Philippians, Colossians—indicated that taking the Gospel into other parts continued as normative. Thus Paul asked that prayer be made on his behalf to declare the Gospel boldly (Eph. 6:19), that God would open a door for the Gospel (Col. 4:3), and that the Gospel would "spread rapidly" (2 Thess. 3:1). He commended the church in Thessalonica for proclaiming the Gospel to the surrounding communities and beyond (1 Thess.1:8). He was glad that Christ was being proclaimed even though the communicators motive was selfish ambition (Phil. 1:17-18). He reminded Timothy that "God our Savior...desires all men to be saved and to come to the knowledge of the truth" (1 Tim. 2:3-4). He pointed out that hardships and sufferings (2 Cor. 4:7-17) are normative if others are to "obtain the salvation which is in Christ Jesus and with it eternal glory" (2 Tim. 2:10).

Each letter presupposed the mandatory, ongoing task of world evangelization. God's mission to the nations was fundamental and accepted, motivating the writers to concern themselves with maintaining the witness and ministry of the churches in world evangelization.

The Revelation of Jesus Christ

Whenever the Church is faithful to its calling of world evangelization and testifies to the Truth, tribulation is bound to follow. It follows that the book of Revelation has been a source of comfort and inspiration to Christians of every generation, for its theme is the victory of Jesus Christ and His Church over Satan (the dragon) and his demonic powers.

Although Revelation speaks primarily of events still to come, the message to the Church in all generations is that things are not what they seem to be. God has not relinquished control of His creation. "The throne rules. The Lamb reigns. As a result, believers need not fear in times of tribulation, persecution and anguish" (Hendriksen 1969:93). He governs the world in the interest of His people. The domain of the beast of darkness may appear to be victorious in its battle against God's people, killing them and not even permitting their bodies to be buried. The enemies of God may rejoice and make merry, sending gifts to each other because the people responsible for their torment have been vanquished (Rev.11:7-10). But their rejoicing is short-lived. God's people will triumph over all powers because Jesus Christ is present with His people and is the Victor. He conquers death, Hades, the world, the dragon, the beast, the false prophet, and all those who worship the beast (Rev.1:18; 6:2; 11:15; 12:9ff.; 15:2-4.; 19:20; 20:2,10-15; 21:4,8). Because He is victorious, so are His people, even when they seem to be hopelessly defeated. God's people are evermore overcomers:

> Look at the great company of believers portrayed in Revelation 7. Are their garments splashed and filthy? They wash their robes, and make them white in the blood of the Lamb (7:14;22:14). Are they in great tribulation? They come out of it (7:14). Are they killed? They stand upon their feet (11:11). Are they persecuted by the dragon, the beast, and the false prophet? In the end you see them standing victoriously on Mnt. Zion....Does it seem as if their prayers are not heard (6:10)? The judgments sent upon the earth are God's answer to their pleading (8:3-5). These very prayers constitute the key that will unlock the mysteries of any sound philosophy of history. Do they seem to be defeated? In reality they reign! Yes they reign upon the earth (5:10), in heaven with Christ a thousand years (20:4), in the new heaven and earth for ever and ever (22:5) (Hendriksen 1969:8-9).

The purpose of Revelation is to call the Church to declare redemption through Jesus Christ and to face the inevitable struggle against all forces of evil with confidence in Christ's victory. The redemption they know and declare "is nothing narrow or national....It is world-wide in its scope and embraces every group; ethnic (tribe), linguistic (tongue), political (people), and social (nation)" (Hendriksen 1969:92).

Revelation is full of encouragement for suffering Christians involved in God's mission, braving Satanic attack. They receive the assurance that God sees their tears (Rev. 7:17; 21:4). Their prayers are influential in world affairs, and even now they reign upon the earth by means of their prayers to the Ruler (Rev. 8:3-4). Their death is precious in His sight. Their final victory is assured (Rev. 15:2); their blood will be avenged (Rev. 19:2). Their Lord and Savior Jesus Christ will come again to take His people to Himself in "the marriage supper of the Lamb" and to live with them forever in a renewed universe (Rev. 21:1-

7; 22:1-5,14). Revitalized by this encouragement, assured of ultimate triumph, the Church can speed on with her task of world evangelization.

The Mission of the Holy Spirit

While on His earthly mission, Jesus cried, in desperation as it were, "I have come to cast fire upon the earth; and how I wish it were already kindled! But I have a baptism to undergo, and how distressed I am until it is accomplished!" (Lk. 12:49-50). His earthly ministry being completed, He was "exalted to the right hand of God, and...received from the Father the promise of the Holy Spirit to enable the evangelization of mankind (cf. Mt. 9:35-37). God's spirit worked in the Old Testament, but there was no permanent residence with His people until the day of Pentecost, when the Holy Spirit came to remain and abide in His Church. He came not only to infill and empower believers for witness (Acts 1:8), but to rest on mankind (Acts 2:17), to "convict the world concerning sin, and righteousness, and judgment" (Jn. 16:8).

The Holy Spirit had the mission of expanding the Church and enabling her to fulfill her missionary mandate. As the Spirit of power, the Holy Spirit brought into being a people of intellectual power, with wisdom and knowledge to meet all the challenges of philosophies, religion and society. They had spiritual power as well, and characterized by great boldness and faith, they accomplished the impossible. They had emotional power, with a deep love one for one another and for all people. They knew how to identify genuinely with believers and unbelievers in their problems. And they had physical strength and endurance beyond normal human capacity. Even amidst physical abuse, beatings, stonings, and imprisonments, they endured, counting it a privilege to suffer for the sake of His name (Acts 5:40-41; 2 Cor. 11:23-27; Col. 1:24; cf. Rom. 8:11).

Furthermore, this God-initiated community was to bring Him the honor by always ministering in faith, expecting His intervention in human affairs (Acts 3:1-26; 4:29-31). They had a divine dynamic, the indwelling Holy Spirit. Because the Church was not a merely human institution, she was characterized by supernatural operations. The Holy Spirit who had empowered believers' salvation also empowered their ministry. Christians attested that it was quite possible to be a believer and not have power in ministry (Acts 18:24-28). But they also knew it was impossible to live the dynamic life Christ intended, and to be a part of His mission, without the daily infilling of the Holy Spirit (Eph. 5:1-18).

The energizing, life-giving Holy Spirit made it possible for the Church to communicate the Gospel and to participate in God's mission in the face of all challenges. Preaching the cross and resurrection was an absolute statement of God bringing into being a new people in a new day. All powers had been defeated, so man need no longer be enslaved. God's people, filled by the Holy Spirit, committed to God's mission, exposed the powers and brought liberation from the slavery imposed on all mankind (Eph. 5:11; cf. Lk. 4:18).

The Holy Spirit's coming was to impart knowledge (Jn.14:26), empower living (Jn. 14:16-17; 16:8-10), and give gifts to His Church for its mission to the nations (cf. Jn. 14:12), that all might participate in world evangelization (Rom. 12:3-9; 1 Cor.12; Eph. 4:7-13; cf. Rom. 15:8-12; 16:25-26). The Church is to mediate the grace and hope of the Gospel to others (2 Cor.4:15). Through personal piety before God and outreach toward man, she is to be as Jesus on earth. What Christ was in microcosm (in that He was one ministering with human limitations), the Church is to be in macrocosm ("greater things than these shall you do") through the power and gifts of the Holy Spirit.

The Confidence of Mission

The commission to evangelize the nations came within the context of principalities and powers constantly opposing the proclamation and representation of the Gospel.

New Testament faith was *a triumphant faith* (2 Cor.2:14) although it was always in severe tension. There were forces creating circumstances which opposed biblical faith disclosing itself: "tribulation, or distress, or persecution, or famine, or nakedness, or peril, or sword, ...[or] death, ...life,...angels,...principalities,...things present,...things to come,... powers,...height,...depth, [or]... other created thing" (Rom. 8:35,38-39). The opposing forces were—and still are—many.

As participants in a triumphant faith, believers knew *a present, victorious reality*. The King is in the midst of His Church (Mt. 28:20). The Messiah has come (Mt. 16:13-19). God's people believed and joyously expected His intervention in life's impossible situations; He had already disarmed all powers in His death and resurrection (Col. 2:14-15; 1 Jn. 3:8). There was also the eschatalogical hope of Christ's universal rule. Still, in the present, He does not always intervene in ways we notice. Jesus had said, "If My kingdom were of this world, then My servants would be fighting" (Jn. 18:36). In the interim the conflict was to be costly and challenging.

A joyous confidence characterized the early Church as biblical faith stimulated confidence. Christ had grappled with the powers of darkness, and Satan had fled ignominiously: "I was watching Satan fall from heaven like lightning" (Lk. 10:18). The disciples knew beyond a shadow of a doubt that the powers of evil had been dealt a decisive blow. Christ's work disarmed and rendered the powers of evil powerless before the power of God (Heb. 2:14). The present struggle between demonic powers and God's people may continue for many years, but victory is sure. The Servant in His "powerlessness" has already won (Rev. 1:17-18; 12:10-11; 19:11-21).

The cross and resurrection signaled a new day. Through God's second Adam, *a new age had arrived and the whole history of mankind since the first Adam had been reversed* (Rom. 5:12-21). The Church was confident that Jesus Christ, by the Holy Spirit, was alive in His people. They were equipped to do what He had done and to do even the "greater things" He had promised (Jn. 14:12).

Christians were confident that even in the present they were *participating in the victory of Jesus Christ,* and they had facts to validate their confidence. They knew the reality of experiential deliverance: they had been delivered "out of this present evil age" (Gal. 1:4). They had "tasted...the powers of the age to come" (Heb. 6:5). They had transferred citizenship: Their citizenship was in heaven and for an age to come (Phil.3:20). They had freedom from the demonic powers (Col. 1:13). Reconciliation to the Father released their spirits to approach God boldly. They were no longer in natural enmity to God, for God's wrath had been assuaged (Rom.5:9-11; 1Thess. 1:10; 5:9). Believers had been adopted into God's family and were now sons and daughters with full family privileges (Rom. 8:15-16; Gal. 4:5-7). They were accounted righteous before God through faith in Jesus Christ (Rom. 5:1-5). God's image in them had been restored as they took on Christ's image (2 Cor. 3:18). They could now become what they were created to be, God's model on earth, His kingdom people.

Because of this assured victory, as His redeemed Church believers knew they were *entrusted with a joyful and triumphant task.* Between Christ's resurrection and His Second Coming they were to proclaim this victory to the entire world. By good deeds (Eph. 2:10; Tit. 2:11-14; 3:8) they were to draw men to the victorious Christ and demonstrate that He is Lord in all spheres of life. They were to summon men to submit to this victory. They had the glorious task of setting the captives free from all kinds of bondage in the authority of Jesus Christ (Lk. 9:1-2; 10:1-20; cf. Lk. 4:18; Jn. 17:18). The principle by which they lived and served was: "Thy Kingdom come, Thy will be done, on earth as it is in heaven" (Mt. 6:10).

Knowing of the coming judgment but also confident of God's love, they were to *persuade people to be reconciled to God*, calling them to a verdict. The Gospel was not a program of reform or social righteousness such as society might have expected, nor was it merely the changing of outward structures. The Gospel transferred people into Christ's death (Rom. 6:6,8) and resurrection (Rom. 6:4-5) and thus into His righteousness (Rom. 3:21-22; 4:25-5:2). Relationship with Jesus Christ was by faith alone (Eph. 2:8,9; Rom. 5:1; Tit. 3:5-7; Gal. 2:20). Their destiny depended upon their response: "But as many as received Him, to them He gave the right to become children of God, even to those who believe in His name" (Jn. 1:12). The Church did not stop there, for "the Gospel" refers to all that Jesus taught (Mt. 7:21; Mt. 28:20). God's people were to announce all that Christ had taught and accomplished. As God's new creatures, they had to respond in obedience and righteousness (Jn. 14:21,23,24; cf. 2 Cor. 5:17). Through them the cultural and evangelistic mandates were to be demonstrated and proclaimed to all men.

Christ's summons to "go therefore and make disciples of all the nations" demanded *a positive and triumphant response* which it received from the early Church: "If God is for us, who is against us?" (Rom. 8:31; cf. Is. 50:7-9). The Church therefore labored in the assurance that God's kingdom would triumph even amid casualties (2 Cor. 4:6-18). She willingly proclaimed His victory at all costs. Though the conflict was sharp, she believed that victory was sure. There would be an unconditional surrender of the enemy and a restoration of all creation under divine dominion (Acts 3:21; Rev.5:13; 19:1-8,11-21). There would be the complete submission of all powers in heaven and on earth to the Christ of Glory (1 Cor. 15:24-28; Eph. 1:22-23; Phil. 2:10). Like her Master-Servant, she, too, suffered persecution and martyrdom, but also like her Servant-Savior, she had the promise that she would never be defeated (Heb.11; 13:5-6).

For the early Church, Christ's commission *demanded urgency*. Time was short: The last days had begun. She was convinced that the Gospel was man's only hope (Acts 4:12). She understood the solemn truth that the world is slated for judgment (Heb.9:27; cf. Rom.6:23): "Knowing...the fear of the Lord" she was obligated to "persuade men" (2 Cor.5:11) to escape God's wrath. She understood her position and purpose: "To Him who loves us, and released us from our sins by His blood, and He has made us to be a kingdom and priests to His God and Father" (Rev. 1:5-6).

The Church's Response to the State

The Church has always lived in tension between the power of Caesar (the state) and her Lord's mandates. Caesar tends to encourage the growth and maintenance of enslaving, dehumanizing structures. To justify what it does the state seeks to develop counterfeit structures of righteousness, maintaining them by implicit or explicit force. The state reacts very negatively when it is called to account for its actions, sensing threats quickly and going to great lengths to safeguard itself. The tendency to persecute those who disagree lies close to the surface.

The early Church had no ordinary means to fight the state, no military, political, economic, or social power. Throughout her history she experienced the truth of 2 Corinthians 4:8-18. From the perspective of outsiders the Church was a powerless and helpless minority. Her members were the disinherited of the empire, the weak and frail, the offscouring of society, a pitiful, helpless minority without any visible power for a hope of victory. Humanly speaking she had no resources to prevail against Caesar (1 Cor. 1:26-28).

The make-up of the Church allowed no hope of being a conquering Church as the world understands the term; the exact opposite was true. As a suffering servant, she was to "drink His cup" (Mk. 10:38,39) and so identify with her Lord in His mission. She, too, was as a lamb led to the slaughter. She was a martyr Church called upon "to take up [her] cross" (Mk. 8:34) and suffer a similar fate if needed. She constantly knew the reality of being a hounded, abused, and persecuted suffering servant—filling up the sufferings of Christ (2 Cor. 11:23-27; Col. 1:24).

The power of the Church was totally unlike that which man normally exercised (Mt. 20:25-28). Her power lay in obedience to her Lord. She understood that she was called to a mission pilgrimage, even facing death (Phil. 1:20-21) if necessary, but she did not yield to despair. Even though she could not humanly produce victory, she was confident that God would make her more than conqueror in every circumstance (Rom. 8:37-39). The truth of Psalm 44 sustained her in times of great trial:

> Through Thee we will push back our adversaries; through Thy name we will trample down those who rise up against us. For I will not trust in my bow, nor will my sword save me. But Thou hast saved us from our adversaries, and Thou hast put to shame those who hate us. In God we have boasted all day long, and we will give thanks to Thy name forever (Ps.44:5-8).

Armed with the power of faith, she was not passive regarding her mission. She believed that the completion of her mission would herald Jesus Christ's return to rule in righteousness (Mt. 24:14; 2 Pet. 3:9-13).

The early Church made no direct attack on abuses in society. Even those utterly contrary to Christ's teachings were dealt with in a non-confrontational way. The apostles urged obedience to the state provided it did not demand a contradiction of Christian faith (Acts 4:18-20; 5:28-29; Rom. 13:1-7; 1 Pet. 2:13-14).

The Church knew she was called to model what it meant to follow Christ in attitude, response, and deed (1 Pet. 2:21; 3:14-16; 4:12-5:3; 2 Pet. 1:3). As followers of Christ, the body of believers sought to maintain its distinct identity (1 Pet. 2:9-12). Christians were urged to remember who they were in Jesus Christ, behave accordingly, and "walk in a manner worthy of the calling" (Eph. 4:1). They were to refute by their lifestyle all charges against them (1 Pet. 2:12,15; 3:16). They were to be confident of God's faithfulness and concern for them, committing their souls to Him, awaiting His reward (1 Pet. 1:7,13).

The Church was engaged in a fearful struggle—portents in heaven, torment and tribulation on earth (cf. Is. 13:4; 2 Thess. 2:9)—as evil hurled itself at the kingdom of God.There were casualties—all but one of the apostles were martyred. She experienced the birth pangs of a new creation, which would come with much pain, agony and distress (cf. Mk.13:8-13). The Church knew constant conflict and confrontation with evil powers in people and institutions who frequently appeared as angels of light (2 Cor. 11:13-15; Gal. 1:8), promising escape from suffering and the necessary confrontation with the powers of darkness. These encounters increased, and will increase until the Lord of the Church returns to establish His visible kingdom (2 Cor. 2:10-11; 2 Tim.3:1-5,13; 4:3-4).

The Church had only one victory—the Servant's victory. This is still *the only way* the Church will conquer in the face of militant religions and the state. The way of the Suffering Servant caused the Roman Empire to crumble; the servant's victory is the most powerful and long-lasting known to man.

The Church in Ministry

Being God's redeemed people was not an end in itself; it was also that a witness would be given to the God of Glory among the nations. God declared, "I am the LORD, that is My name; I will not give My glory to another, nor My praise to graven images" (Is. 42:8);

"You are My witnesses," declares the LORD, "And My servant whom I have chosen, in order that you may know and believe Me, and understand that I am He. Before Me there was no God formed, and there will be none after Me. I, even I, am the LORD; and there is no savior besides Me" (Is. 43:10,11).

With God's support, the Church could count on limitless resources. Pentecost began a new era with a new people of God and with limitless resources to change the whole world (Mt. 28:18; Acts 1:8; Eph. 1:18-23; cf. Lk. 10:17-22).

God had given His promise that, no matter what, He would build His Church; He would never lack messengers to proclaim His glory to the nations. God has sovereignly committed Himself to work through His Church (Col. 1:24-29; Eph. 1:22,23; 3:10). For reasons known to God, He does not work redemptively apart from His Church (Rom.10:14,15; cf. 2 Chron.7:14), yet the church in any given place could limit her own participation in God's mission, even as Israel did.

The Church must resist the temptation to limit God's mission in this world. A person or church may limit God's mission through grieving or quenching the Holy Spirit (Eph. 4:30; 1 Thess. 5:19). Actions which grieve the Holy Spirit may include breaking corporate bonds within the church (Eph. 4:1-6); withholding fellowship God intended for those who are in Christ (Eph.2:13-22; Heb. 10:25); and refraining from exercising one's gifts within the Body of Christ (Eph. 4:16; 1 Tim. 1:18-19;4:14). The Holy Spirit may be quenched when there is deliberate disobedience to the explicit commands of God. The word "quench" has to do with fire, impulse, energy; if a person quenches Him, that one is guilty of limiting Christ in carrying out His mission.

The Church had to constantly resist the tempting misconceptions which plagued Israel. The constant conflict and confrontation involved in Israel's taking the land tempted her to doubt the practicality of warfare and to consider withdrawal from battle. Futhermore, Israel interpreted God's mission to mean that He favored one nation only (Israel), and that He was not the Savior for all nations. In like manner the Church had to recognize her sinful human nature, which desired an exclusive relationship with a "God" concerned only for her personal welfare, fulfillment, and enjoyment. The redeemed people of God knew that Israel's fate was a warning to them; and they had been empowered to resist these temptations (1 Cor.10:1-13).

The redeemed people of God had to accept the commission and purpose in being God's Church. In Christ God had revealed and carried out His redeeming purposes, and now He had committed to His Church the task of proclaiming the message of reconciliation (2 Cor. 5:19-20; cf. 1 Pet. 2:9). The Church must extend the offer of eternal grace through Christ actively, deliberately, and urgently to all peoples. for judgment would not be delayed. Through its proclamation of eternal grace to the nations, the Church prepared for God's glory to cover the earth (Num. 14:21; 2 Cor. 4:15; cf. Is. 45:22-24).

The Engiftment for Missions

Though supported by the visible expression of a redeemed and sanctified life the Church's chief activity was verbal communication. The symbol and instrument of her work was to be the tongue, as Pentecost clearly illustrated.

But the imparting of "tongues" was further accompanied by fire, the symbol of energy, purity, and urgency. As Jesus said: "I have come to cast fire upon the earth; and how I wish it were already kindled! But I have a baptism to undergo, and how distressed I am until it be accomplished!" (Lk. 12:49,50). While the baptism referred to His work on the cross, the casting of fire occurred at Pentecost; His consuming passion ("how distressed I am") was none other than the reconciliation of lost man to Himself. He desired, even demanded that those who were reconciled to Him would declare Him to all those still in darkness. The Church had to commit herself daily to this task and resist anything that deterred her from realizing her God-given mission to the nations.

Knowing she was God's institution through which He would carry on His program for all creation, the Church sought those who had been gifted to communicate the Gospel in special ways, to teach and lead in world evangelization more effectively. The Church quickly recognized that God had given her apostles, prophets, evangelists, pastors, and teachers.

The twelve *apostles*, having been elected for a very specific task in relationship to Israel, the Church, and the nations, spearheaded the early planting and growth of the Church. But they recognized that there were other apostles—"sent out ones"—missionaries, who also carried the Gospel. These messengers were especially gifted to take the Gospel across cultural barriers (Acts 8:5,12,26-39; 14:14; Rom. 16:7). Such apostles were needed to penetrate the remotest parts of the earth.

God gave the *prophets* special revelation to declare to the Church and wisdom in applying the Word of God to daily living, calling the people back to the evangelistic and cultural mandates, and the self-denial, sacrifice, and single-minded dedication to God's purposes these mandates demanded. Prophets moved people into deliberate conflict with the powers of darkness. Where the prophet was at work, conflict was always present!

Whereas prophets were deliverers of the Word, *evangelists* were carriers of the Word. Evangelists confronted unbelievers with the fact that God alone is Lord and tolerates no competition. They spoke of the victory of the cross and resurrection. They called people to repent and confess sin, bringing them to face the claims and invitation of Christ. They spoke in the context of any given culture with a message informed and empowered by the Holy Spirit (Acts 8:5-40).

Pastors and *teachers* ministered to believers, leading them in growth to model Jesus Christ, preparing them for ministry to obey His mandates in encounter with the nations. Whereas pastors shepherded the flock of God and helped them to deal with life, teachers taught the precepts of God's Word, providing the content for Christian living.

The Church was to be involved in purposeful instruction in all her ministry. She had no alternative but to prepare each member, from youngest to oldest, for the work of the ministry. That task was the same as Israel's—that the nations might know that He alone is God, that He desires to bring all to salvation. The Church had to be taught how to participate in this mission. She had to be reminded of man's lost condition, of his pathetic attempts to meet his own spiritual need (Rom. 1:18-2:3), and of God's provision for man's salvation. She needed to maintain a vibrant relationship with Him (Rom. 4:25-5:11). God's purposes and sovereignty over all nations were not to be forgotten (Rom. 9:17-10:15). God's resources, backing, and control of circumstances encouraged her to be faithful to the end (Rom. 15:8-33).

A Community of the King

The Church recognized that both leaders and members must be committed to mutual ministry (Eph. 4:11-16) which would produce a local model of true worship in which God was ascribed worth, praise, and adoration (Eph. 5:18-20; cf. Ps. 100; 145-150).

And Thy godly ones shall bless Thee. They shall speak of the glory of Thy kingdom, and talk of Thy power; *to make known to the sons of men Thy mighty acts, and the glory of the majesty of Thy Kingdom....*My mouth will speak the praise of the LORD; and all flesh will bless His holy name forever and ever (Ps.145:10-12,21, emphasis added).

Having received blessing from God (2 Cor. 1:3-6; 8:9; 9:6-14), the Church was involved in service to all (Mt. 25:34-46; Gal. 6:9-10). As His model, she would know and demonstrate true koinonia. There was a commitment to and demonstration of "familiness" within the membership (Acts 2:44-47; 4:32-37); the Church was the family in macrocosm. In the true family there were no servants or masters. There was freedom to be what God had designed, with mutual acceptance and accountability. There was a genuine caring for each other. There was unity amid diversity (Eph. 4:3; Col. 3:11-14); purity and love (Eph. 4:28-32; Col. 3:12-14); mutual submissiveness and care in interpersonal relationships (Gal. 6:1-3,10; Eph. 5:21-6:6; Col. 3:16-25; 4:1; Heb. 13:16); stability in confronting the principalities and powers (Eph. 6:10-18); and purposeful commitment to bringing all under the headship of Christ (Eph. 6:18-20; Col. 1:16-22,28-29).

While the Church had her citizenship in heaven with the Lord, here on earth she was God's pilgrim people, glorifying God wherever her commission led (1 Cor. 10:31-33). Thus as a community of the King who were redeemed, empowered, and single-minded, she sought to unwrap the potential of all creation for the glory of God. The Church supported herself through different jobs and careers (Acts 9:43; 18:3; 1 Cor. 4:12; 9:11-19), but her true vocation was to make His grace known in all settings and in all lands, until all had heard that Jesus Christ alone is Lord of all (Mt. 24:14).

The Triumphant Church

The Church knew that because Jesus Christ had triumphed in His death and resurrection, the last chapters of history had already been recorded. There was no doubt about the outcome of conflicts and confrontations. Her God of grace, mercy, and power had promised, "As I live, says the Lord, every knee shall bow to Me, and every tongue shall give praise to God" (Rom. 14:11; cf. Is. 45:23-24).

> As we think of the glorious hope of the second coming, our hearts are filled with joy; our souls are consumed with a breathless impatience; our eyes attempt to pierce the dark clouds which veil the future, hoping that the glorious descent of the Son of man may burst upon the view. It is a longing which gushes in the words: "And the Spirit and the bride say, `Come.' And let the one who hears say, `Come.' And let the one who is thirsty come; let the one who wishes take the water of life without cost" (Rev.22:17) (Hendriksen 1969:7-8).

Added to that invitation the Apostle John declared:

> They sang a new song, saying, "Worthy art Thou to take the book, and to break its seals; for Thou wast slain, and didst purchase for God with Thy blood men from every tribe and tongue and people and nation. And Thou hast made them to be a kingdom and priests to our God; and they will reign upon the earth" (Rev. 5:9-10).

The God of promise is indeed the God of fulfillment. What He set out to achieve, He accomplished. "Ah Lord GOD! Behold, Thou hast made the heavens and the earth by Thy great power and by Thine outstretched arm! Nothing is too difficult for Thee" (Jer. 32:17).

What are the themes of both the Old and New Testaments? God is a God for all peoples. He is the God who desires that all peoples should come to repentance and know His deliverance. He is a God who in grace has called to Himself a people who will be witnesses of His great compassion, and also of His holiness, righteousness, and justice. He is the God who has empowered His people to face all enemies, delegating to them His authority to call all powers to account in His all-powerful name.

Is biblical faith unique, distinct from other faiths? Does the Bible detail a theology of missions? How can one fail to see either the difference or the missionary thrust! Are there other purposes for God calling a people to Himself? If so, it is not revealed in the Bible! The Church's task is the same as the Lord Jesus Christ's.

> "The Spirit of the Lord is upon Me, because He anointed Me to preach the Gospel to the poor. He has sent Me to proclaim release to the captives, and recovery of sight to the blind, to set free those who are downtrodden, to proclaim the favorable year of the Lord" (Lk. 4:18).

Although carrying out the task of the God of the nations will bring trials and tears, His victory, and ours, is beyond doubt.

> These have one purpose and they give their power and authority to the beast. These will wage war against the Lamb, and *the Lamb will overcome them, because He is Lord of lords and King of kings, and those who are with Him are the called and chosen and faithful* (Rev. 17:14, emphasis added).

BIBLIOGRAPHY

Adeney, David H. *The Unchanging Commission*. Chicago: Inter-Varsity Press, 1955.

Allen, Geoffrey. *Theology of Missions*. Naperville, IL: Allenson, 1963.

Allen, Roland. *The Ministry of the Spirit*. Grand Rapids: Eerdmans, 1962.

_____. *Missionary Methods: St. Paul's or Ours?* Grand Rapids: Eerdmans, 1962.

Andersen, Wilhelm. *Toward a Theology of Missions*. London: SCM Press, 1955.

Anderson, Gerald K. *Christian Mission in Theological Perspective*. Nashville: Abingdon, 1967.

_____. *The Theology of Christian Mission*. New York: McGraw Hill, 1961.

Barclay, William. *The Letter to the Romans*. Philadelphia: Westminster Press, 1975.

Barth, Karl. "An Exegetical Study of Matthew 28:16-20." *Theology of Christian Mission*. Gerald Anderson, ed. New York: Abingdon, 1961.

Bavinck, J. K. *An Introduction to the Science of Missions*. Philadelphia: Presbyterian and Reformed Publishing Co., 1960.

Berkhoff, Hendrikus. *Christian Faith: An Introduction to the Study of Faith*. S. Woudtsra, trans. Grand Rapids: Eerdmans, 1979.

Beyerhaus, Peter. *Missions: Which Way? Humanization or Redemption*. Grand Rapids: Zondervan, 1971.

_____. *Shaken Foundations: Theological Foundations for Mission*. Grand Rapids: Zondervan, 1972.

Blank, Sheldon. "Prophet as Paradigm," in *Essays in Old Testament Ethics*, J.L. Crenshaw and J.T. Willis, eds. New York: KTAV, 1974.

Blauw, Johannes. *The Missionary Nature of the Church*. New York: McGraw Hill, 1962.

Boer, Harry R. *Pentecost and Missions*. Grand Rapids: Eerdmans, 1961.

Bosch, David J. *Witness to the World: The Christian Mission in Theological Perspective*. Atlanta: John Knox, 1980.

Braaten, Carl E. *The Flaming Center: A Theology of Christian Missions*. Philadelphia: Fortress Press, 1977.

Bright, John. *The Kingdom of God*. Nashville: Abingdon, 1953.

Bruce, Alexander Balmain. *The Training of the Twelve*. New York: Richard R. Smith, 1930.

Brueggemann, Walter. *The Prophetic Imagination*. Philadelphia: Fortress Press, 1978.

Burnett, David. *God's Mission: Healing the Nations*. Kent, England: MARC, 1986.

Carver, William O. *The Bible a Missionary Message*. New York: Revell, 1921.

_____. *Missions in the Plan of the Ages*. Nashville: Broadman, 1951.

Champion, Richard, et al. (eds.). *Our Mission in Today's World*. Springfield, MO: Gospel Publishing House, 1968.

Conn, Harvie M. *Evangelism: Doing Justice and Preaching Grace*. Grand Rapids: Zondervan, 1982.

Culver, Robert Duncan. *A Greater Commission*. Chicago: Moody Press, 1984.

De Groot, A. *De Bijbel over het Heil der Volken*. Roermond, Netherlands: Romens, 1964.

DeRidder, Richard. *Discipling the Nations*. Grand Rapids: Baker Book House, 1975.

Douglas J. D. (ed.). *Let the Earth Hear His Voice: International Congress on World Evangelization, Lausanne, Switzerland*. Minneapolis: World Wide Publications, 1975.

_____. (ed.). *New Bible Dictionary*. Grand Rapids: Eerdmans, 1975.

Dubose, Francis M. *God Who Sends: A Fresh Quest for Biblical Mission*. Nashville: Broadman, 1983.

Dyrness, William A. *Let the Earth Rejoice: A Biblical Theology of Holistic Mission*. Westchester, Pa.: Crossway Books, 1983.

Dyrness, William A. *Themes in Old Testament Theology*. Downers Grove, Il.: Inter-Varsity Press, 1979.

Eichrodt, Walter. *Man in the Old Testament, Studies in Biblical Theology* 4. K. and R. Smith, trans. London: SCM Press, 1951

Fernando, Ajith. *A Universal Homecoming: An Examination of the Case for Universalism*. Madras: Evangelical Literature Service, 1983.

Forman, Charles W. *A Faith for the Nations*. Philadelphia: Wesminster Press, 1957.
Gilliland, Dean S. Pauline *Theology and Missions Practice*. Grand Rapids: Baker, 1983.
Gleason, Archer, Jr. *A Survey of Old Testament Introduction*. rev. ed. Chicago: Moody Press, 1974.
Glover, Robert H. *The Bible Basis of Missions*. Chicago: Moody Press, 1964.
Goerner, H. Cornell. *All Nations in God's Purpose: What the Bible Teaches about Missions*. Nashville: Broadman, 1979.
Gordon, A. J. *The Holy Spirit in Missions*. Harrisburg, PA: Christian Publications, 1968.
Green, Michael. *Evangelism in the Early Church*. Grand Rapids: Eerdmans, 1970.
Griffith, Michael. *God's Forgetful Pilgrims*. Grand Rapids: Eerdmans, 1978.
_____. *Church and World Mission*. Grand Rapids: Zondervan, 1982.
Hahn, Ferdinand. *Mission in the New Testament*. Naperville, IL: Allenson, 1963.
Hendriksen, William. *More Than Conquerors. An Interpretation of the Book of Revelation*. London: Tyndale Press, 1940 reprinted 1969.
Henry, Carl F. H. and Mooneyham. W. Stanley (eds.). *One Race, One Gospel, One Task: World Congress on Evangelism - Berlin 1966*. 2 vols. Minneapolis: World Wide Publications, 1967.
Hodges, Melvin A. *A Theology of the Church and Its Mission: A Pentecostal Perspective*. Springfield: Gospel Publishing House, 1977.
Horner, Norman A. *Protestant Crosscurrents in Mission*. Nashville: Abingdon, 1968.
Howard, David. *The Great Commission for Today*. Downers Grove, Il.: Inter-Varsity Press, 1976.
Jeremias, Joachim. *Jesus' Promise to the Nations*. London: SCM Press, 1967.
Johnston, Arthur P. *World Evangelism and the Word of God*. Minneapolis: Bethany Fellowship, 1974.
Kaiser, Walter. Jr. *Toward an Old Testament Theology*. Grand Rapids: Zondervan, 1978.
Kallas, James. *Jesus and the Power of Satan*. Philadelphia: Westminster Press, 1968.
Kane, J. Herbert. *Christian Mission in Biblical Perspective*. Grand Rapids: Baker, 1976.
Kantonen, T.A. *The Theology of Evangelism*. Philadelphia: Muhlenberg Press, 1954.
Kato, Byang. *Theological Pitfalls in Africa*. Kisumu, Kenya: Evangel Publishing House, 1975.
Kraemer, Hendrik. *The Christian Message in a Non-Christian World*. New York: Harper, 1938.
Ladd, George Eldon. *Jesus and the Kingdom*. New York: Harper and Row, 1964.
Lawrence, J. B. *The Holy Spirit in Missions*. Atlanta: Southern Baptist Home Mission Board, 1947.
Lindsell, Harold ed. *The Church's Worldwide Mission*. Waco, TX: Word Books, 1966.
_____. *An Evangelical Theology of Missions*. Grand Rapids: Zondervan, 1970.
Love, Julian Price. *The Missionary Message of the Bible*. New York: Macmillan, 1941.
Lum, Ada and Genny. *World Mission: 12 Studies for Today*. Downers Grove, Il.: Inter-Varsity Press, 1976.
McGavran, Donald ed. *Eye of the Storm*. Waco, TX: Word, 1972.
McQuilkin, J. Robertson. *The Great Omission*. Grand Rapids: Baker, 1984.
Miller, Donald G. *The Nature and Mission of the Church*. Richmond: John Knox Press, 1957.
Montgomery, Helen B. *Prayer and Missions*. West Medford, MA: Central Committee on the United Study of Foreign Missions, 1924.
Motyer. J.A. in J. D. Douglas ed. in *New Bible Dictionary*. Grand Rapids: Eerdmans, 1975.
Mouw, Richard. *Politics and the Biblical Drama*. Grand Rapids: Eerdmans, 1976.
Murray, John. *The Covenant of Grace*. London: Tyndale, 1953.
Neill, Stephen. *Creative Tension*. London: Edinburgh House Press, 1959.
_____. *The Unfinished Task*. London: Lutterworth Press,1957.
_____. *The Finality of Christ*. Richmond: John Knox Press, 1969.
_____. *The Household of God*. New York: Friendship Press, 1953.
_____. *One Body, One Gospel, One World*. London: William Carling, 1958.
_____. *The Open Secret*. Grand Rapids: Eerdmans, 1978.
_____. *Trinitarian Faith and Today's Mission*. Richmond: John Knox Press, 1963.
Newbigin, Leslie. *A Faith for This One World*. London: SCM Press, 1961.
Niles, Daniel T. *Upon the Earth*. New York: McGraw Hill, 1966.
Orchard, Ronald K. *Missions in a Time of Testing*. Philadelphia: Westminster Press, 1964.
Payne, J. Barton. *The Theology of the Older Testament*. Grand Rapids: Zondervan, 1971.
Perry, Edmund. *The Gospel in Dispute: The Relation of Christian Faith to Other Missionary Religions*. Garden City, NY: Doubleday, 1958.
Peters, George W. *A Biblical Theology of Missions*. Chicago: Moody Press, 1972.

Power, John. *Mission Theology Today*. Maryknoll, NY: Orbis Books, 1971.

Richardson, Alan. *A Theological Word Book of the Bible*. London: SCM Press, 1950.

Rooy, S.H. *Theology of Missions in the Puritan Tradition*. Grand Rapids: Eerdmans, 1965.

Rowley, H.H. *The Missionary Message of the Old Testament*. London: Carey Press, 1944.

Sanders, J. Oswald. *How Lost Are the Heathen?* Chicago: Moody Press, 1972.

Sedgwick, Adam, and William Monk. *Dr. Livingstone's Cambridge Letters*. London: Deighton, Bell and Co., 1858.

Shorter, Aylward. *Theology of Mission*. Notre Dame, IN: Fides Publishers, 1972.

Skoglund, John E. *To the Whole Creation*. Valley Forge, PA:Judson Press, 1962.

Smith, Eugene L. *God's Mission—and Ours*. Nashville: Abingdon, 1961.

Snyder, Howard. *The Community of the King*. Downers Grove, Il., Inter-Varsity Press, 1977.

Soper, Edmund D. *The Biblical Background of the Christian World Mission*. New York: Abingdon-Cokesbury, 1951.

Speer, Robert E. *The Church and Missions*. New York: Doran, 1926.

_____. *The Finality of Jesus Christ*. New York: Revell, 1933.

Stott, John R. W. *Christian Missions in the Modern World*. Downers Grove, Il.: Inter-Varsity Press, 1975.

Stowe, David M. *When Faith Meets Faith*. New York: Friendship Press, 1972.

Sundkler, Bengt. *The World of Mission*. Grand Rapids: Eerdmans, 1965.

Tasker, R.V.G. *New Bible Dictionary*. Leicester, England: Inter-Varsity Press, 1968.

Taylor, John V. *The Go-Between God: The Holy Spirit and the Christian Mission*. London: SCM Press, 1972.

Tenney, Merrill C. ed. *Pictorial Bible Dictionary*. Grand Rapids: Pegency Reference Library, Zondervan, 1967.

Terry, Milton S. Biblical Hermeneutics. Grand Rapids: Zondervan, 1976.

Tippett, Alan R. *Church Growth and the Word of God*. Grand Rapids: Eerdmans, 1970.

_____. Verdict *Theology in Missionary Theory*. Lincoln, IL: Lincoln Christian College, 1969.

_____. *Introduction to Missiology*. Pasadena: William Carey Library, 1987.

Unger, Merrill F. *Unger's Bible Handbook*. Chicago: Moody Press, 1967.

Van Swigchem, D. *Het missionaire Karakter van de Christelijke Gemeente volgens de Brieven van Paulus en Petrus*. Kampen, Netherlands: J.H. Kok, 1955.

Van Til, Cornelius. *The Defense of the Faith*. Philadelphia: Presbyterian & Reformed, 1963.

Verkuyl, Johannes. *Contemporary Missiology*. Grand Rapids: Eerdmans, 1978.

Vicedom, Georg F. *The Mission of God*. St. Louis, MO: Concordia, 1965.

Vidler, Alec. *Christian Belief*. London: SCM Press, 1950.

Visser t'Hooft, W. A. *No Other Name*. Philadelphia: Westminster Press, 1963.

Vos, Geerhardus. *Biblical Theology: Old and New Testaments*. Grand Rapids: Eerdmans, 1948.

Vriezen, T.C. *An Outline of Old Testament Theology*. Oxford: Basil Blackwell, 1960.

Warren, Max A. C. *The Gospel of Victory*. London: SCM Press, 1955.

_____. *I Believe in the Great Commission*. Grand Rapids: Eerdmans, 1975.

_____. *The Uniqueness of Jesus Christ*. London: Highway Press, 1969.

_____. *Yes to Mission*. New York: Seabury Press, 1966.

Webster, Douglas. *Unchanging Mission: Biblical and Contemporary*. Philadelphia: Fortress Press, 1965.

Weiss, G. Christian. *The Heart of Missionary Theology*. Lincoln, NE: Back to the Bible, 1976.

Westermann, Claus. "God and His People: The Church in the Old Testament." Interpretation 17, 1963.

Willis, Avery, Jr. *Biblical Basis of Missions*. Nashville: Baptist Convention Press, 1979.

Winter, Ralph D. ed. *The Evangelical Response to Bangkok*. South Pasadena: William Carey Library, 1973.

Winter, Ralph D. and Stephen Hawthorne eds. *Perspectives on the Christian World Movement*. Pasadena: William Carey Library, 1981.

Wolff, Richard. *The Final Destiny of the Heathen*. Lincoln, NE: Back to the Bible, 1961.

Wright, C. Ernest. *God Who Acts*. London: SCM Press, 1969.

_____. *The Old Testament Against Its Environment*. London: SCM Press, 1968.